SENTIMENT AND SOCIABILITY

Sentiment and Sociability

The Language of Feeling in the Eighteenth Century

JOHN MULLAN

CLARENDON PRESS · OXFORD

*This book has been printed digitally and produced in a standard specification
in order to ensure its continuing availability*

OXFORD
UNIVERSITY PRESS

Great Clarendon Street, Oxford OX2 6DP

Oxford University Press is a department of the University of Oxford.
It furthers the University's objective of excellence in research, scholarship,
and education by publishing worldwide in

Oxford New York

Auckland Bangkok Buenos Aires Cape Town Chennai
Dar es Salaam Delhi Hong Kong Istanbul Karachi Kolkata
Kuala Lumpur Madrid Melbourne Mexico City Mumbai Nairobi
São Paulo Shanghai Singapore Taipei Tokyo Toronto
with an associated company in Berlin

Oxford is a registered trade mark of Oxford University Press
in the UK and in certain other countries

Published in the United States
by Oxford University Press Inc., New York

© John Mullan 1988

The moral rights of the author have been asserted
Database right Oxford University Press (maker)

Reprinted 2002

ISBN 0-19-812252-7

Acknowledgements

THANKS to Rosemary Bechler, Liz Bellamy, Geoff Day, Debbie Hodder, Istvan Hont, Michael Ignatieff, Emma Lilly, Roy Porter, and Gareth Stedman Jones; also to Paul Mclaughlin, for critical acumen, to Michael Keating, for the suggestion that makes the book what it is, and to Tana Wollen, for the best of support and scepticism.

Nick Phillipson gave me important help at an awkward stage of my research, and I thank him for his enthusiasm as well as his ideas. I owe most to Penny Wilson and Tony Tanner, who have always been generous of their time and attentions; I am grateful to them now, even if I did not seem to be so then.

J.M.

Contents

Abbreviations

THE following works are referred to within the text. My choice of editions was a difficult one only in the case of Richardson's novels, and *Clarissa* in particular. The peculiar differences between editions of this novel are discussed in Chapter 2, and I hope this discussion explains why I have chosen the Everyman edition, a widely available, if not always reliable, version of the third (1751) edition of *Clarissa*. References to other editions of this novel are given in footnotes.

Barbauld	*The Correspondence of Samuel Richardson*, ed. Anna Barbauld (6 vols., London, 1804).
Carroll	*Selected Letters of Samuel Richardson*, ed. J. Carroll (Oxford, 1964).
Clarissa	Samuel Richardson, *Clarissa; or, The History of a Young Lady*, 4 vols. (London, 1978). References by volume- and page-number.
Enquiry I	David Hume, *An Enquiry Concerning Human Understanding*, in *Enquiries Concerning Human Understanding and Concerning the Principles of Morals*, ed. L.A. Selby-Bigge, 3rd edn., rev. P.H. Nidditch (Oxford, 1972).
Enquiry II	David Hume, *An Enquiry Concerning the Principles of Morals*, ibid.
Pamela	Samuel Richardson, *Pamela; or, Virtue Rewarded*, 2 vols. (London, 1978). References by volume- and page-number.
Sentimental Journey	Laurence Sterne, *A Sentimental Journey through France and Italy, by Mr. Yorick*, ed. Gardner Stout (Los Angeles; 1967).
Sir Charles Grandison	Samuel Richardson, *The History of Sir Charles Grandison*, ed. J. Harris (Oxford, 1972).
Theory	Adam Smith, *The Theory of Moral Sentiments*, ed. D.D. Raphael and A.L. Macfie (Oxford, 1976).
Treatise	David Hume, *A Treatise of Human Nature*, ed. L.A. Selby-Bigge, 2nd edn., rev. P.H. Nidditch (Oxford, 1978).
Tristram Shandy	Laurence Sterne, *The Life and Opinions of Tristram Shandy, Gentleman*, ed. J. A. Work (1940; rpt. New York; 1981). References by volume, chapter, and page-number.

Introduction

IT is appropriate that the last piece of writing that the philosopher David Hume completed should have been a brief narrative of his life. Some four months before his death, and reckoning on his 'speedy Dissolution', he composed an autobiographical essay, *My Own Life*, which he wished to be prefixed to the first posthumous edition of his works. 'I cannot say, there is no Vanity in making this funeral Oration of myself; but I hope it is not a misplac'd one; and this is a Matter of Fact which is easily cleared and ascertained.'[1] Written without anxiety, it manages to escape narcissism; it is a succinct record of a 'Life . . . spent in literary Pursuits and Occupations',[2] and implicitly of a stoical resignation in the face of death. As Hume's biographer, Ernest Mossner, puts it, it is 'in part, autobiograhy and, in part, manifesto': 'He was a philosopher and was determined to die philosophically, and to convince the public that he had faced death in accordance with his principles—without hope and without fear'.[3] The essay, if we can call it that, was a settling of accounts which brought together the personal and the public life of the philosopher. It brought them together for a death which was itself a publicly controversial event, a test of Hume's secular philosophy which provoked more published attacks on him and his ideas than had appeared during his lifetime. Amongst the flurry of immediate responses, an admirer, who remained anonymous, seized on the significance of Hume's final act of writing:

He sat down to this extraordinary employment, and took up the pen, exactly at the time that hundreds—I might, I believe, extend the number to thousands—were thinking he would begin the bitter groans of recantation . . . the annals of the world cannot possibly produce any instance, whereby philosophy became so much *of a piece* . . . he was calm enough to give

---

[1] *My Own Life*, in E. C. Mossner, *The Life of David Hume* (2nd edn., Oxford, 1980), 611–15; see p. 615. It was written in Apr. 1776, and is reprinted in most collections of Hume's *Essays* (e.g. Indianapolis, 1985).

[2] Ibid. 611.

[3] Ibid. 591. Michael Ignatieff gives a powerful account of Hume's 'philosophical death', and its more than private significance, in *The Needs of Strangers* (London, 1984), 81–103.

a candid account of his literary life, when he *knew* himself to be incurable.[4]

It was the final 'literary' undertaking of a life of writing—a text designed to suit the end of that life.

This lucid biographical conclusion to the pursuits of a self-denominated 'man of letters',[5] the refusal to separate the life from the writings, was also more generally appropriate; Hume's was only one effort to refuse this separation. The biographies of the three very different writers whose works I discuss in most detail in this book all chronicle peculiarly intimate relationships between the texts they produced and the social lives for which they also became known. In an attempt to understand 'sentimentalism', I concentrate upon David Hume, Samuel Richardson, and Laurence Sterne: all are writers committed to the resources of a language of feeling for the purpose of representing necessary social bonds; all discover in their writings a sociability which is dependent upon the communication of passions and sentiments. It is this discovery, I shall argue, which was formative of that fashion of eighteenth-century fiction now called 'sentimental'. For all three of these authors, the conception of harmonious sociability was dramatized not only in the books they produced, but also in their self-conscious efforts actually to live out models of social being. A biography of any of them records the attempt to make exemplary a social life. It might seem a trivial occupation, as the novelistic vogue of sentiment can appear a facile indulgence; both, however, are historically significant, bespeaking the difficulty which a polite culture was having in imagining the nature of social relations.

It is with the particularly social nature of his 'Character' that Hume ends his autobiography, prizing his waning years, despite 'great Decline of my Person', for his continued possession of both 'the same Ardor as ever in Study, and the same Gaiety in Company'.[6] 'I was, I say, a man of mild Dispositions, of Command of Temper, of an open, social, and cheerful Humour, capable of Attachment, but little susceptible of Enmity, and of great Moderation in all my Passions.' Beyond the more superficial temptations of a literary reputation, a final value in his account is the 'Company' he kept and

---

[4] [S. J. Pratt], *An Apology for the Life and Writings of David Hume* (London, 1777), 85–6.
[5] *My Own Life*, in Mossner, 613.   [6] Ibid. 615.

enjoyed. In a letter which his friend Adam Smith wrote to the publisher William Strahan shortly after Hume's death in August 1776, and which was published with *My Own Life* early in 1777, this value is confirmed. The social existence of the philosopher and man of letters is seen to support, even sanction, his projects of enquiry and analysis. It is the compatibility of 'that gaiety of temper, so agreeable in society, but which is so often accompanied with frivolous and superficial qualities' with 'the most extensive learning, the greatest depth of thought' which is seen by Smith as Hume's private and public legacy.[7] In the end—and as an implicit rejoinder to those who attacked Hume throughout his life as a baleful influence, a sceptic, and an atheist—there is this fact of the philosopher's social being.

This social being depended not simply on a personal habit of gregariousness, but also on historically (and geographically) specific forms of social organization. Hume found his particular social identity, and a model for the operation of 'humanity, generosity, beneficence', in the associations of the educated and the enlightened in eighteenth-century Edinburgh. In its clubs and its groups of enquiring men of letters was a kind of paradigm of sociability itself.[8] Yet the relationship between such limited forms of 'society' and a wider world of competing interests and prejudices was problematic. When, in his *An Enquiry Concerning the Principles of Morals* of 1751, Hume addresses himself to the possibility of such a relationship, he leaves us with a question which it is not difficult to read as plaintive: 'But why, in the greater society or confederacy of mankind, should not the case be the same as in particular clubs and companies?'[9] Hume gave some of his own answers to this question, analysing, in the essays that he wrote through the 1740s and 1750s, the fissile effects of religious and political allegiance, or of the desire for acquisition excited by a developing economy. His dissections of

[7] *The Correspondence of Adam Smith,* ed. E. C. Mossner and I. S. Ross (Oxford, 1977), 221.

[8] See Phillipson, 'Culture and Society in the Eighteenth Century Province: The Case of Edinburgh and the Scottish Enlightenment', in Stone (ed.), *The University in Society* (2 vols., Princeton, NJ, 1975), ii. 407–48; and id., 'Hume as Moralist: A Social Historian's Perspective', in S. C. Brown (ed.), *Philosophers of the Enlightenment* (Brighton, 1979), 140–61. The fullest history of the societies of 18th-cent. Scotland is D. D. McElroy, *Scotland's Age of Improvement: A Survey of Eighteenth Century Literary Clubs and Societies* (Washington, 1969).

[9] *Enquiry* I. 281.

social behaviour were not quite to succumb to the pretensions of his polite provincial culture. Standing against the 'Clamour' of superstition and bigotry, and the confused passions of a commercial world, Hume's systems of friendship were necessary, but were not just a reason for complacency. His enquiries into the passions and instincts which, as far as he was concerned, determined social relations were to subdue as often as to uphold his confidence in the prerogatives of his own educated class. His project of generalizing 'particular' forms of sociability was never quite assured; in Chapter 1 I try to chart the obstacles which it encounters.

The proximity of a discourse about the relations on which society depends to a life in which sociability is exemplified was elevated to a principle not by Hume alone. The increasing difficulty, in the eighteenth century, of conceiving of society as a community of moral and material interests, and the resultant premium upon models of social understanding, has been closely described where it applies to the material of a conventional 'history of ideas'.[10] But such ideals were also worked through in types of literature less obviously committed to social analysis or political prescription. The novels of Samuel Richardson, for instance, envisage a responsive feminine sensibility as the best embodiment of social instinct. Richardson's fascination with the potential of this sensibility oddly conditioned the life which the fame of these novels made possible, and in which he showed as great a concern with the enactment of social virtues as any moral philosopher. Quite obsessively, he attempted to reconstruct in his relations with a select group of appreciative friends the bonds of delicacy and feeling which he celebrated in his fiction, and to exploit a literary notoriety for the creation of a social identity. He surrounded himself with predominantly female admirers of his

---

[10] This material has largely been the philosophical and political writing of the period. I have found particularly useful J. G. A. Pocock, *The Machiavellian Moment* (Princeton NJ, 1975); H. T. Dickinson, *Liberty and Property: Political Ideology in Eighteenth-century Britain* (London, 1977); A. O. Hirschman, *The Passions and the Interests: Political Arguments for Capitalism before its Triumph* (Princeton NJ, 1977); D. Forbes, *Hume's Philosophical Politics* (1975; rpt. Cambridge, 1985); I. Hont and M. Ignatieff (eds.), *Wealth and Virtue: The Shaping of Political Economy in the Scottish Enlightenment* (Cambridge, 1983). For the use of more 'literary' material see I. Kramnick, *Bolingbroke and his Circle: The Politics of Nostalgia in the Age of Walpole* (London, 1968); S. Copley (ed.), *Literature and the Social Order in Eighteenth-century England* (London, 1984). The 'literature' that is dealt with in such histories of ideas tends to be explicitly political satire (Swift, Pope), or the periodical and pamphlet texts of authors now better known for less obviously political writings (Defoe, Fielding).

writing. He would correspond with them in letters fixated upon the interpretation of his own works, or would meet them to discuss those works at his house in Fulham—his bourgeois retreat from his London printing business (described slavishly by his friend John Duncombe as 'that mansion of cheerfulness and grotto of instruction').[11] Correspondence was particularly important to him, offering the possibility of a type of communication which could be both rigorously correct and perfectly responsive. His novels had grown out of the 'familiar letters' which he was writing in the late 1730s, and which had offered instructive models for dealing by correspondence with a variety of domestic problems and questions of conduct; in turn the novels always looked back to such models, and to the conflated influences of fastidious moralism and stylistic propriety which they were designed to promote. But this was not just fiction. A certain type of correspondence provided Richardson with a cherished experience of sociability, of 'the ever agreeable and innocent pleasures that flow from social love, from hearts united by the same laudable ties'.[12]

The expression might be one of his heroine Clarissa's descriptions of her correspondence with Miss Howe—but in fact it comes from a letter written by Richardson to a young admirer, Sophia Westcomb, probably in 1746. The letter begins with the celebration of a special communication: 'What charming advantages, what high delights, my dear, good, and condescending Miss Westcomb, flow from the familiar correspondences of friendly and undesigning hearts.' The 'converse of the pen'[13] which fills the pages of his fiction is also the scheme for his own friendships, his own 'society'. It is not surprising that the members of this society should have been predominantly female. It is not just the biographical matter of Richardson's elaborately sublimated affirmation of his own sexuality. It is also that such 'conversation and friendship' logically connected habits of sociability with a body of fiction in which feminine sensibility was represented as the basis of the freest yet most virtuous communication. The young women with whom Richardson corresponded, and to whom he read from his own

---

[11] Duncombe's description comes in a letter he wrote to Richardson in Oct. 1751; see Barbauld, ii. 271. For an account of Richardson's cultivation of an accessible and appreciative readership, see T. C. D. Eaves and B. D. Kimpel, *Samuel Richardson: A Biography* (Oxford, 1971).

[12] Carroll, 64.　　　　　　　　　　　　　　　　　[13] Ibid. 65.

novels in the parlour at Parson's Green, undoubtedly pandered to the author's self-regard. That they were virtuous exemplars of their sex was proved by the attention they were willing to give to the details of Richardson's moralistic texts, the substance of much of the correspondence and conversation into which he enthusiastically entered. But Richardson's development of his society of readers and correspondents was something more significant than the expression of a famous vanity. In a process to whose odd significance for the early development of the novel I return in Chapter 2, he attempted to make his narratives a controlling influence on sociability. By the most wilful cultivation of acquaintance, life and text were made to reflect each other.

Even Richardson though—a writer when his printing business was not taking up his time—allowed more of a gap between the gratifications of fiction and the pleasures of a social existence than Laurence Sterne. On the success of the first two volumes of *Tristram Shandy* (itself something of a feat of self-advertisement) Sterne followed his novel to London and began to adopt, in the fashionable society in which he mixed, the role not merely of the novel's author, but also of one of its characters.[14] The 'Shandeism' which Tristram recommends as the tenor of his narrative, arousing the 'affections' and the 'vital fluids of the body' (*Tristram Shandy*, pp. 337–338), became the principle of what Sterne claimed were his own social pleasures. He declared in a letter to his old friend John Hall-Stevenson that 'the spirit of Shandeism . . . which will not suffer me to think two moments on any grave subject' was what staved off solitude and melancholy.[15] For in the life of society which Sterne made for himself, whimsical wit and tender susceptibilities were compounded. As he wrote to David Garrick from Paris in 1761, 'I laugh 'till I cry, and in the same tender moments *cry 'till I laugh*. I Shandy it more than ever, and verily do believe, that by mere Shandeism sublimated by a laughter-loving people, I fence as much against infirmities, as I do by the benefit of air and climate.'[16] Ephemeral humour passing into the throb of unabashed emotion, and then theatrically back again: a description which fits Sterne's

[14] For Sterne's self-promotional efforts and his enjoyment of his sudden fame, see W. D. Cross, *The Life and Times of Laurence Sterne* (New Haven, Conn., 1929), esp. Ch. 8, or D. Thomson, *Wild Excursions: The Life and Fiction of Laurence Sterne* (London, 1972), Part 3.

[15] *Letters of Laurence Sterne*, ed. L. Curtis (Oxford, 1935), 139.

[16] Ibid. 163.

novels is made by the author to fit his life. Thus is a sociable character displayed, and celebrity exploited.

Just as Sterne's fiction was put together out of much auto-biographical reference and anecdote, so the life of the notorious author was itself another kind of fiction; this much is a truism. But while there was calculation and opportunism in Sterne's projection of himself as Tristram or Yorick into the polite society of London or Paris, there was also the effort (Hume's and Richardson's effort as well) to construct a social persona. In a sense, the only way for Sterne to live out the impulses to benevolence and sympathy described in his novels was for him to pretend to be a character from one of those novels, confessing all the time his tenderness and his whimsicality. It is thus that he was able to represent himself as a man of sensibility, indulging in a series of ambiguous relationships with young women which were modelled on the sentimental flirtations celebrated in his later fiction. Sterne's letters record these relationships in a rhetoric designed to be compatible with the novels—a rhetoric in which the plea of tenderness allows for a writing at once innocent and suggestive. Not infrequently, in fact, Sterne reused passages from his letters in his novels, as well as deriving the matter of much supposedly private communication to his latest 'dulcinea'[17] from the fiction. In Sterne's journals and correspondence we find the pleasures of friendship and society defined through a vocabulary with which the readers of his novels would be familiar; sociability is founded on delicacy of sentiment, on the rush of feeling, on an appreciation of what is 'affection'. The favoured terminology of the sentimental writer spills out from the confines of a literary form. This may illustrate Sterne's opportunism, but it also points to the wider applicability of a vocabulary whose uses it is one of my purposes to describe. In their different elaborations of social being, Hume and Richardson also employ such a vocabulary. Hume believes in the need to moderate 'passions', but equally in the desirability of cultivating 'our sensibility for all the tender and agreeable passions'.[18] Richardson's community of admirers is one of 'feeling hearts' and delicate sentiments. For all three, sociability depends upon the traffic not only of opinions, but of harmoniously organized feelings. Thus the

[17] See ibid. 256.
[18] Hume, 'Of the Delicacy of Taste and Passion', in *Essays Moral, Political, and Literary*, ed. E. Miller (Indianapolis, 1985), 4–6.

particular importance of the term 'sentiment', a word which can
stand for both judgement and affection. When Hume concludes his
Life by declaring himself able to 'speak my *sentiments*' [my italics],
he uses the term, as Sterne and Richardson also do, to conflate
opinion and feeling—to link, in his case, the speculations of the
philosopher and the 'gaiety' of the lover of 'company'.

The types of society that these writers discovered for themselves
were, however, fragile constructions. It is a sense of the limitations
of any expression of sociability (shared, I think, by all three of them)
which determines the forms which that expression finds. Sterne's
self-promoting manœuvres made a virtue of the necessity that the
man of sentiment appear unworldy—valuing types of fellow-feeling
which were always, in the end, to be justified as private and
idiosyncratic. Richardson created a social world turned in on itself,
where feminine delicacy and honour were the abiding principles and
where, therefore, he was always involved in the attempt to make
feminine his own discourse. Hume faced the contradiction between
restricted forms of sociability and the larger facts of conflicting
passions and interests; between special solidarities and usual
competitions. Here, however, the philosopher as man of letters is in
a more difficult position than the novelist, which is the reason (apart
from chronology) that I begin with Hume. To put it at its bluntest,
the contradiction that Hume faced was at the heart of his own
discourse. He confronted the failure of that discourse—of
philosophy itself.

It is important to recognize how, in his questioning of the
authority of reason to explain—let alone to guide—human actions,
Hume broke with what were some of the most influential reflections
of philosophy upon its own activity which were available to him.
Famously, he abandoned the theocentrism of writers like Locke and
Hutcheson, both of them in different ways willing to submit
philosophy to the final verdict of religious belief.[19] But also, and less
famously, he seems to have written directly against Shaftesbury's
confidently aristocratic assumption that philosophy was a discourse
of self-explanatory politeness—a discourse with accepted protocols
which was addressed to a known audience. It was Shaftesbury who
declared that 'To philosophize in a just significance is but to carry

---

[19] On Locke's reference of philosophy to religion see J. Dunn, *The Political
Thought of John Locke* (Cambridge, 1969); on Hutcheson see Forbes, *Hume's
Philosophical Politics*, 32–48.

good-breeding a step higher'.[20] The purpose of his essays, and of their urbanely conversational style, was 'to recommend morals on the same foot with what in a lower sense is called manners, and to advance philosophy (as harsh a subject as it may appear) on the very foundation of what is called agreeable and polite'.[21] He castigated exactly the sceptical analyses whose force Hume could not deny, and characterized as 'whimsical' investigations into 'Nature's remotest operations, deepest mysteries, and most difficult phenomena'.[22] Shaftesbury consistently conflated vocabularies of moral and of aesthetic judgement; in a dominant metaphor, philosophy committed the man of 'good-breeding' to an exercise of 'taste'—a judgement of 'what is harmonious and proportionable' and therefore 'agreeable and good'.[23] This exercise 'perfects the character of the gentleman and the philosopher',[24] the forum for whose 'highest politeness' was seen as the society of conversation.[25] By Shaftesbury's standards, the inordinate ambitions and compulsive self-interrogations of Hume's *Treatise of Human Nature* are signs of a tasteless enquiry—of philosophy pushed beyond politeness.

In fact, Shaftesbury himself, whatever his stylistic assurance, began to encounter problems in theorizing the 'natural' bonds which made society possible; I will return to these problems when I discuss ideas of 'sympathy' in Chapter 1. For now it is sufficient to recognize an assumption that Shaftesbury did not question: the assumption that the philosopher can address 'men' in such a way as to confirm 'their love for society', their 'humanity and common sense'.[26] Hume too was to strive for such polite management of speculation, but was to refuse the notion that philosophy could simply ignore the bait of sceptical self-questioning in order to be urbanely and confidently communicative. For Hume, alongside the persona of philosopher as conversationalist is that of philosopher as solitary sceptic, excluded, most memorably in the final Section of Book I of *A Treatise of Human Nature*, from the normally unconsidered commerce of society, the 'common life' to which the text is compelled to refer. The famous injunction—'Be a philosopher; but, amidst all your

[20] Anthony Ashley Cooper, third Earl of Shaftesbury, 'Miscellaneous Reflections', in *Characteristics of Men, Manners, Opinions, and Times, etc.* (first published in 1711), ed. J. Robertson (1900; rpt., 2 vols. in 1, Indianapolis, 1964), ii. 255.
[21] Ibid. 257.   [22] Ibid. 255.   [23] Ibid. 268–9.
[24] Ibid. 256.   [25] Ibid. 252.
[26] Shaftesbury, 'An Essay on the Freedom of Wit and Humour', in *Characteristics*, i. 65.

philosophy, be still a man'[27]—actually poses a conflict of identities.
Where it appears, near the beginning of Hume's *Enquiry Concerning
Human Understanding*, it is as part of nature's warning to the
philosopher that 'Abstruse thought and profound researches' will be
rewarded only by 'pensive melancholy' and the 'cold reception' any
'pretended discoveries shall meet with, when communicated'. Such,
indeed, was precisely the recompense which Hume felt he had
received for the composition and publication of his *Treatise*, some
ten years earlier. In order to produce a philosophy which naturalized
sociability, the philosopher had become, as he saw it, an 'uncouth
monster', ineffectual because removed from the very processes that
he was trying to describe (*Treatise*, p. 264).[28]

I try to explain the historical significance of this philosophical
reflection on philosophy, and the responsibilities of the philosopher,
when I discuss the relation in the *Treatise* of Hume's scepticism to his
conception of the nature of sociability. It must be acknowledged that
it is always problematic to give any priority to this particular text in
a study which purports to be in any way historical—quite simply
because it had such little impact when it was first published: 'Never
literary attempt was more unfortunate than my Treatise of Human
Nature'.[29] But then, as Hume himself saw it, the failure of this work
was not accidental, but was another symptom of the problem of its
philosophical ambition. It was as if the philosophical text itself could
not be socialized, for it addressed its readers not as social but as
philosophical beings; to understand the promptings of nature and
custom was to be abstracted from the relations and beliefs to which
they gave rise. In its more self-reflective moments, the *Treatise*
worries over this, the problem of whom to address and how. It
distinguishes between 'the opinions and belief of the vulgar' and a
'more philosophical way of speaking and thinking' (*Treatise*,
p. 202), but it cannot hold to this distinction as an easy or
dependable one. For, more radically and self-critically, it has to add
to its characterization of 'all the unthinking and unphilosophical

---

[27] *Enquiry* I. 9.
[28] See D. Forbes, 'Hume and the Scottish Enlightenment', in Brown, *Philosophers
of the Enlightenment*, 94–109, esp. 99–101, where Forbes discusses the 'dichotomy of
"philosopher" seeking truth and "man" active in society' with reference to Hume,
Malebranche, and Smith.
[29] *My Own Life*, in Mossner, 612.
[30] Hume, *An Abstract of a Book lately Published, Entituled, A Treatise of Human
Nature, & c.*, in *Treatise*, 695.

part of mankind' the parenthesis, '(that is, all of us, at one time, or other)' (ibid., p. 205). In the *Abstract* of the *Treatise*, published separately in 1740, Hume celebrates a 'philosophical spirit' which is to produce enquiries more searching and rigorous than those managed by the 'philosophers of antiquity', content as they were, as Hume puts it, with the representation of 'the common sense of mankind in the strongest lights', but unable to anatomize the beliefs which constituted that 'common sense'.[30] The apparent confidence of such a proclamation, designed as an advertising strategy as much as an explanation, should be read alongside Hume's discovery in the *Treatise* itself that beyond the acceptance of 'common sense' is philosophy's 'forlorn solitude' (*Treatise*, p. 264)—an uncommon sense to which few can consistently attend.

What was realized in the *Treatise* as, literally and rhetorically, this problem of address led, in the 1740s, first to Hume's abandonment of this type of philosophical writing and later, at the end of the decade, to the recasting of his early work as the *Enquiry Concerning Human Understanding* and the *Enquiry Concerning the Principles of Morals*. Initially Hume turned to what Nicholas Phillipson calls the 'Addisonian essay', a form of 'polite' and accessible writing designed for 'an audience of men and women of rank, property and position in local and national life, who were preoccupied with questions of social role, personal conduct and private happiness in an increasingly complex, commercially orientated society'.[31] In the Advertisement initially prefaced to his *Essays* Hume explicitly invoked the precedent of the culturally serviceable periodical essay: 'Most of these ESSAYS were wrote with a View of being publish'd as WEEKLY-PAPERS, and were intended to comprehend the Designs both of the SPECTATORS and CRAFTSMEN'.[32] This kind of text lived by its sensitivity to the particular aspirations of its readers. Indeed, it was in terms of the constitution of an audience for the *Essays* that Hume conceived of their form. Their 'end' was, as he wrote, the cementing of a 'League between the learned and conversible Worlds', the bridging of a gap perceived all too clearly in the *Treatise*.[33] So the sceptical lucubrations of the philosopher are

---

[31] Phillipson, 'Hume as Moralist', 141.

[32] David Hume, *Essays, Moral and Political* (2 vols., 2nd edn., Edinburgh, 1742), vol. i, Advertisement, p. iii.

[33] Hume, 'Of Essay Writing', in *Essays Moral, Political and Literary*, ed. E. Miller, 535.

abandoned in favour of an attention to the redeeming conversation and culture of 'such of my readers as are placed in the middle station', uncorrupted by wealth and yet above the 'animal' condition of material need, to whom 'all Discourses of Morality ought principally to be address'd'.[34] Hume now represents himself as an 'ambassador from the dominions of learning to those of conversation':

I shall give Intelligence to the Learned of whatever passes in Company, and shall endeavour to import into Company whatever Commodities I find in my native Country proper for their Use and Entertainment. The Balance of Trade we need not be jealous of, nor will there be any Difficulty to preserve it on both Sides. The Materials of this Commerce must chiefly be furnished by Conversation and common Life: the manufacturing of them alone belongs to Learning.[35]

It is entirely fitting that the governing metaphor here should be one of commercial transaction, for the *Essays* are consistently committed to explaining, and justifying, some of the complexities of commerce. As a socialized form of philosophy, they address themselves not to general principles of 'human nature', not to the nature of 'society' as an eternal human habit, but to the economic and political operations of a specific society. They appeal to their readers' knowledge of those operations, and to the cultural skills, of taste and of manners, which distinguish the polite members of that society, and which innoculate them against the more excessive passions generated by a commercial economy. Because complicit with the exclusivity of a polite audience, the *Essays* can be smug; also, however, they are altogether warier than the *Treatise* about human capacities for disinterested social behaviour. The society they describe is one whose 'harmony' is provided for not by its members' 'passion for public good' but by their animation 'with a spirit of avarice and industry, art and luxury'.[36] It is a society in which the faculty of cultured discrimination in matters of taste and conduct, presumed by Hume in his readers, is a sometimes poor substitute for any deeper solidarity.

The move from *Treatise* to *Essays* was only one in a complex development. It is, though, of a special significance because it is a

---

[34] Hume, 'Of the Middle Station of Life', *Essays Moral, Political and Literary*, 546.
[35] Hume, 'Of Essay Writing', ibid. 535.
[36] Hume, 'Of Commerce', ibid. 263.

clue to the comparability of 'philosophy' and 'literature'. It implies a recognition of the precarious condition of any systematic philosophical project, and a relinquishing of the philosophically conceived models of sociability explicated in Books II and III of the *Treatise*. (I will argue that the retreat from these models is confirmed in Hume's rewriting of parts of the *Treatise* to make the *Enquiry Concerning the Principles of Morals*, and can explain Adam Smith's later reformulation of some of Hume's basic concepts.) Philosophy cannot finally generalize a natural sociability when in doing so it removes itself from society—when it can find no embracing society of readers to address. And yet, where philosophy comes to doubt its own applicability, literature, and particularly the novel, contemporaneously discovers its formal powers. While the novels that I discuss idealize social understanding, and while they imagine such understanding to be supplied by the flow of sentiments and feelings on which philosophers like Hume and Smith also variously rely, they are able to make different kinds of sense of the limitations of sociability, and of the feelings which are its currency.

It is not merely that novels of the eighteenth century could be read as fiction—as transiently entertaining idealization or fantasy. Indeed, novelists themselves went out of their way to deplore the idea that their particular works could be consumed in such a way. (Richardson's lifelong project, for example, was to propose his novels as comparable with the most eternally instructive of religious texts.)[37] It is rather that novelists did not have to find forms of public address. This does not mean that their genre was wholly self-confident; I shall describe how novels were forced always to justify (and sometimes to deny) the private experience of reading which they were reputed to foster. But there was an important resource here too. Novelists were able to concede that habits of sociability were limited or exceptional, only just surviving in a world in which fellow-feeling was rare and malevolence prevailed; but they were able to position each private reader as the exceptional connoisseur of commendable sympathies, and to imply such a reader's understanding of the communication of sentiments and the special capacities of sensibility. It is as if the very form of the novel in the eighteenth century implied a contract, by the terms of which a reader

---

[37] See Chapter 2. Richardson's attitude is exemplified in his delighted citing of his friend Edward Young's characterization of *Clarissa* as '*The Whole Duty of a Woman*' in a letter to Frances Grainger, written in 1749: Carroll, 141.

was set apart from the anti-social vices or insensitivities which the novels were able to represent. This is as true of Fielding or Smollett as it is of Richardson. Novelists were not drawn, as philosophers were, to any exact specification of a world in which narrow self-interest and destructive desires seemed to flourish. In the novels of sentiment which I discuss, those who are part of such a world are typically simply other—unambiguous examples of vice and corruption. The caricatured forms which evil again and again takes, particularly in the most imitative and formulaic fiction from the 1750s to 1770s, can be seen as a displacement into parody of forces which might have menaced schemes of sociability.

Such schemes, in the novels of the mid-eighteenth century, are certainly defensive, as they are in the moral philosophy of the period. Both types of writing register a pressure to produce new and more powerful languages of sociability, and I concentrate upon texts in which that pressure seems most intense. It will obviously not do, however, to assume from common commitments and vocabularies the fundamental equivalence of different discourses.[38] It is important to attend to the different formal aims and capacities of specific kinds of text, and particularly to recognize the distinctive ability of novels of the period to deal with sociability as a desirable but exceptional propensity by addressing as if privately each member of a growing readership. The common concerns with models of social under-standing of such differently organized texts as the philosophical and the novelistic may be a temptation to synthesis, but should not be allowed to produce a history in which difference is forgotten. The projects for showing that there could be social exchange which transcended self-interest were divergent. A comparison of, for instance, the moral philosophy of Hume with the narratives of Richardson, Sterne, or Mackenzie is also a juxtaposition, a testing of the limitations of different types of representation. Sentimentalism has usually been constituted by literary histories as an oddity or a problem—less to be explained than explained away; one of the purposes of my analysis is to suggest that the historical phenomenon of this literature, its vogue and its influence, cannot be clearly

---

[38] I feel this is sometimes a tendency in what is the best literary critical study of sentimentalism, R. F. Brissenden's *Virtue in Distress: Studies in the Novel of Sentiment from Richardson to Sade* (London, 1974). The adjective 'sentimental' is applied to the philosophy of, say, Hutcheson as readily as to the novels of Mackenzie, begging all the difficult questions about what the relations might actually be between these very different types of text. See especially pp. 27–55.

explained by a merely literary criticism. Yet the philosophy of the period cannot serve as a privileged explanatory discourse. I concentrate on Hume in this introduction, and for much of Chapter 1, because his writing acutely probes exactly that incapacity of philosophy—ironically realized for him when philosophy is posing its most searching and ambitious questions.

A language of feeling devoted to the imagining of sociability is not, of course, wholly embraced in the novels and moral philosophy of the period. If sentimentalism in the novel derives from the attempt to conceive of an uncorrupted social being—and thus connects the fiction to the works of philosophy which I discuss—then this is an attempt whose implications are worked through in other types of writing. It would be possible, for instance, to make a description of developments and experiments in English poetry of the mid-eighteenth century a part of this account. The private sensibility and high-minded reclusiveness celebrated in many novels has its parallels in the poetic postures of wounded melancholy and solitary meditation typical of many of the fashionable odes, elegies, and laments of the period. A consideration of the uses of sentiment in such poetry would involve a description of poetic traditions of retreat, for this metaphorical movement in the writings of Thomson, Gray, or Young was achieved only with studied reference to literary precedent. There is not room for such a description here, and it is anyway appropriate that we should look first to the novel for the signs of sentimental fashion, and for the development of new representations of social instinct. This is not merely because the novel came to dominate the market for books—the market for representations—in the eighteenth century; it is also because the disconnection of its form from precedent (as it was perceived) allowed it to explore most extravagantly the powers of a language of feeling. Indeed, I think it will be seen that the novelistic fashion for sentiment should be understood in relation to the anxieties and the opportunities of a literary form which appeared unprecedented.

This said, there is one particular tendency which much of the contemporary poetry could be shown to share with the novels and the philosophy which I discuss: this is the tendency for a desired generalization of social instincts to be countered by a need to look inwards upon resources of sensitivity which are considered as private and exceptional. Yet, if these resources are what provide for social understanding, how can particular experiences of society, pàrticular exchanges of feeling, ever be more than particular and private? How can a language of feeling explain social relations as such? These problems are encountered in whatever kind of text elevates sentiment as the very matter of communication. In novels, the articulacy of sentiment is produced via a special kind of inward attention: a concern with feeling as articulated by the body—by its postures and gestures, its involuntary palpitations and collapses. Here sensibility is both private and public, and here, transcending the influences of speech, the novelist finds an eloquence which promises the true communication of feelings. In its construction of the body—its fixation upon tears, sighs, and meanings beyond words—novelistic convention is, again, of more than literary significance. For the construction of a sensitive and socialized body—the site where the communicative power of feeling is displayed, but also where sensibility can become excessive or uncontrollable—is not only a project of novels. In the medical discourse of the mid-eighteenth century, discussed in my final chapter, feeling and sensibility are equally important (and fashionable) terms, and in the writings of physicians, the body also displays the effects of a privileged sensitivity which is set against the unfeeling and unsocial habits of a larger world. Not that such writings are the only others influenced by the cult of sentiment and sensibility. However, in their concern with the inner world of a particular type of malady (hypochondria, hysteria, nervous disorder), they elicit most clearly the uncertain effects of the powers of feeling. A privileged delicacy or refinement can forebode illness. With the description of a passage from sensibility to physical incapacity we have the strange confirmation of an ambiguity which was always inherent in the celebration of an exceptional susceptibility to feeling.

If sensibility is an exclusive and defensive faculty, then it is perversely logical that its finally fashionable form should be that of the private subjection to nervous disorder. As I shall try to show, novelists of the eighteenth century actually found it increasingly difficult to distinguish between the figure of the virtuous hero or, more especially, heroine, and that of the sadly distracted and isolated hysteric. Illness became the last retreat of the morally pure. Indeed, here biography can be invoked again. Those supposedly personal records which writers left behind them confirm the configuration. The correspondences of Hume, Richardson, and

Sterne detail, alongside their particular lives of society, their various dispositions to melancholy, hypochondria, or 'spleen'. For as all three were determined to experience social affections, all three were to acknowledge (as fashion seemed to dictate) the private susceptibilities which were the price of their capacities for feeling. The sensitive and penetrating writer was held to be more at risk than most—a solitary epicure of sentiment. The spectre of illness is but a sharp reminder of the ambiguity of that sensibility which it became a vogue for the refined and the educated to cultivate in the eighteenth century. What was originally posed as a capacity for sociability was eventually realized in the most private of experiences. If nothing else, I hope I can explain this paradox.

1

Sympathy and the Production of Society

DAVID HUME's reputation as the sardonic analyst of common beliefs, and of religious commitment in particular, has survived his own time to symbolize the iconoclasm of a retrospectively construed 'Enlightenment'. Yet he is not merely the reasonable expositor of irrational prejudice, for his earliest and most ambitious work, the *Treatise of Human Nature*, addresses itself above all to the limitations of reason. In describing these limitations, it is also a text which has to confront the incapacities of its own 'reasonings'. It is this confrontation which provides the *Treatise* with its most gripping phases, producing a work in which what came to be called 'Enlightenment' philosophy discovers the narrowness of its own boundaries. In this context, however, there is something surprising about the more polemical moves in Hume's argument concerning reason, and concerning the constraints within which it is supposed to operate. What is odd is the very assurance of the polemical style: 'Tis not contrary to reason to prefer the destruction of the whole world to the scratching of my finger' (*Treatise*, p. 416). This is meant to surprise, however fleetingly. The audacity of the style is calculated, and in its way confident as well. Hume is arguing against what he considers to be common and insupportable presuppositions; but he is also arguing for a new scheme of 'the influencing motives of the will' which will enable him to show how desires and judgements are shared and communicated—how they are socialized.

Hume's tactic is to give priority to 'the passions'. He represents 'the greatest part of moral philosophy, antient and modern' as built upon an assumption of the 'suppos'd pre-eminence of reason above passion', and an insistence on the 'blindness, unconstancy, and deceitfulness of the latter' (p. 413). He then sets out 'to·shew the fallacy of all this philosophy', to demonstrate that 'reason alone can never be a motive to any action of the will'. As Hume sees it, passions are what drive humans to all action and achievement; reason and passion cannot even properly be seen as contending for domination with each other: 'Since a passion can never, in any sense, be call'd unreasonable, but when founded on a false supposition, or when it chuses means insufficient to the design'd end, 'tis impossible that reason and passion can ever oppose each other, or dispute for the government of the will and actions' (p. 416). It is 'passion' that is absolutely primary. Though Hume's polemical formula is often cited, sometimes the polemicism of the cadence is forgotten: 'We speak not strictly and philosophically when we talk of the combat of passion and reason. Reason is, and ought only to be the slave of the passions, and can never pretend to any other office than to serve and obey them' (p. 415). It is a notorious passage, to which interpreters of Hume's philosophy have constantly returned. It continues to disconcert, as it was no doubt meant to, because here scepticism about the powers of reason seems so unreserved and destructive—because reason is here removed from all estimations of human motivation. But Hume's argument at this point has also, I think, proved puzzling because of its peculiar (if last-ditch) assurance. Its oddity is the calculated risk and hyperbole of its rhetoric. If this is scepticism, it is not the melancholy scepticism of Book I of the *Treatise*, where the philosopher is locked in an epistemological combat in which there can be neither victory nor a useful report of defeat. Indeed, the critique of reason in the discussion 'Of the Passions' can best be understood contrasted, rather than continuous, with the evaluation of scepticism in Book I.

In Book I, 'Of the Understanding', 'philosophy', the activity in which Hume self-consciously indulges, and 'nature', that which dictates the forms of human knowledge, cannot finally be reconciled. 'Human nature' is not merely the object of philosophical enquiry, but is a limit and a rejoinder to that enquiry. In Hume's epistemological discussions, philosophy is put to the analysis of a prevailing blindness of 'human nature' to the guidance of any 'reasonings'. Philosophy describes how illusion and imagination are the supports which nature requires, but it is led to admit that nature will always win out in the end. The question of whether scepticism is justified is thus, in the end, something of a non-question; this is Hume's only real response to those who accused him of being a Pyrrhonian—one who subversively refuses the grounds for any sort of belief. As he writes in his *Abstract* of the *Treatise*, 'By all that has been said the reader will easily perceive, that the philosophy contain'd in this book is very sceptical, and tends to give us a notion of the imperfections and narrow limits of human understanding . . . Philosophy wou'd render us entirely *Pyrrhonian*, were not nature too strong for it.' Several years later, in a footnote to his *Enquiry Concerning Human Understanding*, Hume was to characterize sceptical arguments in these terms: *'they admit of no answer and produce no conviction*. Their only effect is to cause that momentary amazement and irresolution and confusion, which is the result of scepticism' (*Enquiry* I. 155). In the *Treatise* the irresolution is something more than momentary. In this text the possibilities of scepticism are pursued to the Conclusion of Book I, where the predicament of philosophical melancholy is outlined. It is really a logical resting-place—a Conclusion which is no conclusion at all. Here Hume recognizes that nature is too strong to be curbed by philosophical questioning, but that 'sceptical doubt, both with respect to reason and the senses, is a malady, which can never be radically cur'd, but must remain upon us every moment, however we may chace it away' (*Treatise*, p. 218).

Thus the peculiar statement of scepticism in the first Book of the *Treatise*. As John Wright puts it, 'scepticism is a philosophical attitude which is self-consciously adopted by Hume';[1] scepticism is cited rather than argued. Indeed, Hume almost literally puts quotation marks around the propositions of 'sceptical systems of philosophy' in Part IV of Book I of the *Treatise*. And this is not a tactic unique to the *Treatise*. The second volume of Hume's *Essays, Moral and Political*, published in 1742, contains four essays ('The Epicurean', 'The Stoic', 'The Platonist', and 'The Sceptic') designed, as Hume's own note has it, 'to deliver the sentiments of sects, that naturally form themselves in the world, and entertain different ideas of human life and happiness'.[2] Each of these has philosophy making sense 'of human life and of happiness', but only in inverted commas. As if Hume's note were not enough, the prefatory Advertisement to the volume finds it 'proper to inform the READER, that, in those ESSAYS, intitled, *The Epicurean, Stoic,* & c. a certain Character is personated; and therefore, no Offence ought to be taken at any Sentiments contain'd in them'.[3] Each of the essays speaks in its own

---

[1] J. Wright, *The Sceptical Realism of David Hume* (Manchester, 1983), 4 and *passim*.

[2] Hume, *Essays Moral, Political, and Literary*, ed. E. Miller (Indianapolis, 1985), 138.

[3] Hume, *Essays, Moral and Political* (Edinburgh, 1742), vol. ii, Advertisement, p. iii.

voice, self-contained in the matter of its argument, but also in the particular literary style of its address. Yet each in sequence contends with the one before it. Hume appears to have domesticated philosophical argument to a polite irony, an exercise in mimicry. But then none of the essays puts forward arguments which, by the standards of the *Treatise*, are simply ludicrous or wrong. And, most of all, they veer, as if despite themselves, to the decisions of the final one in the sequence, 'The Sceptic'. This essay declines the partiality of any philosophical 'sect' even as it is itself supposed the voice of such a 'sect'. The Advertisement's apology cannot but draw attention to the coherence of this essay in particular, and alert us to its reconstitution of the doubts entertained in the *Treatise*: 'The empire of philosophy extends over a few; and with regard to these too, her authority is very weak and limited'.[4]

The ventriloquism of the essay writer allows him to restate (as if wittily) the paradox insisted on in the *Treatise*: 'scepticism with regard to reason' cannot be argued away, yet those who adhere to any '*total* scepticism' are merely ridiculous, members of a 'fantastic sect' (*Treatise*, p. 183). Sceptical argument is unanswerable in its own limited philosophical terms, and insupportable outside them:

Shou'd it here be ask'd me, whether I sincerely assent to this argument, which I seem to take such pains to inculcate, and whether I be really one of those sceptics, who hold that all is uncertain, and that our judgement is not in *any* thing possest of *any* measures of truth and falsehood; I shou'd reply, that this question is entirely superfluous, and that neither I, nor any other person was ever sincerely and constantly of that opinion (*Treatise*, p. 183).

Hume is caught between the identities—of 'philosopher' and 'man'—to which I referred in the Introduction. 'Nature, by an absolute and uncontroulable necessity has determin'd us to judge as well as to breath and feel'—and the philosopher must also be one of 'us', a creature with natural needs and appetites which reflection cannot dispel. He pursues 'a subtle reasoning' whose conclusions he must habitually contradict (*Treatise*, p. 186). The dark fatalism of Hume's epistemological enquiry is a product of this contradiction, rather than of scepticism as such. It is the articulation of an impossible dilemma: 'We have . . . no choice left but betwixt a false reason and none at all. For my part, I know not what ought to be done in the present case. I can only observe what is commonly done;

---

[4] Hume, *Essays*, ed. Miller, 169.

which is that this difficulty is seldom or never thought of' (*Treatise*, p. 268).

So how is Hume's critique of reason in Book II of the *Treatise*, his discourse 'Of the Passions', to be distinguished from this fatalism? What is his assertion of the enslavement of reason to passion more than a restatement of the same troubling theme? The beginning of an answer is signalled by the immediate direction in which the assertion leads Hume in his discussion of 'the influencing motives of the will'. For he goes on to distinguish, at some length, between 'calm and violent passions', and to redefine what are 'very readily taken for the determinations of reason' as in fact the impulses of 'calm passions' (*Treatise*, pp. 417–18). In this formula, 'calm passions and tendencies, which, tho' they be real passions, produce little emotion in the mind, and are more known by their effects than by the immediate feeling or sensation', are separated out from the 'reason' with which they are habitually 'confounded'. The 'struggle of passion and reason, as it is call'd' is restated as a conflict between 'calm' and 'violent' passions; the appearance of reasoning in the government of 'the will' is an illusion. At this particular point, Hume's argument seems uncharacteristically contorted, his rewording of the language in which motivation can be described at its most opportunistic. It is the least subtle tactic of what Alisdair MacIntyre refers to as 'emotivism . . . dedicated to characterizing as equivalent in meaning two kinds of expression which . . . derive their distinctive function in our language in key part from the contrast and difference between them'.[5] But Hume's forced vocabulary of 'weak' and 'violent' passions is the consequence of his determination to address questions of motive and judgement through a discourse 'of the passions', and it is this determination which is formative. As is made clear in the *Abstract*, the very 'foundation' of 'morals, criticism and politics' is laid in an 'account of the passions'.[6] This account is crucial, and can in a sense redeem scepticism, because it allows for a description of sociability. It is Hume's reliance upon this that sanctions the famous polemic against reason.

MacIntyre argues that Hume's commitment to the influence of the passions is anchored to an implicit moral and political conservatism, an 'unacknowledged view of the state of the passions in a normal and

---

[5] A. MacIntyre, *After Virtue: A Study in Moral Theory* (1981; rpt. London, 1982), 12.

[6] 'Abstract', *Treatise*, 646.

what we might call, but for Hume's view of reason, reasonable man'.[7] He emphasizes that 'Hume is already covertly using some normative standard' of acceptable passion, and for confirmation refers us to Hume's later condemnation of the heightened passions of 'enthusiasts' as dangerous or absurd. But while such unsurprisingly ideological content can be extrapolated, the difficulty with which this is achieved should be recognized. In the *Treatise* at least, standards of judgement and behaviour specific to the ruling class of Hanoverian Britain are only ever implicit.[8] This does not mean that they played no part in determining Hume's project; it does mean that the point of the project was to be the scope of its generalization and abstraction. Unlike the *Essays*, in which the particular historical and cultural context of judgement is quite explicit, the *Treatise* is committed to a philosophical description of 'human nature'. To take this commitment seriously is not to refuse its historical context. It is to recognize that, in its own terms, the discussion of the passions is secured not by any appeal to the influence of particular ranks and institutions, but by a sociability which is conceived of as an absolutely natural propensity. I have already mentioned something of the social history to which we can refer Hume's conception of this tendency—notably the experience of the 'society' of the polite and educated in eighteenth-century Edinburgh.[9] But Hume's effort in this early work is to generalize any such model of social relations; it is this effort which is the ideological strategy of the *Treatise*.

Hume's reliance on 'the passions' is possible and purposeful because they are not seen merely to promote private interests and desires. Though Hume was later to retreat from this position, in the *Treatise* the passions are socialized. Their tendency to possess subjectivity—traditionally regarded as disruptive of social and moral order—enables them to be the very currency of society: 'The

---

[7] MacIntyre, *After Virtue*, 46–7.

[8] The best analysis of such standards is to be found in D. Forbes, *Hume's Philosophical Politics* (Cambridge, 1985); see especially 'Political Obligation for "Moderate Men" ', 91–101.

[9] I have, though, made no real reference to the national self-consciousness of those who constituted such society, or to the mixed ingredients of fervour for improvement and cultural anxiety which made for the intensified self-images of this new ruling class. For more on this see N. Phillipson, 'Culture and Society in the Eighteenth Century Province', in L. Stone (ed.), *The University in Society* (Princeton, NJ, 1975), D.D. McElroy, *Scotland's Age of Improvement: A Survey of Eighteenth Century Literary Clubs and Societies* (Washington, 1969), and D. Craig, *Scottish Literature and the Scottish People 1680–1830* (London, 1961).

passions are so contagious, that they pass with the greatest facility from one person to another, and produce correspondent movements in all human breasts' (*Treatise*, p. 605). The mobility of passions permits the communication upon which society is founded, the 'agreeable movements' which bind its members together. Whatever the passion, it is distinguished by its communicability: 'Hatred, resentment, esteem, love, courage, mirth and melancholy; all these passions I feel more from communication than from my own natural temper and disposition' (*Treatise*, p. 317). 'Reason' becomes wholly commanding of only limited and specialized projects such as those of mathematics; a description of a social and moral world must be a description of the movements of passions.

Hume here gives a new twist to an old argument. As several studies, of which J.G.A. Pocock's *The Machiavellian Moment* is perhaps the best known, have shown, political discourses of the eighteenth century habitually identified passion with narrow interest and socially destructive fantasy. In the domain of philosophy, much intellectual labour was expended in attempts to refute Hobbes's description of the passions as dominant and competitive primal 'appetites' and Mandeville's depiction of a world in which 'public benefits' flow not from human virtues but from the inevitably self-interested operation of private passions. It was a conventional necessity to demonstrate that passions were conquerable, not merely by some theoretical reason, but by the actual practices of virtue, politeness, or religion. Yet in the *Treatise* Hume, while theorizing a sociability which transcends self-interest, embraces the passions. He turns on its head Mandeville's characterization of passion as unconquerable by reason,[10] his assertion that 'strong habits and inclinations can only be subdued by passions of greater violence'.[11] He does so by arguing that passions can represent not the divisive forces of private desires, but the very currency of sociability. Passion actually becomes interchangeable with a set of other terms—'feeling', 'affection', 'sentiment'—which constitute this currency. Hume's blurring of any distinction between the terms is in itself an advertisement of his project: passion is not appetite but sentiment; the proximity of feeling and judgement, impression and idea. It is the movement of 'passion' and 'feeling'

---

[10] See Bernard Mandeville, *The Fable of the Bees*, ed. D. Gurman (London, 1934), 157.

[11] Ibid. 202.

which registers the fact of social being, and this movement is made possible by a principle at the very centre of Hume's analysis of society and morality. This principle is 'sympathy'.

To examine the history of ideas of 'sympathy' in eighteenth-century philosophy, up to and after the *Treatise*, is not merely to write an episode in the history of philosophy. For the philosophical project of theorizing sociability, that which sympathy makes possible, is not an isolated one. The work of producing—of modelling or staging—society as a scheme of consensus and unanimity, and of warning against the forces or habits which threaten such a scheme, is an undertaking common to different types of writing. In the mid-eighteenth century, moral philosophy and narrative fiction engage in the description of forms of society—and I will argue that this is the determining concern of the novel of sentiment in particular. But neither type of text simply reflects social conditions or relations: both *produce* society; both seek to make society on the page. A result and a measure of this is a common ideological complexity—writings confusingly caught between description and projection, between the results of an analysis and the temptations of an ideal. In this respect, the texts of philosophers like Hume or Adam Smith are not necessarily less contradictory, nor more ideologically apposite, than those of Richardson or Sterne. While the moral philosophy and the novel of sentiment deploy in common certain key terms, these do not specifically or primarily belong to a philosophical vocabulary. In novels as much as treatises, social habits and virtues depend upon the influences of 'feeling', 'passion', and 'sentiment'. Indeed, it could be argued that the common currency of these forms of expressiveness precisely indicates a wider concern to fashion and explain sociability than could be articulated within philosophy alone. This concern is manifested in different ways, of course, and in no type of text is it unproblematic to resort to passions and sentiments as the stuff of social understanding. Any description, for instance, of how, in the novel of sentiment, sympathy and the articulacy of feeling hold the promise of unfettered communication must refer also to how this prospect, for novelists like Richardson and Mackenzie, is often remote, oppositional, and even despairing. In the moral philosophy of the period, meanwhile, there is the problem of projecting a sympathetic alignment of feelings seen as the rule in limited companies of the enlightened on to a more inclusive model of

society. Hume's *Treatise* is the most thoroughgoing attempt to make
sympathy describe all social relations, permitting the thesis of a
natural sociability. To understand how it falters, it is necessary to
give some attention to influential treatments of the theme before
Hume, and to the later retrenchments of both Hume himself, and
Adam Smith.

When Hume, in a passage cited above, describes passions as
'contagious', having previously rejected reason as any actual
regulator of action or judgement, he capitalizes perversely on a
conventional association. In previous discussions of the topic, it was
the infectious spread of passions—capricious emotions igniting each
other—which had subverted or travestied the proper forms of
sociability. So a writer like Shaftesbury was suspicious of sympathy,
willing to trust to the gentlemanly fellowships of which he was a
member, but not to the mobs and factions whose disordered
passions he saw as more generally the rule. In his *Characteristics*,
sympathy can stand for either a pleasurable 'sharing' of 'sentiments'
or a 'contagion' which is dangerous and disruptive: 'One may with
good reason call every passion panic which is raised in a multitude
and conveyed by aspect or, as it were, by contact of sympathy'.[12]
Sympathy can be that which puts people 'beyond themselves' and
which causes 'their very looks' to be 'infectious'. It can take the form
of 'enthusiasm'.[13] It breaks down proper restraints and exceeds
proper distinctions. It allows 'passions' to spread 'from face to face'.
It conjoins 'men' in a way which is not desirable: 'Such force has
society in ill as well as in good passions: and so much stronger any
affection is for being social and communicative'. Yet it is the
'sympathy' of the 'magistrate' which is also the 'cure' for this
'passion', this 'disease'. 'The magistrate, if he be any artist, should
have a gentler hand . . . and with a kind sympathy entering into the
concern of the people; and taking, as it were, their passion upon him
should, when he has soothed and satisfied it, endeavour, by cheerful
ways, to divert and heal it.'[14]

Sympathy, then, expresses two aspects of the 'social and

[12] Anthony Ashley Cooper, third Earl of Shaftesbury, *Characteristics of Men, Manners, Opinions, and Times, etc.*, ed. J. Robertson (1900; rpt. Indianapolis, 1964), 13.

[13] Indeed, throughout the century, 'sympathy' could be synonymous with 'enthusiasm'. See, for instance, Richard Graves, *The Spiritual Quixote, or the Summer's Ramble of Mr. Geoffrey Wildgoose*, ed. C. Whibley (London, 1926), 48.

[14] Shaftesbury, *Characteristics*, 14.

communicative' capacities of humans, and revealingly does so according to the social positions of those who experience it. First there is the possibly 'infectious' nature of 'passions' and 'affections' and the 'panic' which is their spread; then there is the assertiveness of an authority which finds in sympathy a means for the re-establishment of social order and harmony. Sympathy, which is the mutuality of 'affections', can bring people together, but there is always the risk that it can do so in the wrong way. When it is merely a 'herding principle' it brings 'disorder . . . to the general society of mankind'.[15] The 'close sympathy' which enables 'the force of the confederating charm' to be felt can, 'by a small significance of the affection', be productive of division and conflict. 'Division' comes with the wrong kind of 'association', 'For sedition is a kind of *cantonising* already begun within the State. To *cantonise* is natural; when the society grows vast and bulky'.[16] The complexity of 'the society' alienates or confounds its members, who seek to satisfy their need for sociability by attaching themselves to partisan companies. The 'spirit of faction' stems from 'the abuse or irregularity of that social love and common affection which is natural to mankind'. Conflict within 'society' arises not so much from anti-social tendencies as from a 'wrong social spirit'. In an age of bitter political faction—and an age in which the deprecation of faction was readily to hand for the convenience of any political grouping—Shaftesbury was attuned to the dangers of limited allegiance. His was a search for a more inclusive vocabulary of social coherence than political discourse could provide; it was also the search for an exclusive group that could be entrusted with the application of that vocabulary.

His theme and his terminology continued to exert an influence on the pioneering works of the Scottish Enlightenment. Attempts to detect the fundamental principles of sociability were liable to have to deal with expressions of solidarity which were disruptive of social cohesion. Indeed, Hume himself was to revert, in some of his texts, to Shaftesbury's double sense of 'sympathy'. His use of this term in the *Treatise* is the more distinctive when set against his return to Shaftesbury's rhetoric in his later *Enquiry Concerning the Principles of Morals*. In this text he qualifies and retreats from a dependence on sympathy; more pessimistic than in his earlier work concerning 'the narrow attachments of self-love and private interest', he writes that

---

[15] Ibid. 75.   [16] Ibid. 76.

'Popular sedition, party zeal, a devoted obedience to factious leaders; these are some of the most visible, though less laudable, effects of this social sympathy in human nature' (*Enquiry* II. 224). As Shaftesbury has done previously, Hume here sees sympathy as an alienated faculty, productive only of the coherence of opposing, even warring, groups. In this guise it has the potential to bring about political instability. In the *Enquiry* II, an emphasis, not present in the *Treatise*, is given to the tendency of passions and emotions to spread in ways regarded as inordinate or dangerous. 'From instances of popular tumults, seditions, factions, panics, and of all passions, which are shared with a multitude, we may learn the influence of society in exciting and supporting any emotion' (*Enquiry* II. 275). A human requirement of solidarity, if it finds no constructively social expression, can be the basis for nothing better than shared 'enthusiasm'. In this phase of his argument, Hume draws out the more worrying implications of Shaftesbury's analysis of sympathy.

The implications are worrying because, for Shaftesbury, sympathy is also that which describes the coherence of 'natural Affections'—those 'Affections' 'which lead to the Good of THE PUBLICK'.[17] This is the coherence which allows society to be represented as 'company', a domain of agreement and mutual understanding. 'The difference we find between Solitude and Company, between a common Company and that of Friends; the reference of almost all our Pleasures to mutual Converse, and the dependence they have on Society either present or imagin'd; all these are sufficient Proofs on our behalf.'[18] They are 'Proofs' that 'the natural *Affections are in themselves the highest Pleasures and Enjoyments*'. 'Company' involves '*sharing Contentment and Delight with others*'. This 'sharing' proceeds with the 'gathering' of such 'Delight'

From the very Countenances, Gestures, Voices and Sounds, even of Creatures foreign to our Kind, whose Signs of Joy and Contentment we can any-way discern. So insinuating are these Pleasures of Sympathy, and so widely diffus'd thro our whole Lives, that there is hardly such a thing as Satisfaction or Contentment, of which they make not an essential part.[19]

This is 'society' under a special political, as well as semantic, heading; it is the bonding of those educated into a tasteful

---

[17] Shaftesbury, *An Inquiry Concerning Virtue, or Merit*, ed. D. Walford (Manchester, 1977), 54.
[18] Ibid. 63.   [19] Ibid. 67.

appreciation of shared privilege. The 'looks' which, elsewhere in the *Characteristics*, can connote 'enthusiasm' and induce 'panic' have become the 'Countenances' whose intelligibility sympathy permits and relies on. The very same mechanism which can produce a dangerous overflow of passion or a divisive spirit of sedition also, in a different context, produces the pleasure which can be taken in the appearance of society as a 'mutual Converse'. The ambiguity of sympathy in Shaftesbury's account proceeds from an uneasy sensitivity to the limitations of such 'Company' and 'mutual Converse', from an awareness of the necessary separation of polite society from society at large.

In Hume's effort to rid his discourse of such ambiguity, sympathy in the *Treatise* takes centre stage: 'No quality of human nature is more remarkable' (*Treatise*, p. 316). The coherence of society, and 'communication' within society, are made possible by the fact that 'nature has preserv'd a great resemblance among all human creatures, and that we never remark any passion or principle in others, of which, in some degree or other, we may not find a parallel in ourselves' (*Treatise*, p. 318). Sympathy realizes this 'resemblance'. It is a 'natural' principle of the affinity of different positions and interests. It is what enables us to know that local differences and particular disputes are just local and particular. The 'propensity we have to sympathize with others' is one with the ability 'to receive by communication their inclinations and sentiments, however different from, or even contrary to our own' (p. 316). This 'propensity' is theorized (made 'natural') in the *Treatise* as the general principle of social being: not just existence in society, which necessitates self-interested calculation and allegiance, but a fundamental sociability which is proved in every encounter with 'others'. In the *Treatise*, it is through sympathy that 'we', the pronoun which Hume characteristically employs, become infused with the passions of others. Hume's scheme of the 'double relation of impressions and ideas' (p. 381), of their interchangeability, allows for 'us' not merely to 'imagine' another's passion, but for there to take place 'a transition of passion' (p. 385). There is an 'instantaneous' transformation of 'idea' into 'impression' so as to become 'the very passion itself, and produce an equal emotion, as any original affection' (p. 316). Understanding the affection of another involves 'feeling', reproducing, the very same affection. Crucially, Hume asserts that the 'ideas' of the 'passions and sentiments of others' are 'converted into the very impressions they represent'. He proceeds to sketch a set of examples of this conversion in order to demonstrate that the way in which 'sentiments' pass from one person to another is 'an object of the plainest experience, and depends not on any hypothesis of philosophy' (p. 319). In outlining the natural operations of sympathy, Hume can presume what was impossible amidst his abstracted reasonings on cause and knowledge—namely that philosophy here simply illuminates what is everywhere known and practised. The possibility of such transitions of sentiment or passion radically distinguishes Hume's scheme of 'ideas', and of the 'association of ideas', from previous theories—and specifically that of Locke —by producing the possibility of immediate and complete communication.[20]

Sympathy is not selflessness; its operation does not guarantee that our actions will be adapted to the sentiments of others. What it provides for is the accessibility of those sentiments, and therefore a sociability not explicable in terms of political or material necessity. 'This principle of sympathy is of so powerful and insinuating a nature, that it enters into most of our sentiments and passions, and often takes the place under the appearance of its contrary' (*Treatise*, p. 593). Even a particular conflict or 'contradiction' is overshadowed by the realization of a 'sentiment on the other side', and is represented only within the context of a ruling compatibility: 'The sentiments of others can never affect us, but by becoming, in some measure, our own' (p. 593). The very possibility of intelligible contradiction depends upon the 'principle' of sympathy. It is only thus that 'we enter so deep into the opinions and affections of others, whenever we discover them' (p. 319). The 'sentiments' of 'others' are always available, different positions unavoidably comparable.

So, in the *Treatise*, sympathy is a 'natural' principle by which different positions and interests are socialized. This type of formulation has its parallels in other philosophical texts of the period, but in none does sympathy enable the effacement of difference which it promises in the *Treatise*. Some comparison with such texts gives a sense of the unique thoroughness, and therefore perhaps the unique failures, of Hume's theory of sympathy. In David Hartley's *Observations on Man* of 1749, for instance, sympathy is invoked to explain what appears to be a type of

---

[20] For the differences between 'ideas' in Locke and in Hume see M. Kallich, *The Association of Ideas and Critical Theory in Eighteenth-Century England* (The Hague, 1970), especially p. 87.

incompatibility—such as 'envy'—as the sub-category of a more general principle of compatibility: even rivalry depends upon a bond, a sympathetic appreciation of another's pleasure or privilege. But here, sympathy is based on 'the general resemblance of the *circumstances* of all mankind to each other' [my emphasis], rather than on the fundamental mutuality of passions and sentiments.[21] Sympathy for Hartley is what we are, or should be, educated into. His is a language of sociability in which he attempts to describe how we *learn* to perform elaborate calculations of pleasure against pain, of the benefits of 'sociality' against the gratifications of apparent self-interest. His faith in the process of an education into sympathy is founded on religiosity, on individuals' perception of 'their common relation to God as their creator, governor, and father; their common concern in a future life'.[22] Necessarily paired with sympathy is 'Theopathy'—the relation to God that allows narrow interests to be transcended. While he needs to explain sociability, Hartley's reliance on the theses of educability and religious perception lead him away from an encounter with the problem of contradictory desires and interests.

Another whose theories of society remained bound to religious instinct was Francis Hutcheson, Professor of Moral Philosophy at Glasgow, and a friend and correspondent of Hume's. For Hutcheson, sympathy is more or less equivalent to 'benevolence', the product of a naturally inherent 'publick Sense'.[23] For him, '*Sympathy* with others' is 'the Effect of the Constitution of our Nature, and not brought upon ourselves by any Choice, with view to any *selfish Advantage*'. This may sound close to what Hume proposes in the *Treatise*, but it differs in important respects. It presumes a natural 'publick Sense', and asserts that 'Benevolence and Compassion . . . are *Determinations of our Nature*, previous to our Choice from Interest'.[24] Sympathy does not harmonize 'Passions and Affections'; rather it is set against them, educating and restraining their influences. Sympathy, Hutcheson conventionally suggests, makes us aware of the need to discipline passions—to aim for the goal of '*the best* Management of *our Desires*'.[25] Indeed, in his

---

[21] See David Hartley, *Observations on Man* (1749; rpt. London 1791), 284–6.

[22] Ibid. 286.

[23] Francis Hutcheson, *An Essay on the Nature and Conduct of the Passions and Affections with Illustrations on the Moral Sense* (1st edn. 1728, 3rd edn. 1742; rpt. Gainesville, Fla., 1969), 14.

[24] Ibid. 92.   [25] Ibid. 167.

final work, published posthumously, Hutcheson explicitly excluded the kind of sympathy about which Hume writes from his 'System of Moral Philosophy'. Here religious belief sanctions the assertion that 'our nature is susceptible of affections truly disinterested in the strictest sense'.[26] In this 'System', to accept that sympathy induces 'us' to be interested in the 'pleasure or pain' of 'others' because it becomes our own 'pleasure' or pain is unacceptably close to naturalizing a 'selfishness' which Hutcheson is concerned to deny.[27]

The differences between Hutcheson and Hume (who culturally and socially had so much in common) are important to observe—the more so as their theories are sometimes conflated. In fact, the two philosophers recognized their differences quite clearly, even if in terms which might seem unfamiliar to us now. Their relative attitudes to the function of moral philosophy, and implicitly to the concept of sociability, are neatly represented in an exchange of letters which took place in 1739. Hutcheson wrote to Hume, worrying about the tendency of the *Treatise* to avoid the recommendation of duty or virtue in favour of description and analysis. Hume homed in on this anxiety: 'What affected me most in your Remarks is your observing, that there wants a certain Warmth in the Cause of Virtue, which, you think, all good Men wou'd relish, & cou'd not displease amidst abstract Enquiry'.[28] His response was to describe the separation of two types of moral discourse—his and Hutcheson's. Where Hutcheson was 'a Painter', he was 'an Anatomist'; where Hutcheson was engaged in 'examining the Mind' in order 'to describe the Grace & Beauty of its Actions', he sought 'to discover its most secret Springs and Principles': 'I imagine it impossible to conjoin these two Views'. As Hume saw it, Hutcheson was a 'moralist', legislating for the management of the passions, while he was an 'anatomist', analysing the affects of passion and feeling, but unable to pretend that he could alter them. Hutcheson's intervention left its mark on the Conclusion to the *Treatise*, where Hume returns to the same imagery in insisting on the 'accurate dissections' of his philosophy. However, his apparent concession, here, to Hutcheson's rationale of moral exhortation reads like nothing more than a gesture of routine tact: 'An anatomist, however, is admirably fitted to give advice to a painter; and 'tis even

---

[26] Francis Hutcheson, *A System of Moral Philosophy* (London, 1755), 49.
[27] Ibid. 47.
[28] *The Letters of David Hume*, ed. J. Y. T. Greig (2 vols., Oxford, 1932), i. 32.

impracticable to excel in the latter art, without the assistance of the former' (*Treatise*, p. 621). Not only the exchange with Hutcheson, but, more obviously, the whole analytical organization of his 'science' of 'human nature', undermines this assurance.[29]

But for the fundamentally friendly nature of the exchange, Hume might have added that whereas Hutcheson's moralism could look to the final proofs of religion, his own 'experimental' philosophy recognized only the facts of a world without eternal sanctions or purposes.[30] Of course, Hume's facts, and the 'human nature' which he anatomizes, are constructed in his theory. In this sense it can be said that his representation of sympathy, his naturalization of the capacities of feeling, is as prescriptive as Hutcheson's moralisms. But the point is that he is able to represent his text as anatomical—built on an enlightened acceptance of a world of passions in which, beyond the failings of reason and religion, sympathy is the saving fact, 'the chief source of moral distinctions' (*Treatise*, p. 618). Hutcheson needs to posit a natural 'moral sense', and to declare a very un-Humean confidence in the compatibility of eternal moral truths with *'what passes in our own Hearts'*. Hume, at least in the *Treatise*, resorts to a sympathy by which judgements and inclinations, while they cannot be referred to any absolute standard, can at least be shared.

For Hume, 'Every human creature resembles ourselves, and by that means has an advantage above any other object, in operating on the imagination' (*Treatise*, p. 359). In theory, this seems easily said. But then, as Hume acknowledges, this resemblance manifests itself in a world of particular contacts and relations, and this leaves him with a problem. The society which is a fellowship of feeling, proved in these contacts and relations, is not the same as political society, in which property is secured by 'Justice', and 'submission to government' is made necessary by the criterion of 'public interest' (see pp. 545-6). Hume wants to explain the necessity of the 'artificial virtues' which justify the conventions of political society; but also, and more importantly, he wants to show how what is necessary to 'civilized' existence also comes to be morally approved. His effort is

---

[29] On the relevance of the metaphor of the 'anatomist' to 'The Study of Human Nature', see B. Stroud, *Hume* (London, 1977), Ch. 1, pp. 1-16. I disagree, though, with Stroud's version of Hume's project as 'an expression of the unbounded optimism of the enlightenment'.

[30] See M. Ignatieff, *The Needs of Strangers* (London, 1984), 87-8.

to use a moral discourse to demonstrate, outside considerations of utility or self-interest, how judgements and habits are socialized. The 'rules of justice' may be practical, but in excess of this *we annex the idea of virtue to justice, and of vice to injustice'* (p. 498). If a discourse 'Of Morals' is to explain what social identity is, it must attend to this annexation of 'the idea of virtue' to rules which serve the 'public interest'. Sympathy is used to fashion such an explanation, but only by means of obscuring the potential disparity between the immediate experience of sociability (conversation, the flow of affections, the communication of sentiments) and the implications of belonging to a political society. Two distinct meanings of 'society' (the experience of particular contacts and the consistency of a political structure) are elided. Sympathy with 'another' is made congruent with sympathy with 'the interest of society' (p. 579).

Hume introduces this application of sympathy in his discussion of the 'moral approbation' of 'justice': *'self-interest is the original motive to the establishment of justice: but a sympathy with public interest is the source of the moral approbation which attends that virtue'* (p. 499). Previously sympathy was a principle of identification which involved sharing 'passions' or 'sentiments' with those we encountered. Now 'we partake of' the 'uneasiness' of any victims of injustice, though they may not be known to us, 'by sympathy'. From saying that sympathy is that which 'takes us so far out of ourselves, as to give us the same pleasure or uneasiness in the characters of others as if they had a tendency to our own advantage or loss' (p. 579), Hume proceeds to argue that this 'pleasure or uneasiness in the characters of others' is equivalent to an 'extensive concern for society'. The principle which unifies 'the minds of men' is now that which interests us in 'the public good'; a description of local understanding has become one of generalized (and moralized) social coherence. Hume's account of sociability is here under a significant pressure—a pressure which is a determinant not only of philosophical enquiry. As will be made clearer, the novel of sentiment in the eighteenth century, committed as it might be to the celebration of fellow-feeling, elaborates pathos from exactly the disconnection of special experiences of sympathy from dominant patterns of social relationship.

Hume has not the simply conventional resources of either fatalism or fantasy available to novelists, but we will find these resources deployed in narrative fiction in response to the same kind of problem that the moral philosopher faces. In the *Treatise*, the problem is the gap between a limited sympathy dependent upon the commerce of sentiments and a 'sympathy with public interest'. In his discussion of 'our sense of beauty', Hume writes, 'The minds of all men are similar in their feelings and operations . . . As in strings equally wound up, the motion of one communicates itself to the rest' (*Treatise*, p. 576). Sympathy facilitates something more than vague fellow-feeling. It involves the direct and immediate reproduction of another's 'sentiments'. The mind 'is actuated with a like emotion'. But Hume goes on to suggest that sympathy is not necessarily, as it seemed in Book II of the *Treatise*, the sympathy whose characteristic forum is 'company' or 'conversation', the sympathy with a known person. When he writes of the sympathy with the possessor of what we might judge beautiful, it is 'the pleasure or advantage of some other', of an imagined 'stranger, for whom we have no friendship', which constitutes 'our pleasure'. It is the sympathy which is based on the imagining of an owner for each object surveyed. Sympathy here need not involve any actual transference of passion or sentiment; if sympathy can reach beyond the immediate contact of friendship and conversation, it can be suggested that 'the good of society . . . pleases by sympathy'.[31] If feeling prevails, there are, in the end, no strangers.

Hume, however, does not, in the *Treatise* at least, reproduce Shaftesbury's thesis that 'virtue' is a function of social utility. Indeed, it is a stress on 'utility' outside the conditions of sympathy which, in part, distinguishes the *Enquiry* II from the *Treatise*; the employment of utility as a criterion of virtue marks the threshold of a retreat from sympathy. In the *Treatise*, 'there are other virtues and vices besides those which have this tendency to the public advantage and loss' (p. 577). What is more, it is only through sympathy that the 'public interest' and 'the good of society' can be realized. This realization rests upon the ability to posit, in all circumstances, 'some other person' with whom such sympathy can be felt. This is not a matter of any calculation of general advantage; what counts is the natural bond which renders others' interests and pleasures immediately accessible. Hume makes the very institutions of society

---

[31] But for the wider significance for Hume of 'friendship' as denoting obligation which can be political or financial, see D. Miller, *Philosophy and Ideology in Hume's Political Thought* (Oxford, 1981), 138–41.

understandable according to the imagined 'affections' of those who benefit from them. It is sympathy that permits this. For sympathy is the principle according to which 'the ideas of the affections of others are converted into the very impressions they represent' (p. 319): 'an idea of a sentiment or passion, may by this means be so inliven'd as to become the very sentiment or passion'. 'Ideas' are mutable forms, and through their mutability sentiments can be replicated as 'the passions arise in conformity to the images we form of them' (p. 319). Perhaps Hume's best-known image for the workings of sympathy is represented thus: 'the minds of men are mirrors to one another, not only because they reflect each other's emotions, but also because those rays of passions, sentiments and opinions may be often reverberated, and may decay away by insensible degrees' (p. 365). After a while it inevitably becomes 'difficult to distinguish the images and reflexions', but what is at stake is the principle which allows the 'reflexions' to take place and to substantiate each other.

In his *An Enquiry Concerning the Principles of Morals* of 1751, Hume's reverberating strings and his infinite regress of reflections are gone. In this text, sympathy is, generally, either omitted or represented according to a new model. The model for the operation of sympathy now is the theatre, where 'every movement . . . is communicated, as it were by magic, to the spectators' (*Enquiry* II, 221). These 'spectators' are 'inflamed with all the variety of passions, which actuate the several personages of the drama' (p. 222). Sympathy still involves a 'communication' of 'passions', but the representation of that communication is now a function of the subject's position as spectator (a metaphor to which I shall return in my discussion of Adam Smith's *Theory*). It is a position still calculated to defy the spectre of 'self-interest', but through an image of dissociation, a necessity of separation. The sympathy of the *Treatise* rendered all interests compatible by positing the immediate mutuality of passions and sentiments within society. This then became a general sympathy with 'the good of society'. In the *Enquiry* II, the rejection of 'self-interest' or 'self-love' no longer depends upon such an apotheosis of sympathy. Now 'we must renounce the theory, which accounts for every moral sentiment by the principle of self-love. We must adopt a more public affection, and allow, that the interests of society are not, even on their own account, entirely indifferent to us' (*Enquiry* II. 219). A concern for 'the happiness of society' is no longer mediated through sympathy. The scheme for the reproduction of the 'passions and sentiments' of 'others' is replaced by a 'natural sentiment of benevolence' (*Enquiry* II. 230). It is still the case that the representation of society as coherent and harmonious depends upon the overcoming of differences of interest, but these possible differences are no longer consistently effaced by sympathy. It is 'necessary for us, in our calm judgements and discourse concerning the characters of men, to neglect all these differences, and render our sentiments more public and social' (*Enquiry* II. 229). Now Hume relies upon a resolution of position and interest into 'some general unalterable standard, by which we may approve or disapprove of characters and manners'; now a preferential regard for 'private connexions' is corrected by reflection on 'the universal abstract differences of vice and virtue'. Such reflection qualifies the 'regard to self' according to 'a general standard of vice and virtue, founded chiefly on general usefulness'. Compare this with the discussion of 'the esteem, which we pay to all the artificial virtues' in the *Treatise*: 'Thus it appears *that* sympathy is a very powerful principle in human nature, *that* it has a great influence on our taste of beauty, and *that*, it produces our sentiment of morals in all the artificial virtues' (*Treatise*, p. 577). It is, above all, a notion of 'utility' that, in the *Enquiry* II, has displaced the emphasis on sympathy, reconstituting the basis on which all positions and interests can find a place within a coherent image of society.

In the *Enquiry* II, Hume writes that whatever 'the writers on the laws of nature' might speculate upon, they are sure to terminate here at last, and to assign, as the ultimate reason for every rule which they establish, the convenience and necessities of mankind' (p. 195). Argument terminates with what is '*beneficial* to human society', the fact of a '*useful* purpose'. In the *Treatise*, however, 'utility', to which the whole of Section V of the *Enquiry* II is devoted, is never more than a function of sympathy. Thus the 'pleasure' at the design of a fortified town which 'arises from the utility, not the form of the objects, can be no other than a sympathy with the inhabitants', a sympathy which transcends the particular interest of the person who observes the design (*Treatise*, p. 450). So too, the 'utility' of 'justice', its conduciveness to 'the good of society', 'where our own interest is not concern'd, or that of our friends, pleases only by sympathy' (p. 577). In the *Enquiry* II, the formulation of 'those rules, which are, on the whole, most *useful* and *beneficial*' (p. 195) needs, it appears, no such recourse to sympathy. What is 'useful' is itself held out as a sufficient criterion, and the idea of society as 'company', as the unanimity of mutually overflowing affections, recedes further into the background.

In the *Enquiry* II, justice and its 'institutions' 'arise merely from the necessities of human society' (p. 202), and the satisfaction of these 'necessities' is taken as a sufficient basis for moral approbation: 'The necessity of justice to the support of society is the sole foundation of that virtue; and since no moral excellence is more highly esteemed, we may conclude that this circumstance of usefulness has, in general, the strongest energy, and most entire command over our sentiments' (p. 203). But in the *Treatise*, to return to a passage that I have already discussed, *'the source of the* moral approbation *which attends that virtue'* of *'justice'* is specifically 'a sympathy *with public interest'* (pp. 499–500). It is the role of sympathy in the earlier work which distinguishes this formula from the discussion of justice in terms of 'necessity' and 'utility' in the *Enquiry* II.[32] In the *Treatise* sympathy is that which allows society to be represented as both the government and the compatibility of positions and interests. Even 'when the injustice is so distant from us, as no way to affect our interest, it still displeases us; because we consider it as prejudicial to human society, and pernicious to every one that approaches the person guilty of it. We partake of their uneasiness by *sympathy'* (p. 499). In the *Enquiry* II, on the contrary, justice is referred to a 'political society' in which 'the sole foundation of the duty of allegiance is the *advantage* which it procures to society, by preserving peace and order among mankind' (p. 205). Throughout Book III of the *Treatise*, sympathy plays a crucial role in the identification of justice as a 'virtue'. In the Appendix on 'Justice' in the *Enquiry* II, sympathy is seen to explain only the limited instincts which bind a person to friends or family (pp. 303–4). Any wider loyalty to 'the social virtues of justice and fidelity' is explicable only with reference to their 'public utility'.

---

[32] It also distinguishes this formula from Locke's influential political analysis of the institutions of justice. For Locke, justice arises out of conventions recognized as essential to the stability of power and possessions, and thus of society itself: 'Men unite into Societies, that they may have the united strength of the whole Society to secure and defend their Properties, and may have *standing Rules* to bound it, by which every one may know what is his', John Locke, *Two Treatises of Government*, ed. P. Laslett (New York, 1965), 404. See generally 'The Second Treatise of Government', Chs. 9–11, pp. 395–409. Though I do not investigate the inheritance from Locke, it is clear that Hume's *Enquiry* II sticks much more closely than the *Treatise* to a Lockian conception of justice.

With the detachment of utility from sympathy comes also the production of a 'natural', inherent, 'benevolence' or 'humanity', no longer dependent on the understanding, the mutual reverberations, which sympathy excited in the *Treatise*. In the Appendix 'Concerning Moral Sentiment' of the *Enquiry* II, utility is declared the 'foundation of moral praise' with the qualification that 'a *sentiment*' (opposed here to 'reason') 'should here display itself, in order to give a preference to the useful above the pernicious tendencies. This sentiment can be no other than a feeling for the happiness of mankind, and a resentment of their misery' (p. 286). We have a naturalization of 'benevolence'; this both fills and reveals the gap left by the displacement of sympathy. For in the *Treatise*, 'the good of society, where our own interest is not concern'd, pleases only by sympathy' (p. 577). The fact that 'there is no human, and indeed no sensible, creature, whose happiness or misery does not, in some measure, affect us . . . proceeds merely from sympathy, and is no proof of such an universal affection to mankind' (p. 481).[33] In the *Enquiry* II, however, the key element in Hume's attempt to repudiate the tyranny of 'self-love' is 'a general benevolence in human nature' (p. 300). Sympathy, where it appears, is not the condition of, but merely another synonym for, 'a general benevolence, of humanity' (p. 298). As P.H. Nidditch points out in his Introduction to the *Enquiries*, whereas Hume stated in the *Treatise* that 'there is no such passion in human minds as the love of mankind merely as such, independent of personal qualities, of services, or of relation to oneself' (p. 481), 'benevolence' has become in the *Enquiry* II a primary feature of 'human nature', a 'natural philanthropy'.[34] Hume, as Duncan Forbes puts it, 'retreated from the suggestive and original analysis of sympathy in the *Treatise* to the classical "humanity" or "fellow-feeling" of the *Enquiry* as the "origin of morals."[35]

The at least uneven use of 'benevolence' in Hume's writings is enough of a demonstration that this concept is not always or necessarily integrated into eighteenth-century descriptions of

[33] For the distinction between sympathy and a more general tendency to compassion or benevolence, see G.R. Morrow, 'The Significance of the Doctrine of Sympathy in Hume and Adam Smith', *The Philosophical Review*, 32 (1923), 60–78.

[34] P.H. Nidditch, Introduction to David Hume, *Enquiries Concerning Human Understanding and Concerning the Principles of Morals* (Oxford, 1979), p.xxv. See also Philip Mercer, *Sympathy and Ethics* (Oxford, 1972), 42.

[35] Forbes, *Hume's Philosophical Politics*, 15.

sociability based on sympathy—on the confluence of 'sentiments'. The point needs making because the supposed influence of ideologies of benevolence has particularly interested those who have sought to connect the discourses of moral philosophy with those of narrative fiction in this period. Brissenden's *Virtue in Distress* is perhaps the most lucid and knowledgeable version of an account which sees a belief in benevolent human capacities at the roots of both types of writing.[36] To understand the language of sympathy and sentiment it is necessary, I think, to question the plausibility of such an account. Later chapters of this book will describe the ways in which much of what is called 'sentimental' fiction actually depicts benevolence as a limited and exceptional propensity. Within moral philosophy, meanwhile, Hume's *Treatise* seems precisely committed to finding an alternative to a naturalized benevolence. Even if this is an attempt which meets with only limited success, despite all the philosopher's ingenuity, and even if it is negated by Hume's later writings, at this stage it is central to his experimental science of human nature.[37] Apart from anything else, it distinguishes Hume's steadfast adherence to secular argument from the final religiosity of many contemporary discussions of benevolence.

The absence of religious reference from Hume's accounts of fellow-feeling precludes the kind of naturalization of benevolence to be found in the work of some of his contemporaries. For a writer such as David Hartley, 'Benevolence' as 'the grand design and purport of human life, of the present probationary state' could receive religious sanction.[38] For him the final effacement of difference which is the goal and the imperative of benevolence is found when 'all become members of the mystical body of Christ'.[39] Hutcheson, too, constructed what Duncan Forbes calls 'a profoundly religious system' in which benevolence and happiness could only properly be understood with reference to God as 'the supreme objective good'.[40] Having turned away from religious hypothesis, Hume cannot seek such sanction. Yet, in the *Enquiry* II,

---

[36] See, for instance, Brissenden, Chs. 2 and 3.

[37] Alasdair MacIntyre addresses this issue, but seems to me to have given an influentially mistaken account of the transition from *Treatise* to *Enquiry*, and of the importance of sympathy for Hume. This is because he conflates sympathy and benevolence, which may fit the *Enquiry* II, but misrepresents the *Treatise*. See *After Virtue*, pp. 47-8, and MacIntyre, Introduction, *Hume's Ethical Writings* ed. MacIntyre (New York, 1965), 15.   [38] Hartley, *Observations on Man*, 477.

[39] Ibid. 476.   [40] See Forbes, *Hume's Philosophical Politics*, 58.

he must try to represent benevolence as in excess of any imputation of 'selfishness': 'It is sufficient for our present purpose, if it be allowed, what surely, without the greatest absurdity cannot be disputed, that there is some benevolence, however small, infused into our bosom' (p. 271). The qualifications of this prose are a measure of the awkwardness with which the philosopher surrenders the territory which the *Treatise* has set out to colonize. Here, 'where every thing else is equal', 'benevolence' appears from behind the normal bulk of 'interest' and involvement to induce 'a cool preference'. When all else, we are told, is removed, forgotten, or suppressed, it remains. Now 'the principles of humanity' must 'have *some* authority over our sentiments, and give us a general approbation of what is useful to society, and blame of what is dangerous or pernicious' (*Enquiry* II. 226).

This possibility of 'cool preference' is linked to a revision of Hume's earlier 'account of the passions'. Without a controlling sympathy, the passions cannot be allowed to govern as before. In the *Enquiry* II, the separation of passion and reason, a separation which allows passion to be the very stuff of sympathy, is no longer absolute. Now it is possible that 'The judgement . . . corrects the inequalities of our internal emotions' (*Enquiry* II. 227); it may well be 'requisite to employ much reasoning, in order to feel the proper sentiment' (p. 173). In the *Treatise*, 'Moral distinctions . . . are not the offspring of reason. Reason is wholly inactive, and can never be the source of so active a principle as conscience, or a sense of morals' (p. 458). In the *Enquiry* II, however, Hume writes that the 'arguments on each side'—for either 'reason' or 'sentiment' as 'the general foundation of Morals'—'are so plausible, that I am apt to suspect, they may, the one as the other, be solid and satisfactory, and that *reason* and *sentiment* concur in almost all moral determinations and conclusions' (p. 172). With the marginalization of sympathy in the latter work, passion and sentiment lose their force and their synonymity. For it is when Hume writes of sympathy or communication in the *Treatise* that passion and sentiment become interchangeable. So 'the pleasure which we receive from praise, arises from a communication of sentiments', whilst the shock of 'contempt' stems from 'the passion . . . receiv'd by sympathy' (p. 324). As P. S. Ardal says, sympathy in this text is not equivalent to 'compassion' or 'pity'; it is a 'principle of communication' which is not itself a passion, but which stands for the spread and articulation of passions.[41] In the *Enquiry* II, sympathy, when mentioned, has become merely a member of the general class of 'beneficence and humanity, friendship and gratitude, natural affection and public spirit' (p. 178). With this marginalization, passion and sentiment cease to be the very materials of sociability. The inescapably *social* identity which sympathy produces in the *Treatise* gives way to a conventional list of social virtues in the *Enquiry* II; these must stand against the forces of self-interest that, with sympathy relinquished, threaten once again.

The alterations in Hume's account of sociability can be seen most clearly in the transformation of Book III of the *Treatise* into the *Enquiry Concerning the Principles of Morals*, where sympathy is marginalized or abandoned. Notable also, though, is the fact that the discourse 'Of the Passions' which constituted Book II of the *Treatise*, and which was to be the basis for 'morals, criticism and politics', plays no really important role in Hume's later arguments. It is not that Hume was never to discuss 'the passions' again, for a wry or cautionary attention to the kinds of 'passion' that condition material and political ambitions in a commercial society is a characteristic of his *Essays*, it is rather that 'the passions' are never again to be the currency of social intercourse. Indeed, it could be argued that it is the description, in the *Essays*, of passions as potentially divisive appetites peculiarly excited in a commercial society which bars any later appeal to the socialized passions of the *Treatise*. Book II of the *Treatise* was not just left behind, and was recast as 'Of the Passions', the second of the *Four Dissertations* of 1757. But here the substance of the earlier description of the workings of sympathy, the communication of passions or sentiments, is simply absent. Missing entirely is the emphasis on sympathy as a principle demanding fundamental explication, that 'remarkable . . . phaenomenon' which 'merits our attention, and must be trac'd up to its first principles' (*Treatise*, p. 317). The discussion of sociability is ruthlessly abbreviated, and reference to sympathy condensed to what, at the time, could have been little more than truism: 'Our opinions of all kinds are strongly affected by society and sympathy, and it is almost impossible for us to support any principle or sentiment, against the universal consent

41 P.S. Ardal, *Passion and Value in Hume's Treatise* (Edinburgh, 1966), 51. See also Mercer, *Sympathy and Ethics*, 21.

of every one, with whom we have any friendship or correspondence.[42]

In the writings of the 1750s, the intercourse of feeling persists only as a kind of residual ideal. In the *Enquiry* II, for instance, Hume declares, as a parenthesis to his main argument, that the 'merit of benevolence, arising from utility' is not the only source of 'that esteem, which is so universally paid to it':

> It will also be allowed, that the very softness and tenderness of the sentiment, its engaging endearments, its fond expressions, its delicate attentions, and all that flow of mutual confidence and regard, which enters into a warm attachment of love and friendship: it will be allowed, I say, that these feelings, being delightful in themselves, are necessarily communicated to the spectators, and melt them into the same fondness and delicacy. The tear naturally starts in our eye on the apprehension of a warm sentiment of this nature: our breast heaves, our heart is agitated, and every humane tender principle of our frame is set in motion, and gives us the purest and most satisfactory enjoyment. (p. 257)

This moment of rhapsody (from which any explicit reference to sympathy is absent) is actually rather close to the language of the novel of sentiment. Such heavings and agitations are the usual manifestations of sociable instinct in much of the fiction discussed in following chapters. So it is perhaps appropriate that Hume goes on to represent the arousal of such 'warm sentiment' as a peculiarly literary capacity, most often to be identified with 'the great charm of poetry' (*Enquiry* II. 259). In the influences of sentiment are to be found a special, but also an occasional, pleasure: the connoisseur's enjoyment rather than the experience of a universally evident process. Hume's metaphor tells the story. Even in this rhapsody, the delight of this 'sentiment' is the privilege of 'spectators'; even here is a distance from the '*immediate* sympathy', the 'correspondent movements', of the *Treatise* (pp. 604–5).

In the early work of Hume's friend and admirer Adam Smith this distance is keenly exploited; spectatorial aloofness is made the condition of the operation of sympathy. In Smith's *Theory of Moral Sentiments*, first published in 1759, sympathy may be, as one eighteenth-century reader put it, 'a general principle, like that of gravity in the natural world';[43] it is, however, much altered from the

---

[42] Hume, *Four Dissertations* (London, 1757), 149.

[43] James Wodrow, quoted in D.D. Raphael and A.L. Macfie, Introduction, *Theory*, 3.

Treatise. Through the elaborate and exhaustive model-making of the *Theory* the overflowing of feeling is subjected to an inflexible rule of example, and sympathy is tethered to a concept of 'communication' based upon a specific distinction; this distinction, the basis of relations within society, is that between 'spectator' and 'agent'. Sympathy, for Smith, operates only in the space of this distinction, only according to the stability of two positions which are, of course, neither equivalent nor opposite, for the 'spectator' must always 'know' more than the 'agent'. For the young Hume, sympathy involved a direct reproduction of the 'passions' of 'others'. For Smith it is 'the thought of his situation, in the breast of every attentive spectator' which leads to an 'analogous emotion' (*Theory*, p. 10). This 'emotion' can be produced most accurately as 'our imagination's copy', by 'changing places in fancy' (p. 9). But no longer can 'the very passion itself' (*Treatise*, p. 316) be produced: 'Our heart must adopt the principles of the agent and go along with all the affections which influenced his conduct, before it can entirely sympathize with and beat time to, the gratitude of the person who has been benefited by his actions' (*Theory*, p. 73). Sympathy is conditional on the spectator having the necessary information, and on 'his' subsequent reflections and efforts. In certain cases, the superiority of the spectator is such as to allow sympathy to be a corrective rather than a reproductive mechanism:

Sympathy . . . does not arise so much from the view of the passion, as from that of the situation which excites it. We sometimes feel for another, a passion of which he himself seems to be altogether incapable; because, when we put ourselves in his case, that passion arises in our breast from the imagination, though it does not in his from the reality. (*Theory*, p. 12)

In facilitating communication, Smith's sympathy must also organize relations within society. It cannot allow passions and sentiments to flow absolutely freely, as they do in Hume's *Treatise*, but must subject them to the controlling distinction between spectator and agent.

Such a distinction is not implicit in Hume's treatment of sympathy in the *Treatise*, though the spectatorial point of view has become a useful reference for him by the time of the *Enquiry* II.[44] Indeed, in this later work, the reference to a spectatorial standard of judgement

---

[44] Here I disagree with D. D. Raphael, 'The Impartial Spectator', *Proceedings of the British Academy*, 58 (1972). See also Ardal, *Passion and Value*, 151.

actually implies a move away from sympathy. In the *Enquiry* II, 'The hypothesis which we embrace . . . defines virtue to be whatever mental action or quality gives to a spectator the pleasing sentiment of approbation; and vice the contrary'. In the *Treatise*, the formula is slightly, but importantly, different. 'All morality depends upon our sentiments; and when any action, or quality of the mind, pleases us *after a certain manner*, we say it is virtuous' (p. 517). In this work, all discussion of the nature and movement of sentiments is governed by the deployment, not of the figure of the spectator, but of the pronouns 'we', 'you', and 'us'. 'Nothing can be more real, or concern us more, than our own sentiments of pleasure and uneasiness' (p. 469). 'We' are bound together by sympathy—the principle that makes explicable shared judgements without any absolutely disinterested imposition of moral criteria. The metaphor of spectatorial scrutiny is simply at odds with a version of sympathy which allows for the natural mutuality of passions and sentiments.

This point is clarified in an indirect exchange between Hume and Smith issuing in a footnote which Smith added to the second edition of the *Theory*. In 1759 Hume wrote to Smith praising the *Theory* but objecting to the proposition that 'all kinds of Sympathy are necessarily Agreeable'.[45] Surely 'there is a disagreeable Sympathy, as well as an agreeable'—the sympathy with pain or distress. If this were not so, Hume remarked in his letter, 'An Hospital would be a more entertaining Place than a Ball'. In his footnote Smith rejects the charge of incoherence: 'I answer, that in the sentiment of approbation there are two things to be taken notice of; first, the sympathetic passion of the observer; and, secondly, the emotion which arises from his observing the perfect coincidence between this sympathetic passion in himself, and the original passion in the person principally concerned' (*Theory*, p. 46). Sympathy becomes in itself a principle of pleasure, whether it be sympathy with 'pleasure' or with 'pain'. It is the 'observing' of the 'perfect coincidence', rather than the 'coincidence' itself, which is all-important. The pleasure derived from sympathy, in the *Theory*, confirms distinction (between spectator and agent) as well as coincidence. So distance facilitates judgement. As P.S. Ardal writes, 'it seems approval does not just consist in noting the coincidence of

---

[45] *The Correspondence of Adam Smith*, ed. E.C. Mossner and I.S. Ross (Oxford, 1977), 43.

emotions: it consists in an emotion that arises when this coincidence is noted'.[46] This secondary 'emotion' is determined by the possibility of 'observing', a possibility which strictly controls the 'sympathetic passion' of the 'observer'. The 'sentiment of approbation', which consists in an 'emotion' which is 'always agreeable and delightful', stems from this observation, rather than from any immediate action of 'the sympathetic passion'. Sympathy consistently articulates and regulates the representation of 'the original passion in the person principally concerned'. So passions are no longer allowed, as they were in the *Treatise*, to reverberate freely. Sociability is moderated—a product of distance carefully maintained, self-control cannily preserved.

So, when Smith describes sympathy according to the estimations of a 'spectator', he radically corrects a central proposition of Hume's *Treatise*. He seeks, in fact, to remove sympathy from the realm of contending passions and interests: a willed uninvolvement precedes sympathetic identification. Although, for Smith, humans are 'naturally sympathetic', and despite 'some correspondence of sentiments', the spectator must 'endeavour, as much as he can, to put himself in the situation of the other', must 'strive to render as perfect as possible, that imaginary change of situation upon which his sympathy is founded' (p. 21). Smith's subsequent discussion of the conditions of power and applicability of sympathy is notably more elaborate and qualified than Hume's precisely because sympathy has become a propensity conditional upon the realization of the respective positions of 'spectator' and 'the person principally involved'. Examples have to be given and carefully differentiated because sympathy has to be controlled, the positions of spectatorship have to be identified and secured. No longer does sympathy denote an automatic and immediate movement of affections. While Hume likened 'the minds of all men' to 'strings equally wound up', which 'communicate' their vibrations to each other, Smith writes, 'the great pleasure of conversation and society, besides, arises from a certain correspondence of sentiments and opinion, from a certain harmony of minds, which like so many musical instruments coincide and keep time with one another' (p. 337). Smith pictures a unanimity which involves not a direct and unmediated relation between 'motions' but a generally 'delightful

46 Ardal, *Passion and Value*, 141.

harmony', an arena of possible 'unison' and concord rather than an all-embracing overflowing of sentiments.[47]

The shifting of position which Smith refers to in the *Theory*—a shifting which can only ever be 'imaginary', which is posited only on the very separation of 'spectator' and 'agent'—also becomes a means whereby sympathy facilitates self-judgement. In another appropriation of one of the images of Hume's *Treatise*, Smith introduces this topic by writing not of 'the minds of men' as 'mirrors to one another' but of society itself as a 'mirror'. Smith writes that a human being who, hypothetically, had had no 'communication with his own species' would not be able to think of 'his own character, or of the propriety or demerit of his own sentiments or conduct'. 'All these are objects which he cannot easily see, which naturally he does not look at, and with regard to which he is provided with no mirror which can present them to his view. Bring him into society, and he is immediately provided with the mirror which he wanted before' (p. 110).

More important than the similarity between Hume's and Smith's respective images is the difference between the two. For Hume there is a series of endless reflections, diminishing and finally untraceable reverberations which constitute a mutuality of sentiments without distinction, a continuous passing from one 'mind' to another. For Smith society itself is a 'mirror' which is 'placed in the countenance and behaviour of those he lives with'. The mirror is that which allows the subject to observe whether there is a sympathy between 'his' sentiments and those of others. In Humes's image, subject and object are different minds conjoined in an infinite regress of 'reflexions'; in Smith's image, the 'mirror' allows the one mind to become both subject and object, both 'agent' and 'spectator'. In the 1759 edition of the *Theory* 'we must imagine ourselves not the actors, but the spectators of our own character and conduct'

[47] See N. Phillipson, 'Adam Smith as Civic Moralist', in I. Hont and M. Ignatieff (eds.), *Wealth and Virtue: The Shaping of Political Economy in the Scottish Enlightenment* (Cambridge, 1983), 179–202. Phillipson distinguishes the operation of 'sympathy' in the *Theory* from a process which he calls 'empathy'. The former is the 'warier principle' (p. 185), enabling a 'system of social bonding' proper to a commercial age; the latter is seen to belong to a world 'associated with ideas of partriarchal authority and "dependence" and with the servile values of feudal civilization' (p. 188). The distinction is suggestive, but depends uneasily on the term 'empathy', which Smith himself never employs, and which does not seem precise enough to allow an accurate description of Hume's and Smith's different emphases upon sympathy.

(p. 111). In the 1761 edition, and all later editions, this is represented as the process whereby 'I divide myself, as it were, into two persons . . . the first is the spectator . . . the second is the agent' (p. 113). It is in terms of this construction that even processes of introspection are depicted.

Smith is concerned to demonstrate that 'we examine' our conduct 'as we imagine an impartial spectator would' (p. 110). We judge of our conduct as we judge of another's towards us when, 'upon placing ourselves in his situation, we thoroughly enter into all the passions and motives which influenced it'. So, in order to 'survey our own sentiments', we must 'remove ourselves, as it were, from our own natural station'. The aim is that 'we' should become spectators. It is sympathy which enables us to 'view' our 'sentiments and motives . . . with the eyes of other people or as other people are likely to view them' (*Theory*, p. 110). What, in Hume's *Treatise*, was a 'principle' devised not to negate self-interest but to transcend it, is now one which subordinates self-interest to the possibility of 'impartiality'. To become the spectator is not to be possessed by the passion of others, but to be the arbiter of all sentiments. In the 1790 edition of the *Theory*, the sixth, and the last edition to have been revised by Smith himself, the identification of 'judgement', and self-judgement, with the attitude and resources of 'impartiality' is asserted more than ever. The logic of sympathy leads to the replacement of 'conscience' by 'the man within the breast', the construction of a necessary fiction whereby 'we conceive ourselves as acting in the presence of a person quite candid and equitable' (p. 129). In order to judge ourselves 'we must view . . . from the place and with the eyes of a third person . . . who judges with impartiality between us' (p. 134). This designation, first included in the edition of 1761, makes clear that 'consulting this judge within' involves a 'change' of 'position', an 'imaginary' movement, made in 'the light in which he is conscious that others will view him'. It does not involve the shared passions of the *Treatise*.

The Theory of Moral Sentiments does not only displace Hume's early theory of sympathy (a propensity subject to such restraints in Smith's work as to be on the threshold of redundancy); it also revives a deeply cautious and suspicious approach to the influences of passion. For Smith, the tendency of passion to act upon and overpower its subjects must be guarded against. At the very least, passion must be tutored and watched over. Even 'the man who acts according to the rules of perfect prudence, of strict justice, and of proper benevolence' is subject to its blandishments: 'his own passions are very apt to mislead him; sometimes to drive him and sometimes to seduce him to violate all the rules which he himself, in all his sober and cool hours, approves of' (*Theory*, p. 237). There are 'social and agreeable passions' which, when properly regulated, are not disruptive of the orders of society or language: 'Joy, grief, love, admiration, devotion, are all of them passions which are naturally musical' (*Theory*, p. 37). But the mechanisms of regulation provide the key to their promotion of sociability. The spectator is not to be drawn into just any palpitation of feeling or desire; passions and sentiments must be moderated if they are to arouse a justifying sympathy. Not for Smith the natural society of responsive subjectivities described in the *Treatise*. A person may only obtain sympathy 'by lowering his passion to that pitch, in which the spectators are capable of going along with him. He must flatten, if I may be allowed to say so, the sharpness of its natural tone, in order to reduce it to harmony and concord with the emotions of those who are about him' (*Theory*, p. 22). Only such an exercise in self-control can provide for a 'correspondence' of 'sentiments' which 'is sufficient for the harmony of society'.

It is not reason which is to govern passion. Smith is scarcely less sceptical than Hume about the capacities of reason, even if his phrasing is typically more diplomatic. His discussion of 'those Systems which make Reason the Principle of Approbation' (*Theory*, pp. 318–21) is written as a wry exercise in intellectual archaeology. He represents such 'Systems' as responses to Hobbes's 'doctrine' that standards of judgement 'were mutable and čhangeable, and depended upon the mere arbitrary will of the civil magistrate'. His own attitude to this 'doctrine' seems one of calculated ambivalence. A sense of his view of Hobbes depends, at this point in the text, on whether we think that Smith accepts his characterization of that philosopher's argument as 'odious', or merely quotes it as a conventional, but not necessarily correct, opinion. Certainly, however, there is no ambiguity in what follows 'Pleasure and pain are the great objects of desire and aversion: but these are dis- tinguished not by reason, but by the immediate sense and feeling' (*Theory*, p. 320). Against the dictates of passion Smith sets not reason, but impartiality; the 'fury of our own passions' is limited by the prospect of entering 'more coolly intò the sentiments of the

indifferent spectator' (*Theory*, p. 157). The figure of this spectator
permits the restraining and the interrogation of the passions.

Supporting Smith's distinction between spectator and agent,
therefore, is his recourse to the language of Stoic philosophy.[48] It is
the Stoic virtue of 'self-command' which, throughout Smith's
writings, answers the riddle of seemingly limitless passions and
desires: 'Self-command is not only itself a great virtue, but from it all
the other virtues seem to derive their principal lustre' (*Theory*,
p. 241). It is, as Michael Ignatieff says, 'a language of the will, a
Stoic's language' which enables Smith to propose that 'men . . . can
keep their distances from the "great scramble of society" by learning
to judge their own conduct from the vantage point of an impartial
spectator'.[49] In this respect, the bond of sympathy has ceased to
unify the particular passions or sentiments of sociable individuals; it
does not provide in any simple way for the assurance of shared feeling. Instead it is the basis of the regulation of behaviour according
to an abstracted standard—'by regard to the sentiments of the supposed impartial spectator': 'Without the restraint which this principle
imposes, every passion would, upon most occasions, rush headlong,
if I may say so, to its own gratification' (*Theory*, pp. 262–3).

Yet the invocation of Stoic self-command is the sign of what can be
interpreted as either a point of weakness or a moment of resignation
in Smith's text. By his own account, such control and renunciation
require the exercise of exceptional discipline, and are liable to fail
even the most scrupulous of their practitioners. Smith's description,
with its constant stress on the intoxicating powers of passion, reads
more like the outline for a style of propriety to be observed by the
polite and far-seeing few than the scheme for an inclusive society of
discriminating spectators. By his own apparent definition, not all
will be able to perform such calculations. Thus we have a blurring of
the status of spectatorial judgement when Smith moves from the
notion of a sociability dependent upon one person's distanced
understanding of another, to that of judgement with reference to a
projected 'impartial spectator'. In fact, the standard that Smith
invokes implies an act of imagination. When he writes 'We must . . .
view ourselves not so much according to that light in which we may
naturally appear to ourselves, as according to that in which we

---

[48] See Raphael and Macfie, Introduction, *Theory*, 5–10.
[49] Ignatieff, *The Needs of Strangers*, 122. See also the rest of his chapter 'The
Market and the Republic', ibid. 105–31.

naturally appear to others', he requires the availability of a necessarily hypothetical viewpoint (*Theory*, p. 83). A 'man' 'must . . . humble the arrogance of his self-love, and bring it down to something which other men can go along with', in order to 'act so as that the impartial spectator may enter into the principles of his conduct, which is what of all things he has the greatest desire to do'. It is the 'supposed' criterion of impartiality that is paramount; it is the ambiguity of Smith's 'must'—indicating either natural necessity or Stoic moral duty—that registers the intangibility of this criterion.

Unable to conceive of any natural community of sentiments such as that initially supposed by Hume, Smith actually extends sympathy beyond any idea of the immediate transference of feeling, beyond—it might be said—any practical contact. He requires the saving presumption that the 'moral sentiments' of any person 'suppose the idea of some other being, who is the natural judge of the person that feels them; and it is only by sympathy with the decisions of this arbiter of his conduct, that he can conceive either the triumph of self-applause, or the shame of self condemnation' (*Theory*, p. 193). He constructs a subjectivity whose behaviour and judgements are inherently socialized, and yet one which is raised above the passions which dominate 'the game of human society' (*Theory*, p. 234). That game itself is played according to rules which are not explicable in a language of sentiment and sympathy alone. Though Smith remains wedded to a discourse of moral philosophy, he has begun to glimpse its ideological limitations. These limitations are encountered in the periodic necessity for him to refer to the specifically political constitution of society—to the purposes of justice and the practices of government. For while such reference allows Smith to avoid the reliance upon sympathy of Hume's *Treatise*, or the naturalized benevolence of the *Enquiry* II, it produces its own kind of contradiction. Take as an example Smith's discussion of justice. He provides a basically political analysis suggesting that the structural necessity of justice is in excess of considerations of benevolence:

Society may subsist among different men, as among different merchants, from a sense of its utility, without any mutual love or affection . . . Beneficence . . . is less essential to the existence of society than justice. Society may subsist, though not in the most comfortable state, without beneficence; but the prevalence of injustice must utterly destroy it. (*Theory*, p. 86)

Yet he also wants to argue that a consideration of social utility does not itself constitute our approval of 'the enforcement of the laws of justice' (p. 87): 'few men have reflected upon the necessity of justice to the existence of society, how obvious soever that necessity may appear to be' (p. 89). He simply does not believe in the capacity of 'men' to calculate and recalculate the social utility of particular actions. This, however, leads to the possibility that the 'concern which we take in the fortune and happiness of individuals'—and which is the basis of a judgement of any given operation of justice—is no more than a convenient illusion. For according to this analysis, the moral discourse by which an interest in the workings of justice is articulated does not actually explain the structural necessity of those workings.

In the event, Smith vacillates. He goes on to assert that 'Upon some occasions . . . we both punish and approve of punishment, merely from a view to the general interest of society, which, we imagine, cannot otherwise be secured' (p. 90). Indeed, he invokes, the 'firmness and resolution' by which a 'man of humanity' may have to correct his benevolent tendencies in order to agree with the demands of justice. As elsewhere in the *Theory*, the Stoic effort of self-command is the only guarantee of an understanding superior to the compulsions of particular feeling. But as such effort is exceptional, it is also uncertain. It is not the process always underlying an individual's judgements and allegiances. Smith's political analysis discovers a clarity of vision as apparently uncommon and implicitly momentary as Hume's philosophical scepticism. The prudence and self-command which allow such an analysis to be acted upon cannot be assumed to be generally available. So the purpose of the analysis becomes a stringent political conservatism. In Hume's *Treatise*, the tendencies of 'human nature' in themselves guaranteed, albeit by some stretch of the imagination, an allegiance to the institutions of justice; in the *Theory*, where fluctuating passions and desires are above all mistrusted, the stability of political society, the preservation of a status quo, becomes a fundamental value in itself, separated out from the customs of moral discourse. A respect for 'established powers and privileges' and a resistance to schemes of political innovation or improvement is a prerequisite for the reliability of moral judgement (see *Theory*, pp. 232–4). Human beings are not always (or not only) the unreflecting toys of interest and affection, but only in a commercial society whose political forms are secured, even though in a state of imperfection, can moral judgement be purposeful or sympathetic identification be trustworthy.[50]

It is not surprising, then, that Smith's construction of sympathy is strained. The reign of feeling and passion proclaimed in Hume's *Treatise* is over, but at a cost. The moral and the political descriptions which are supposed to be complementary in the *Theory* are found to contend with each other as well. Such strains show up more clearly still if we set the *Theory* alongside Smith's *Inquiry into the Nature and Causes of the Wealth of Nations*, published in 1776. Obviously Smith did not see the later, and more famous, analysis of 'police, revenue, and arms' as invalidating or superseding his arguments about moral judgement; indeed, he continued revising and republishing the *Theory* up to 1790.[51] Yet the retrospect which the *Wealth of Nations* inevitably suggests does now allow for a clearer realization of the incapacities of his writing on 'moral sentiments'. In the *Theory*, for example, Smith uses this conceit in his discussion of how 'every man' pursues 'his own happiness' over that of others:

In the race for wealth, and honours, and preferments, he may run as hard as he can, and strain every nerve and every muscle, in order to outstrip all his competitors. But if he should jostle, or throw down any of them, the indulgence of the spectators is entirely at an end. It is a violation of fair play, which they cannot admit of . . . They readily, therefore, sympathize with the natural resentment of the injured, and the offender becomes the object of their hatred and indignation. He is sensible that he becomes so, and feels that those sentiments are ready to burst out from all sides against him. (*Theory*, p. 83)

In *The Wealth of Nations*, the race may be the same still, but no such supposition of restraining spectatorial judgement is necessary to the workings of society. In this work interests are arranged and organized according, most importantly, to the concept of 'the

[50] In a crude fashion, I have used Donald Winch's analysis in his *Adam Smith's Politics: An Essay in Historiographical Revision* (1979; rpt. Cambridge, 1979); see pp. 167–177.

[51] See the Advertisement to the 6th edition, reprinted in the Oxford edition of the *Theory*, for Smith's confirmation of the two works as distinct yet non-contradictory projects. For a contemporary account of this, see Dugald Stewart, *Biographical Memoirs of Adam Smith, of William Robertson, and of Thomas Reid* (1793; rpt. Edinburgh, 1811).

division of labour', and are described in a writing which divorces itself from an allegiance to any of the 'orders of . . . civilized society', the interests of which it can distinguish more clearly than the members of such 'orders' themselves.[52] Benevolence and sympathy have no place in this text. The relations enacted in patterns of exchange and the division of labour are in excess of 'friendship' or 'benevolence'. 'Man' in 'civilised society' 'stands at all times in need of the co-operation and assistance of great multitudes, while his whole life is scarce sufficient to gain the friendship of a few persons'.[53] As Istvan Hont and Michael Ignatieff have said, 'the whole burden of the analysis of the *Wealth of Nations*' is committed to a demonstration that, via the stimulation of 'agricultural production in a system of competitive markets', a society could evolve in which the material well-being of all would depend on 'neither the generosity of individuals nor the interventions of the magistrate'.[54] Fellow-feeling might ornament such a society, but would not be intrinsic to its proper functioning.

Hont and Ignatieff describe Smith as transposing 'the question of justice' from 'the terrain of jurisprudence and political theory' to 'the terrain of political economy';[55] it is not the purpose of this study to follow Smith across such territory, nor is it to propose a teleology in which *The Wealth of Nations* is the foreordained end of a consistent project. It should be recognized, though, that the *Theory of Moral Sentiments*, in its earliest form, is already moving away from Hume's moral theory; it is trying to find alternatives to either the pure sociability of the *Treatise* or the naturalized benevolence of the *Enquiry* II. Some of the time it attempts to stretch the language of such moral theory to fit a description of how passions are regulated by individual self-command; some of the time it introduces metaphors of society which could have no place in a text like the *Treatise*. So society, according to the 'political view' available to Smith, can be represented as 'an immense machine, whose regular and harmonious movements produce a thousand agreeable effects' (*Theory*, p. 316); it is the task of the public-spirited legislator to manage, rather than to amend, the workings of this machine. Here,

---

52 *The Wealth of Nations*, i. 276.
53 Ibid. i. 34.
54 Hont and Ignatieff, 'Needs and Justice in the *Wealth of Nations*: An Introductory Essay', in id., *Wealth and Virtue*, 24.
55 Ibid. 25.

as elsewhere, Smith's model recalls the writings of Mandeville as much as those of Hume. As Mandeville declared himself interested in society only as 'a body politic', in which 'man' 'is become a disciplined creature',[56] so Smith is committed to society as a 'system' dependent upon 'the several wheels of the machine of government', and not just as the forum for the action of sympathy. Smith's metaphors lead two ways because he is able to rely solely on neither a theory of sociability nor one of the political and expedient organization of social relations. He adheres to the discourse of moral philosophy, but cannot put his whole faith in it. Even when his vocabulary does appear to be closest to that previously employed in Hume's elaboration of morals, his theory is not one of unreserved sociability.

In a sense, then, Smith's sympathy works in the opposite direction to Hume's. Hume generalizes the model of particular contact or connection to explain all social relations; Smith insists on all specific interactions or conflicts being referred to an abstract and universal standard. In Hume's *Treatise*, sympathy is crucial as that which promises to harmonize interest. The 'tendency' of a person's 'passions' can be judged, '*not* with impartiality, but' 'by a sympathy with the sentiments of those, who have a more particular connexion with him' (*Treatise*, p. 602). For Hume, sympathy can always invent or elaborate a contact which can transcend particular interests and render passions intelligible. 'We are oblig'd to forget our own interest in our judgements of this kind by reason of the perpetual contradictions, we meet with in society and conversation, from persons that are not placed in the same situation, and have not the same interest with ourselves' (*Treatise*, p. 602). Society, for Hume, is stable and harmonious in as much as sympathy permits its constitution as an 'intercourse of sentiments' which 'in society and conversation, makes us form some general inalterable standard, by which we may approve or disapprove of characters and manners' (p. 603). For Smith, such an 'intercourse of sentiments' cannot generally be available outside the production of certain positions for a socialized subjectivity—and the fixity of these positions is incompatible with the flow of affections which the *Treatise* had envisaged.

In his *Treatise* Hume attempts to outline a theory of morals and a

---

[56] Mandeville, *The Fable of the Bees*, 213.

theory of sociability which are inextricable; in Smith's *Theory*, the two are becoming unstuck. One way of putting this is to say that Smith does not trust in sociability: thus the transformation of the workings of sympathy, a concept at the centre of their theories of both society and morals. When Hume writes that 'morality' is 'more properly felt than judged of' (*Treatise*, p. 469), he puts his faith in neither an innate moral sense nor a prevailing tendency to benevolence; his later retrenchments only make this clearer. He rests his case on the unhinderable flow of feeling and passion, and on the sympathy that makes it possible. Smith's insistence, on the contrary, that feeling be regulated and chastened draws on strands from Stoic philosophy and political theory to order rather than to celebrate feeling and passion. His use of Stoic concepts involves a rhetoric of recommendation and admonishment, a prescription for conduct; his habits of political description are more clinically 'anatomical' than anything in the *Treatise*. These approaches may seem opposed, but they have in common a narrative strategy. In both cases, the philosopher removes himself from the world of passions, whether to correct or merely to describe what he sees. The ease of this removal perhaps most fundamentally distinguishes the *Theory* from the *Treatise*. For what the *Treatise* above all interrogates is a problematic relationship between 'philosophy' and 'nature', a distance between the two which is a worry. One of the points, on the contrary, of Smith's *Theory* is to construct a social subject ideally able to pose passion and feeling as other, safely experienced only vicariously. Its narrator has no qualms about cleaving to this ideal.

Hume's *Treatise*, then, is central to an account of the language of sentiment and feeling in the eighteenth century not merely because of its insistent vocabulary and its attention to the nature of social instinct. It is not just that Hume sets out more rigorously than any other philosopher to analyse the basic processes of sociability. It is also, and finally, because of the pressure that Hume's project is under—the pressure, above all, to generalize a society of particular contacts—that his moral philosophy is singular. It is because of this that it intersects with the prevailing concerns of the novelists to whose works I will now turn. For the universality of social understanding which Hume's philosophy of 'human nature' proposes is precisely what is questioned (and typically rejected) in the novel of sentiment.

2

Richardson: Sentiment and the Construction of Femininity

Instruction . . . is the Pill; Amusement is the Gilding.
(Samuel Richardson, Letter to Lady Echlin, September 1755)[1]

IN his *Life of Johnson*, James Boswell records several instances of a dispute with his mentor over the respective merits of the novels of Fielding and Richardson. On one occasion, Boswell's admiration for Fielding's 'very natural pictures of human life' is met by Johnson's dismissal of the novelist as 'a barren rascal' and his declaration that 'there is more knowledge of the heart in one letter of Richardson's, than in all *Tom Jones*'.[2] When it is suggested that Richardson is 'tedious', Johnson retorts, 'Why, Sir, if you were to read Richardson for the story, your impatience would be so much fretted that you would hang yourself. But you must read him for the sentiment, and consider the story as only giving occasion to the sentiment.' When this judgement is cited now, it is usually at Richardson's expense. If his novels are famous for anything, it is the slow rate of their fastidious analyses and accretions. Yet there can be no doubt that Johnson meant it as praise—that he considered 'sentiment' in some sense superior to 'story'. If his comment has become a well-worn literary joke about some of the lengthiest and least obviously eventful novels in the language, it is in part because it is no longer clear what the practice of reading might be that Johnson recommends in prefering Richardson over Fielding. What is it (or was it) to read 'for the sentiment'?

In one way, the currency of 'moral sentiments' in the philosophy of the period can serve as a clue to this meaning. What Hume and Smith describe when they use this phrase are at once feelings and

[1] Carroll, 322.
[2] James Boswell, *Life of Johnson*, ed. R. W. Chapman (1904; rpt, Oxford, 1980), 480.

judgements—instincts and opinions. In a similar usage, Johnson, when he advises his companions to read 'for the sentiment', conflates the morally instructive content of Richardson's narratives and the 'knowledge of the heart' which they display. That the latter is not simply a matter of naturalistic technique is made clear in Johnson's deprecation of the 'low life' to be found depicted in Fielding's novels. The replication of what is taken to be 'life' is not in itself a value; the matter of a text's 'knowledge' is not to be separated from its moral intent. The truths of sentiment are held for inspection by a narrative thought haughty of impropriety. The 'knowledge' to be gained from Richardson is supposed available precisely because of the scrupulous refinements of his texts, because of their avoidance (even if at a cost to the 'story') of all that might be 'low'.

Throughout the eighteenth century, those who extolled Richardson's novels as paragons of their form emphasized two things: these texts inculcated virtue, and they staged exquisite scenes of feeling and distress. The relationship between these two capacities of the novels, a relationship which continually preoccupied both Richardson and his readers, distinguishes the texts' 'sentimentalism'. If Richardson's writings have become in some ways alien or inaccessible to us, one reason is that their moral didacticism and their indulgence in cameos of lachrymose emotion together invite a practice of reading now forgotten. These preoccupations of the narratives have become foreign, or even embarrassing; for Johnson and for Richardson's other supporters, however, they raised the texts above the normal level of the novel's aspirations. They lent the form a new moral and stylistic density.

Whatever our judgements of their merits or sophistication, Richardson's novels can lay claim to a historical importance beyond dispute. They excited more contemporary admiration, and subsequent emulation, than those of any other novelist of the century. Crucially, Richardson made what we now call the novel respectable.[3] The fixation of his texts upon virtue, and upon the association of sensibility with moral rectitude, made plausible the deliverance of narrative fiction from the category of 'romance'—connotative of irresponsible fantasy and disreputable titillation. Indeed, it is difficult now to overestimate Richardson's

---

[3] As R. A. Day writes, '*Pamela* was something new in fiction, a novel which one need not be ashamed of reading', *Told in Letters: Epistolary Fiction Before Richardson* (Ann Arbor, Mich., 1966), 208.

influence on writers, and readers, of the eighteenth century. It is significant that Johnson should have been an advocate for Richardson's writing, for he was as suspicious as any of the supposed allure of romance.[4] Not all went so far as Diderot, who proclaimed the author of *Clarissa* the equal of Homer, Euripides, and Sophocles,[5] but scarcely any English novelist for at least thirty years after 1748—the publication date of the last volume of *Clarissa*—produced work which did not testify to admiration for, and often adulation of, Richardson's writing. Yet Richardson's texts, more influential than any others in directly validating the 'rise of the novel', have since become the objects of only specialist enthusiasm. They are often known at one remove—for their reputations alone. The last of Richardson's three novels, *Sir Charles Grandison*, has a borrowed place in literary history as the favourite of both Jane Austen, who worked on adapting it as a play, and George Eliot, who 'was sorry that the long novel was not longer'.[6] Despite its immense popularity and unrivalled prestige among eighteenth-century readers, even *Clarissa* has, until recently, remained at the margins of most literary canons. In the nineteenth century George Eliot bemoaned this: 'It is a solace to hear of any one's reading and enjoying Richardson. We have fallen on an evil generation who would not read "Clarissa" even in an abridged form.' In the twentieth century, Richardson's novels have often fallen victim to types of literary criticism willing to separate out a text's value from the history of its reception and influence. Q.D. Leavis's dismissive description of *Clarissa* as of 'almost entirely historical' interest (a pejorative use of 'historical' that historians might find rather odd) was one of the better known examples of a recoil from, rather than an explanation of, that novel's distance from modern tastes.[7] F.R. Leavis's declaration that 'it's no use pretending that Richardson can ever be made a current classic again' was for some time a self-fulfilling prophecy; there was little attention to the reasons for the gap between his texts' 'classic' status in their own age and their apparent inaccessibility in ours.[8]

---

[4] *The Rambler*, No. 4, (Mar. 1750), in *The Yale Edition of the Works of Samuel Johnson*, vol. iii, ed. W. J. Bate and A. B. Strauss (New Haven, Conn., 1969), 21–2.

[5] D. Diderot, *Eloge de Richardson*, in *Œuvres* (Paris, 1962), 1059–74.

[6] For Jane Austen's adaptation see *Sir Charles Grandison*, ed. B. Southam (Oxford, 1980). George Eliot's comment comes in a letter of 1876; see *The Yale Edition of the George Eliot Letters*, ed. G. S. Haight (7 vols., New Haven, Conn., 1954–5), vi. 320.

[7] Q. D. Leavis, *Fiction and the Reading Public* (1932; rpt. London, 1965), 99.

[8] See F. R. Leavis, *The Great Tradition* (1948; rpt. Harmondsworth, 1977), 13.

Most of the best-known attempts to revivify interest in
Richardson have actually gone along, to some extent, with the
Leavisite criteria, and have tried to argue for the neglected literary
merit of his works.[9] They have called attention to what are seen as
his powers of psychological analysis and naturalistic description.
Yet the 'sentiment' for which Johnson advised his companions to
read, the 'sentiment' which is moral reflection and insistent pathos,
has been left out of these accounts. It is possible to make a case for
Pamela and *Clarissa* as works of attentive realism, or for *Sir Charles
Grandison* as an innovative (if somewhat ponderous) drama of
manners. However, to make such arguments is, at some point, to
ignore Richardson's own evident concerns. Indeed, one of the
problems of rescuing the novels from the archive—of making them
readable again—has been their author's fastidious prescriptions for
their interpretation. Richardson attempts, in many ways, to show
how his books should be read. His editorial revisions, his
supplementary publications, the whole apparatus of introductions,
notes, and appendices: these are all directed at the explication of the
texts' moralism, and I will return to them later. The awkward fact
has been that the novels try to teach how to read 'for the sentiment',
and that their educative mechanisms are inseparable from their
resources of precision and intensity.[10] They are narratives in fact
built out of internalized parables of reading and writing—out of an
extraordinary specialization of epistolary forms—but they are not
abstract or disinterested meditations on what Richardson calls the
'converse of the pen'. They are texts committed to the least pluralistic
of projects: the teaching of virtue.

Johnson's implied disdain for those who read 'for the story' echoed
a conventional refrain; it was one which Richardson, when he
emphasized the commitment of his narratives to the cause of virtue,
reiterated with a new severity. In his Preface to the third edition of
Clarissa, he states that

considerate readers will not enter upon the perusal of the piece before them,
as if it were designed only to divert or amuse. It will probably be thought

9 The two most significant literary-critical recuperations of Richardson's
reputation are M. Kinkead-Weekes, *Samuel Richardson: Dramatic Novelist*
(London, 1973), and M. A. Doody, *A Natural Passion* (Oxford, 1974).

10 The embarrassment about Richardson's instructionalism lives on, even where
that trait is productively analysed: 'In Richardson's novels . . . art got the better of
moral instruction': R. Goldberg, *Sex and Enlightenment: Women in Richardson and
Diderot* (Cambridge, 1984), 28.

tedious to all such as dip into it, expecting a light novel, or transitory romance; and look upon story in it (interesting as that is generally allowed to be) as its sole end, rather than as a vehicle to the instruction. (p. xv)

Of course, in Richardson's awkwardly impersonal parenthesis is his recognition that he is to use the traditional tactics of the novel for his moral purposes—that his text must be as 'interesting' and engaging as any 'transitory romance'. But the 'instructive' potential of that text remains the guarantee of its aesthetic and moral value. Richardson sets out to be, as Hume would have put it, a 'painter' of virtue, and none of the actual ambiguities of his texts should allow us to forget this. The virtue he describes is realized in the capacity to feel and display sentiments, a capacity that is called 'sensibility'. This sensibility is not so much spoken as displayed. Its instrument is a massively sensitized, feminine body; its vocabulary is that of gestures and palpitations, sighs and tears. The vocabulary is powerful because it is not spoken (but only spoken of); it is everything that punctures or interrupts speech. All the later novelists of sentiment resort to this repertoire of wordless meanings; most reveal an obvious debt to Richardson when they do so. But for no novelist as ominously as for Richardson can speech be a terrain of possible conflict and imposition, blandishment and deceit. It is a consequence of his celebration of the currency of sentiment and feeling that the dangers and inadequacies of conversational protocols are thereby acknowledged. The special powers of feeling, the exceptional reaches of sympathy, are set against a world of twisted or broken communications.

* * *

If there were Sex in Heaven, good Women would be angels *there*, as they are *here*.
(Samuel Richardson, Letter to Sophia Westcomb, September 1746)[11]

In 1751, Richardson wrote in a letter to Lady Bradshaigh:

I own that a good woman is my favourite character; and that I can do twenty agreeable things for her, none of which would appear in a striking light in a

---

[11] Carroll, 69.

man. Softness of heart, gentleness of manners, tears, beauty, will allow of pathetic scenes in the story of one, which cannot have place in that of the other.[12]

An idea of feminine virtue—of the 'good woman'—ruled his relations with his predominantly female friends and admirers; it also conditioned his representation of the 'pathetic scenes' for which his narratives were renowned. His heroines record their virtuous sufferings in stories of 'the heart'—stories of rectitude and sensibility, of moral discernment and a noble capacity for feeling. At the centre of all three of his novels he has women writing with a 'Softness of heart' and a rigour of judgement—writing, in other words, of their 'sentiments'. The heart from which writing flows is a principle of constancy, inviolable and virtuous, but also of a keen susceptibility to ennobling feeling. Its pulses throb through the correspondence of Richardson's paragons of feminine virtue.

In *Pamela, or Virtue Rewarded*, Richardson's enormously successful first novel, the heroine describes a world of 'overflowing', 'aching', responsive hearts. Her correspondence with her parents ('such worthy hearts', i. 6) presumes a mutuality of finely attuned sensibilities—'Indeed, my dearest child, our hearts ache for you' (i. 3); 'Don't your heart ache for me? I am sure mine fluttered about like a new caught bird in a cage' (i. 21–22). The heart is the true, and 'honest', self, guiding Pamela's pen; she tells Mr B, 'I don't remember all I wrote, yet I know I wrote my heart, and that is not deceitful' (i. 203). The desire which drives Mr B to his attempts on Pamela's honour is that which temporarily dulls him to the ways of the heart: 'This love', declares Pamela's fellow servant, Mrs Jervis, 'is the d——l! In how many shapes does it make people shew themselves! And in some the farthest from their hearts' (i. 36). The triumph of Pamela's virtue involves a restoration of the rule of the heart, which is made to embrace the previously wicked or infatuated. In one of the more unprecedented transformations in any eighteenth-century novel, the lascivious predator becomes the solid man of virtue. Mr B is converted from insensibility, and learns, as he says, to 'speak the sentiments of my heart' (i. 365). He learns to acknowledge the source of Pamela's moral and descriptive eloquence: 'I love to hear this honest heart of yours speaking at your lips' (i. 269). The crisis is resolved, and full hearts and tearful eyes are the unchallenged

---

12 Carroll, 180.

condition of domestic felicity: 'I wonder not, my dear Pamela's father, that your honest heart springs thus to your eyes, to see all her trials at an end' (i. 275–6). This state of a heartfelt unanimity (where the plot, notoriously, stops dead) is the ideal envisaged in Richardson's first novel; it is not, however, always to be guaranteed in his fiction, or that of his many subsequent imitators. For a reliance on sentiment, on the promptings of the heart, comes with narratives not just concerned to describe virtue, but also preoccupied with metaphors of a virtue shown to be exceptional, defensive, beleaguered.

All Richardson's novels purport to reproduce, in the letters of their heroines, a decorous yet guilelessly tremulous language of feeling. The text which supposes such transcription relies on the image of the heart as the source of writing itself. The organ whose urgings were traditionally associated with romantic delusions has become a guarantee of truthfulness. The misunderstandings and prejudices which undermine social harmony can be comprehended only as they are set against such truth. Thus Clarissa's lament in Richardson's second novel: 'O! that my friends knew but my heart!—would but think of it as they used to do. For once more I say: If it deceive me not it is not altered, although theirs are!' (*Clarissa*, i. 411). While *Pamela* effects a reconciliation between the virtuous dictates of a young woman's heart and the practices of a social world, *Clarissa* envisages a heartfelt language cast off from the moorings of social habit. 'I know my own heart', asserts Clarissa (i. 404); its urgings sustain her against the tyranny of her family and then of her abductor. It has become the principle of the heroine's resistance to the insufferable demands with which she is beset. Unsupported by—indeed, contending against—the inclinations of the family on which she should be able to rely, Clarissa has only her heart.

For much of the book, her correspondence with Miss Howe is also the record, amidst catastrophe, of a dialogue with herself. It would seem a suitably Puritan model of what she calls 'close self-examination' (ii. 306) for Richardson the devout bourgeois, and the mode of a devotional exercise, a devout inspection of the self, does, of course, structure the confessional cadences of all his heroines' correspondences. In *Pamela*, where the heroine's exposition of her 'feelings' is often a soliloquy, the model is closest to the surface. But there is more to these stories of the heart than conformity to a religious pattern. The scrutiny of conscience is inextricable from an acquaintance with involuntary feeling, exquisite delicacy, suffering sensibility. It is 'a *feeling heart*' that Clarissa's sister is said to lack: 'The highest joy in this life she is not capable of: but then she saves herself many griefs by her impenetrableness' (i. 218). Clarissa herself, on the other hand, prizes her susceptibility to affection and distress. Indeed, she values her capacity for 'suffering'—the sign both of that susceptibility and the strictly moral resolution which controls it: 'the school of affliction' is 'an excellent school . . . in which we are taught to know ourselves, to be able to compassionate and bear with one another, and look up to a better hope' (iv. 2). In the 'sensible' passivity of such suffering, she holds to an unwavering habit of judgement, which is also sanctioned by the heart. Thus she writes in order to correct Miss Howe's suggestion that she has been over-modest:

Be pleased then to allow me to think that my motives on this occasion arise not *altogether* from maidenly niceness . . . they arise principally from what offers to my own heart; respecting, as I may say, its own rectitude, its own judgement of the *fit* and the *unfit*; as I would, without study, answer *for* myself *to* myself, in the *first* place, (ii. 306)

In the promptings of the heart are combined will, judgement, and feeling.

The terminally acquisitive Harlowes demand control over this mysterious organ. It is with trouble within the family that the narrative begins, and it is the attempt of the family to exercise power over Clarissa for the sake of its material and social aggrandizement that sets her tragedy in motion. This attempt involves the usurping of the very language of Clarissa's heart; constantly her mother resorts to the innuendo that that heart is improperly 'engaged'—that her resistance to the family's schemes is prompted by an infatuation with Lovelace: 'if your heart *be really free* . . .' is the reiterated and increasingly sardonic prologue to their 'dreadful' reasoning (see i. 70–7). By an extraordinary concentration of vocabulary (the property of a text which typically works through repetition and increment) the words which would allow Clarissa to speak her sentiments are denied her; as long as she remains in her parents' house, her imprisonment is more than physical. Though her body is to be made a token of exchange, her family want even more. In this drama of cupidity and possessiveness, the power over will and desire is as much at stake as the command of material destiny. 'The heart,

Clary, is what I want', insists her mother (i. 90); 'Your heart, not your knees, must bend' (i. 71). So Clarissa's only resourse is an almost silent resistance—'sobs still my only language' (i. 70). She is exiled from the society of familial conversation; speech brings only more demands: 'Since silence is your choice, hearken to me, and *be* silent'. Her mother decrees that she should not speak 'unless what you have to say will signify to me your compliance' (i. 96): 'Will you not, *can* you not, speak as I would have you speak?' With the 'freedom' of her heart questioned or derided, she has nothing but the choice of a negation: 'I offer only to preserve to myself the liberty of *refusal*, which belongs to my sex' (i. 226). The signs of her heart are maligned or ridiculed, and in the end cannot be spoken. So she trembles and swoons, her body the manifestation of her sensibility: 'I sighed. I wept. I was silent' (i. 82). Her resolute passivity is realized in the signs that are not speech: 'I wept. I knew not what to say; or rather how to express what I had to say' (i. 96). Her correspondence records—at length and repetitively—the situations of her silent resistance: 'I was speechless, absolutely speechless. Although my heart was ready to burst, yet could I neither weep nor speak' (i. 97).

But her silence and her passivity are also meaningful and assertive. Refusal has become the expression of necessary moral resolution. Clarissa concedes the economic power which her grandfather's will has vested in her to her family's avaricious plans, but her virtue cannot be given up. Richardson makes that virtue, in all his novels, synonymous with virginity. In *Clarissa*, it is to be inflexibly so, with not even the reconciling institution of marriage a possibility. Her resistance to her family is to be only the preparation for her resistance to the demands of Lovelace, her abductor. In the attempt to preserve her 'will' 'unviolated' (iv. 186), 'the charming sufferer' (iii. 424) relies on a heart which knows itself—a passivity which finally, if self-sacrificially, triumphs over all imposition. Though Richardson is scarcely renowned for his irony, it is the bitterest of ironies that only after death can Clarissa's 'will' take positive and literal form in a testament that comes from beyond the grave to haunt her tormentors.[13]

There is no room for compromise on the part of the heroine in the desperate conflict which *Clarissa* depicts. This is one of the most

---

[13] On the various forms and implications of 'will' in *Clarissa*, see T. Tanner, *Adultery in the Novel: Contract and Transgression* (Baltimore, Md., 1979), 100–12.

important points on which Richardson refused to take advice from his coterie of readers, many of whom responded to the early volumes of the novel (the first four volumes were published before he had completed the concluding ones) by requesting their favourite author to provide a 'fortunate' (matrimonial) ending.[14] In attempting an absolute vision of virtue, Richardson produced a narrative which refuses, along with Clarissa herself, such felicitous manipulation of fate. It is a text for a fallen world—written, as Richardson puts it in his Postscript, by an author who 'has lived to see scepticism and infidelity openly avowed' (iv. 553). The 'great end' of representing an exemplary virtue issues in the apotheosis of a sensibility too pure to be reconciled to the world. Clarissa is the 'angel' who has come to earth to face desires whose destructiveness is represented as implicit in their masculine agency. Her sacrifice to those desires is also her triumph. With her 'honour' stolen, she assumes a 'majestic composure', while Lovelace's once smooth loquacity gives way to 'broken sentences and confusion': 'O Belford! Belford! whose the triumph now! HERS or MINE?' (iii. 221). Her sensibility, her capacity for feeling, is seen to outlive the libertine's specious articulacy. 'Clarissa has the greatest of Triumphs even in this world. The greatest I will venture to say, even *in*, and *after* the Outrage, and *because* of the Outrage that ever Woman had', wrote Richardson to Lady Bradshaigh in 1748, justifying the 'Catastrophe' of his bourgeois tragedy.[15] *Pamela* relied on an extraordinary transformation of desire into virtue; *Clarissa* stages a virtue which soars as it renounces practical involvement in the world. This is certainly a paradox for a supposedly 'instructive' text, but it is a stringent one. Clarissa's refusals are inescapable; the heart compels them.

In *Pamela*, with Mr B returned to 'goodness', the heart comes to command all discourse, all forms of expression. In *Clarissa*, no such reconciliation is provided, and the situation of Clarissa's throbbing and resistant heart is one of isolation. She has only her correspondence with Miss Howe—'my other self' (i. 281); she has only the 'sympathizing love' which that correspondence enacts, unrealized in any other available social exchange. Sociability founded on shared sentiment is narrowed down to the form of this desperate correspondence—one which is impeded and interfered

[14] See Richardson's Postscript (iv. 552-3), and his letters to Aaron Hill, Jan. 1747 (Carroll, 78-80), to Lady Bradshaigh, Oct. 1748 (Carroll, 89-97) and Dec. 1748 (Carroll, 103-9), and to Elizabeth Carter, Dec. 1748 (Carroll, 117).

[15] Carroll, 108.

with by both Clarissa's family and her would-be lover. In this exchange only, two hearts beat as one. 'My heart, as I have heretofore said, is a sincere sharer in all your distresses', writes Miss Howe (i. 342); 'Nothing less than the knowledge of the inmost recesses of your heart, can satisfy my love and my friendship' (i. 188). Only in this exchange can Clarissa's sensibility find an echo and a support: 'You know best your own heart; and what that will let you do' (i. 299). Yet though this sympathy can never be refuted, it is no practical defence against ruthless and ingenious schemes. The very material of communication is insecure. As a prelude to his invasion of her body, Lovelace invades Clarissa's correspondence —intercepting, stealing, and even forging letters. Sympathy and shared feeling, as they are attested in the correspondence of these two young women, are exemplary and yet cruelly severed from the ways of the world. The ability to 'compassionate' belongs, in what many of the novel's readers recognized as a pessimistic association, only to the most exceptional and beleaguered incarnation of what Richardson called 'the fairer and better sex'.[16]

This emphasis upon a specifically feminine correspondence, residue of value in a world of ravening desires, should not be mistaken for any kind of proto-feminism. Richardson mythologizes femininity—and, like many male writers before and since, he isolates virginity as its essential representation. Inasmuch as he creates, in all his novels, a woman to fulfill his ethical and religious ideals, his elevation of femininity cannot be understood to be 'radical'.[17] Though his attitudes to the roles and prerogatives of women may have been more liberal than those of some men of his age, Richardson does not provide, in his novels, any actual analysis of the condition of women in eighteenth-century society. The politics of his representations is wholly ambiguous. What we get is

---

[16] Carroll, 49.

[17] For this argument, see K. Rogers, 'Richardson's Empathy with Women', in A. Diamond and L. R. Edwards (eds.), *The Authority of Experience: Essays in Feminist Criticism* (Amherst, Mass., 1977). For a more equivocal version, in which Richardson is 'no feminist' but still writes 'from the point of view of a woman', see E. Figes, *Sex and Subterfuge: Women Writers to 1850* (London, 1982), 4–20. Terry Eagleton's emphasis on a 'feminization of values', and a correspondence between Clarissa and Miss Howe of 'sisterly solidarity', also produces an incongruously radical Richardson: see T. Eagleton, *The Rape of Clarissa* (Oxford, 1982), 14–15 and 77–9. Nancy Miller's discussion of 'feminocentric fictions' is more useful: 'it is not altogether clear to me that these novels are about or for women at all', *The Heroine's Text: Readings in the French and English Novel, 1722–1782* (New York, 1980), 149.

not a depiction of women's alienation, but an incarnate symbol of the
separation of value from effective action. It is in this sense that the
heroine has to be shown to be acted upon, shown as palpitating
object of scrutiny, the property of a spectacle. His investment in
femininity is in an impossibly angelic sensibility. In the resort to the
good woman's heart, so important to all Richardson's narratives, is a
retreat away from social criticism—an obsessive lament, most
unrelenting in *Clarissa*, for the marginalization of virtue.

The transparency of the heart is both Clarissa's understanding of
her own motives, and that which enables a reader finally to
comprehend the semantics of gesture and the certainties of virtue. It
is a formal device as well as a moral resource. In all the talk of the
heart, it is easy to mistake a moral didacticism as a psychological
investigation. But the heart is not a principle of characterization, so
much as a principle of writing, of the coherence of narrative itself.[18]
These are not narratives of unconscious impulse or introspective
ambivalence; they are novels of sentiment, depicting rigorous
judgement supported by acute sensibility. Indeed, the heart is a
general principle; though Clarissa's heart is the most important locus
of assurance and resistance, none of the main correspondents truly
lacks a heart. Every voice, every pen, must finally acknowledge its
movements. Thus Richardson, in his Preface to the third edition
writes:

All the letters are written while the hearts of the writers must be supposed to
be wholly engaged in their subjects (the events at the time generally
dubious): so that they abound not only with critical situations, but with
what may be called instantaneous descriptions, and reflections (proper to be
brought home to the breast of the youthful reader) (*Clarissa*, p. xiv).

None of Richardson's letter-writers can completely escape the
demands of the heart; even his 'rakes' engage in correspondence in
which the confession of those demands cannot be avoided. To write
is to have the heart engaged—by definition; Richardson presumes
that, for the reader, the truth of feeling is revealed in the moment of
this engagement. In the event, this 'writing to the moment' provided

18 Probably the most painstaking description of Richardson's novels in terms of
their psychological realism is M. A. Doody's *A Natural Passion*. For other such
analyses see, for instance, D. Van Ghent, 'On Clarissa Harlowe', in J. Carroll (ed.),
Samuel Richardson: A Collection of Critical Essays (Englewood Cliffs, NJ, 1969); L.
A. Fiedler, *Love and Death in the American Novel* (New York, 1960); and, for a case-
historical approach, J. A. Dussinger, *The Discourse of the Mind in Eighteenth-
century Fiction* (The Hague, 1974).

no such guarantee of unclouded judgement; I shall return later to Richardson's attempts to deal with the undesirable ambiguities that it generated.

The gravest of Clarissa's misgivings about Lovelace is her suspicion of his heartlessness. The man who has 'his passions unsubdued' (i. 200) is, for her, liable to be beyond the reach of finer sentiment: 'I still am of opinion, that he wants a *heart*: and if he does, he wants everything. A wrong *head* may be convinced, may have a right turn given it; but who is able to give a *heart*, if a heart be wanting' (i. 202). But, in supposing a reader's privileged access to Lovelace's own compulsive correspondence, the novel produces the privately acknowledged pulses of *his* heart. The rake, plagued by '*honest* sensibilities', 'ever of a party against myself' (ii. 469), confesses a sensitivity which he must continually strive to conquer: 'what would be her thoughts, did *she* know my heart as well as I know it; when I behold her disturbed and jealous, and think of the *justness* of her apprehensions, and that she cannot fear so much as there is *room* for her to fear; my heart often misgives me' (ii. 399). In Richardson's world, 'vice' is not to be allowed to escape the language of the heart—not to be allowed beyond the call of 'virtue'. Lovelace must be torn: 'Am I not all this time arraigning my own heart? I know I am, by the remorse I feel in it, while my pen bears testimony to her excellence. My heart, Belford, *is not to be trusted*' (ii. 470). The heart is a principle of homogeneity for a text which unifies different voices and different writings even as it points up their differences. The recourse to the urgings of the heart determines Lovelace's self-descriptions as much as Clarissa's. He must tell of how his judgement is pulled to the elaboration of her virtue.

But this presents a problem. In emphasizing Lovelace's potential for feeling, and drawing the reader into a complicity with the villain's confession of this susceptibility, Richardson was to produce a 'devil' that many of his readers found all too alluring. Because Lovelace's compulsive desires are not allowed to justify themselves in any alternative world to that of refined sentiment and 'sensible' virtue, desire and sentiment are apt to become confused. Lovelace's confessions can be ambiguous, referring to excitement and to guilt—'How my heart went *pit-a-pat!*' (iii. 68). So it is with reference to a capacity for feeling in excess of all 'dissimulation' that Lovelace describes the frisson experienced as he prepares to surprise Clarissa, when she has fled from him and is in hiding: 'Never was there a more

joyous heart . . . fluttering in secret, ready to burst its bars for
relief-ful expression' (iii. 36). Sensibility and desire have drawn
together here: 'Oh! how my heart bounded again! It even talked to
me, in a manner; for I thought I *heard*, as well as felt, its unruly
flutters; and every vein about me seemed a pulse' (iii. 40).

Richardson runs the risk of making his rake too much a man of
sensibility in order to construct a narrative that, even as it depicts the
disruptive force of improper desire, regulates and delimits that
desire. Libertinism is not just a subservience to over-insistent sexual
drives. It is a 'vice' which acknowledges the consistency of virtue and
feeling; it is a proclivity most readily excited by what is apparently
inimical to its declared purposes: 'Her virtue, her resistance, which
are her *merits*, are my stimulatives. Have I not told thee so twenty
times over' (ii. 491). Lovelace's desire is determined by, and
dependent on, the virtue which resists it, the virtue which will,
eventually, triumph over it. Following the rape, Lovelace writes of
Clarissa, 'so much has grief stupefied her, that she is at present as
destitute of will as she always seemed to be of desire' (iii. 201).
Neither the male power of will nor the male symptoms of desire
belong to Clarissa, but she retains unviolated *her* will, the
unflinching effort of her resistance. Lovelace, as the rake, represents
and enacts desire, but it is a desire which has to acknowledge its
negation. Lovelace claims, 'I love opposition. As gold is tried by fire,
and virtue by temptation, so is sterling wit by opposition' (ii. 185);
this 'wit', however, is to evaporate in the face of Clarissa's suffering
virtue. A pointed confirmation of this comes with a reversal of what
have previously been the relations of power over correspondence in
this epistolary drama. Her virginity stolen from her, Clarissa is
shown, by Belford, one of Lovelace's letters to him. She scans its
oaths and apostrophes, diagnosing both the 'libertine froth' that
passes for 'wit and spirit', and the fatality of the rake's guilt and
torment (iii. 461-2). She is able to confirm, as a reader, what the text
has gone out of its way to demonstrate: that she does not offer the
required and amusing 'opposition'; that, instead, she has come to
negate the very confidence of 'vice' in its own powers. Before she is
given such literal opportunity to declare this, before Lovelace has
given ground to her completely as 'a *true heroine*' (iv. 523), she has
forced Lovelace to celebrate what he schemes to destroy. Though
Clarissa may not see through the complexities of Lovelace's plotting,
his vice is articulated always with reference, indeed deference, to her

virtue. He trembles before her look even as he is convinced of her ignorance of his plans. He states in his last letter to Belford that, as he enacted these plans, he was 'all the while enabled to distinguish and to adore her excellences, in spite of the mean opinion of the sex which I had imbibed from early manhood' (iv. 522). He recognizes retrospectively that he was always in the grip of virtue personified.

Virtue, in fact, is the very obsession of Lovelace and Belford, who discuss its shapes and powers endlessly in their correspondence (especially ii. 318–30). Libertinism is obsessive, and it is a function of this obsessiveness that Lovelace should write of it as clearly as he does. 'All my vice is women, and the love of plots and intrigues' (iv. 36). His letters show him engrossed by his own diabolical theatricality, his wild and unfulfilled schemes as exciting as his actual disguises and contrivances. The intriguer can best be impassioned by the recognition of his own destructive potential, which is also the recognition of the transcendent merit and power of virtue. 'What a horrible thing that my talents point all that way—when I know what is honourable and just; and would almost wish to be honest', writes Lovelace (ii. 15). Like Mr B before him, Lovelace recognizes, indeed loves and desires, what is 'virtuous' and 'honest'. He erects no alternative system of values, but knows himself to be a 'varlet'. He who breaks families and destroys honour, he who shows contempt for the marriage contract, eventually confirms the integrity of what he seeks to destroy. Michael Foucault describes the transgressive compulsion of the literary libertine in terms which illuminate this paradox:

Underneath the great violator of the rules of marriage—stealer of wives, seducer of virgins, the shame of families, and an insult to husbands and fathers—another personage can be glimpsed: the individual driven, in spite of himself, by the sombre madness of sex. Underneath the libertine, the pervert. He deliberately breaks the law, but at the same time, something like a nature gone awry transports him far from all nature; his death is the moment when the supernatural return of the crime and its retribution thwarts the flight into counternature.[19]

The 'sombre madness of sex' is about right for Lovelace's manically pretentious celebrations of his desires, but while *Clarissa* is, of course, all about sex, it is a narrative in which sex is to be

---

[19] Michel Foucault, *The History of Sexuality: vol. i. An Introduction*, trans. R. Hurley (London, 1979), 39.

conquered. Richardson cannot allow perversion to have its own values. He must turn the private language of the libertine to a (dangerous) conformity with the impulses of sensibility, delicacy, nature. This is not just a matter of the conclusion that Foucault describes (Lovelace brought to repentance and death, the exhaustion of all his scheming) but also of the private correspondence in which Lovelace confesses, admits, concedes to the power of sensibility— and tries to steel himself for another assault on what he venerates. Lovelace can propose what Foucault calls a 'counternature' only according to the signs of virtue, only through an obsession with the 'nature' which is Clarissa's feminine heart. His 'madness', if such it be, is a terminal reflection and confirmation of the status of that femininity. He is driven to it, in the desperate irony which is the triumph of sensibility, by Clarissa's virtue. Clarissa herself recognizes that 'even persons who have bad hearts will have a veneration for those who have good ones' (iii. 386). Lovelace's letters bespeak, beyond veneration, an absolute dependence.

In *Clarissa*, then, desire acts out its intrigues at great cost, but the self-knowledge of the libertine is strangely bent to the magnetism of imprisoned feminine virtue. In *Pamela* the crisis is suppressed. Desire exists to be thwarted. As Pamela's parents say, 'temptations are sore things; but yet, without them, we know not ourselves, nor what we are able to do' (i. 15). But while virtue's abilities of introspection develop in tribulation, so also, as in *Clarissa*, desire acknowledges virtue. Mr B confesses to Pamela, 'I see you so watchful over your virtue, that . . . I cannot but confess my passion for you is increased by it' (i. 188). He prizes her for precisely those qualities for which all the other characters declare their value. In this narrative of providential conversion, all those who do not already esteem her are transformed by her example, or merely by her appearance. She has the effortless power to bring about 'strange reformations' (ii. 132) in all from the lowest servant to the grandest relative of Mr B. Where necessary, this power is rendered as the facility for socially licensed expression which Clarissa is denied. Pamela can stand before an approving company of those who admire her as a peerless 'example' (i. 255), an 'improving' and 'edifying' model (i. 368)—who listen to her story of past distress with 'rapture' and 'tears'. Once her would-be seducer has been brought back to 'goodness', her very sighs and hesitancies are guaranteed the response of sympathetic hearts: 'your language is all wonderful, as your sentiments: and you most abound, when you most seem to want' (i. 328). Her every breath is exemplary, and her admirers unanimous.

Of course, what all this harmony, this unanimity of throbbing hearts and dewy eyes, produces is a strangely plotless narrative. While there is smugness in Richardson's continuation of his novel to represent life after marriage, there is also unease. This is partly the unease of trying to make a masterfully proper and benevolent Mr B contiguous with the potential rake of what was originally the first volume of *Pamela*. It is also the unease of a language become utterly homogeneous and foreseeable—the formlessness of a story into which Richardson eventually has to import some conflict, by suggesting that the reformed Mr B is still drawn to improper flirtation. Much of the novel is eventless by the standard of the assaults and escapes of its first part; inevitably so, if we are to be given 'Virtue Rewarded', if we are to be shown a world of united sentiments. Whilst Clarissa's sensibility must operate defensively and desperately, Pamela's articulations of 'feeling' are unproblematically acceptable at all levels of the social hierarchy in which she has gained promotion. Lady Davers writes to her that 'what we admire in *you*, are truth and nature, not studied or elaborate epistles' (ii. 32). Pamela bestows 'the pleasure of sentiments flowing with that artless ease, which so much affects when we read your letters'. The servant-girl become mistress enacts virtue in the guise of nature—education and innocence conflated.[20] The other characters exist to recognize this 'artless' integrity of expression. A dominant oxymoron of natural refinement cements the influence of Pamela's sensibility: 'your talent is nature' (ii. 279).

The figure of the innocent moralist, the untutored representative of 'honest' feeling, is to recur in many of the novels of the mid-eighteenth century. The powers of sentiment are justified in a myth of *natural* sensitivity and judgement. In *Pamela*, these faculties are supposed to be demonstrated in the writing ('to the moment') itself: these are, according to Richardson's Preface to what were Volumes iii and iv of the novel, 'Letters . . . written to NATURE' (ii, p. v).

---

[20] The implications of Pamela's change of status seem to have been more problematic for French than for English readers. Voltaire and Goldoni wrote plays based on the novel, and both felt it necessary to blunt any radical edge by raising the social standing of the heroine; see T. C. D. Eaves and B. D. Kimpel, *Samuel Richardson: A Biography* (Oxford, 1971), 126.

When Mr B, whilst still the predator, intercepts Pamela's letters it is to recognize what is at once the moral sophistication of her style and the natural flow of her self-expressions (which are, of course, Richardson's expressions): 'I . . . am quite overcome with your charming manner of writing; so free, so easy, and many of your sentiments so much above your years' (i. 69). The letter is the form in which, as even the would-be seducer admiringly observes, sentiment is displayed as vivid sensation married to pressing moral discrimination: the letter is easeful yet polite; intimate yet distant; sententious yet from the heart. The most 'natural' expression of all, though, is the one which does not need words. Throughout Richardson's novels, sentiment displays itself in a repertoire of conventionally involuntary signs—tears, sighs, palpitations. These signs of sensibility, signs which Richardson's heroines constantly reproduce, are the most obviously distinct features of 'sentimental' writing. One might call them *symptoms*, as it is according to an idea of the body (and particularly the female body) as a visible and describable register of effects that these signs appear. In *Pamela* the clarity of sentiment is made one with the organization of social relations, and of the narrative itself; it underpins a conceptual and conversational harmony. Here the feminine heart enters into an eternal contract with a reformed male authority, and here the gestures which bespeak the dominance of that heart are unapologetic and universally accepted. The clearest signs are tears, tears which initially join Pamela with the other servants to the exclusion of Mr B. 'I was overwhelmed with tears, at the affecting instances of their esteem' (i. 83), writes Pamela as, unwittingly, she leaves for her spell of incarceration. Sympathy is as liable to arouse these tears as distress. More so, indeed, as the speechless chorus of sobs, the silent communication of moist eyes, is presented as the irrefutable evidence of social or domestic harmony.

Pamela falls to her knees or weeps with a regularity easily parodied—indeed, we can later see such parody in some of Lovelace's supplications to Clarissa—but to unerring effect. And though she acts out the gestures and postures of feeling with the greatest intensity, all characters and voices are conjoined in sentimental demonstration. So Pamela writes to Lady Davers, 'what could Mrs. Jervis or I say to him?—Why, indeed, nothing at all!—We could only look upon one another, with our eyes and our hearts full of a gratitude that would not permit either of us to speak'(ii. 56). The heart is beyond and above speech, and so are the signs of its integrity. What is 'felt' is liable to express itself here 'at last in a manner he was pleased to call more elegant than words—with uplifted folded hands, and tears of joy'. Whether she narrates sorrow or joy, Pamela elicits these signs—arouses sensibility through her writing: 'you make our hearts and eyes so often overflow, as we read'. (ii. 82). Here is the harmony, and the righteous bliss, which comes from the communication of sentiments. Here is the model of 'affecting' correspondence (which is also, of course, obsessive and repetitive) enacting the most 'natural' instincts of virtuous sociability.

Mistress and servant, former servant and aristocratic sister-in-law, feminine virtue and recently redeemed male authority; all pairs of opposites are reconciled in the confluence of sentiments demonstrated in the universality of certain signs and gestures. A figure such as Mr Adams may have little to say, 'but joy danced in his silent countenance for all that' (ii. 153). The system of signs articulates feeling beyond words: 'his countenance, and eyes gave testimony of a gratitude too high for further expression'. Only the countenance, eyes, and heart are required to ensure sympathy. Weeping, particularly, becomes an indication of an always intelligible pleasure, both an overflowing and a carefully defined refinement of feeling. Pamela's tears are 'the escaped fugitives that would start unbidden beyond their proper limits, though I often tried, by a twinkling motion, to disperse the gathering water, before it had formed itself into drops too big to be restrained' (ii. 172). The eyes are the portals of sentiment, and this is as true for the servant as it is for her recently promoted mistress: 'Mrs Jervis's honest heart . . . shewed itself at her eyes' (ii. 208). But Pamela's is a femininity capable of the strongest possible expressions of such feeling: 'Struggle not, my beloved Pamela, for words to express sentiments which your eyes and your countenance much more significantly express than any word *can* do' (ii. 222). Mr B confirms the eloquence, beyond speech, which is Pamela's particular facility.

In *Clarissa*, too, ready tears are recommended. Belford, his past sins eclipsed by his penitent probity, advises the dying rake Belton, 'I ever honoured a man that could weep for the distresses of *others;* and ever shall . . . such a one cannot be insensible of *his own* . . . Tears, my dear Belton, are no signs of an unmanly, but, contrarily of a humane nature; they ease the overcharged heart, which would burst but for that kindly and natural relief' (iv. 145). Belford has

learned the signs of feeling—taken them to heart, we might say. So
he can be admitted, as if a worshipper, to another deathbed, that of
the 'divine', the 'heavenly creature' herself. He is part of the fixated
audience that witnesses a '*Death from grief*'—that mixes tears with
tears in a special ritual of sensibility, in the religious society of the
deathbed. Indeed, this is the only society that Clarissa is allowed to
discover, and whose composition and manners she can control. It is
one of lachrymose unanimity, ceremonially organized wonder.
When Clarissa offers her 'last tear' for Lovelace, 'him by whom I die',
Belford and the attendant minister know that speech is not enough:
'Our eyes and hands expressed for us both what our lips could not
offer' (iv. 307). Nothing, after all, can express true sentiment like the
'melting' eye.

Previously, Clarissa's tears have been scorned, ignored, or shed
only in isolation. Though her heart's promptings may escape the
snares of language, she does not have the privilege of the tears of
affection which Pamela can share with those who surround her.
Instead, eyes convey another kind of control over meaning, the
'gaze' or 'look'. The non-verbal is deprived of the demonstrative
signs of sentiment proposed in *Pamela*. There is no practicable
society of feelings that Clarissa can live out before the one that her
death produces. While she is in the custody of Lovelace, she has
something more singularly defensive, her gaze: unknowing but
unchallengeable, a look which cannot save her but which is reported
as the piercing expression of her virtue. Clarissa is one, Lovelace
warns his fellow rakes, 'whose eyes will pierce to the bottom of your
shallow souls the moment she hears you open' (ii. 217). Where she
cannot unravel the mendacity she faces, she can only look. Her gaze
is unseeing, and yet all-penetrating: 'I have felt half a dozen such
flashes, such eye-beams, in as many different conversations with this
soul-piercing beauty' (iii. 112). The power of 'a sudden flash from
her eye, an *eye-beam*' is described in Lovelace's always confessional
letters; for all his schemes, the rake is riveted to the gaze of virtue:
'She looked at me as if she would look me through: I thought I *felt*
eyebeam after eyebeam penetrate my shivering reins. But she was
silent. Nor needed her eyes the assistance of speech' (ii. 433).
Sensibility is this pure expression—and a perturbation at the heart of
even the most diabolical of Lovelace's scheming. In *Pamela*,
mutually affecting looks awaken contagious tears; the gazes in
Clarissa—where Lovelace and Clarissa are become 'great watchers

of each other's eyes' (ii. 93)—signify suspicion, resistance, dread. The possibility of a harmonious commerce of supportive sentiments, of sociability visibly enacted in bodies and countenances, has been perverted by Lovelace's ruling desire. Richardson's second novel pictures the value of sensibility *in extremis*, cut off from social application.

Initially, it is Clarissa's family which, in its concern with accumulation, refuses sensibility. Only when she is sinking into death do her relations begin to discover their hearts and the ennobling contagion of feeling: Colonel Morden's display of a 'humanity' that 'no brave heart should be ashamed of' arouses in the Harlowes some kind of sentimental response—'The eyes of everyone but the hard-hearted brother caught tears from his' (iv. 282). All this is, of course, belated; lessons are learned too late for application. Until they succeed in martyring virtue, the members of Clarissa's family are distinguished by their insensibility. Indeed, intoxicated with the prospect of aggrandizement, they are further from sensibility than Lovelace, who knows the outflowings of feeling well enough to contemplate exploiting them. Thus his observation on the flawed duplicity of the so-called Captain Tomlinson, his partner in crime: 'The villain Tomlinson looked at me with a rueful face, as if he begged leave to cry for company. It might have been as well, if he *had* cried. A feeling heart, or the tokens of it given by a sensible eye, are very reputable things, when kept in countenance by the occasion' (iii. 125). But this is still ambiguous. In order to traduce sensibility, the rapist must know it. And to know it is to believe it. To report his confrontations with Clarissa is to encounter, to admit to, the buried vibrations of his own sensibility: 'I trembled between admiration and love . . . free as my clasping emotion might appear to her apprehensive heart, I had not, at the instant, any thought but what reverence inspired . . . all the motions of my heart were as pure as her own' (ii. 383). Lovelace is not just a trickster, and it is not just triumphantly that he transcribes Clarissa's exclamation on his maligned potential for feeling:

What *sensibilities*, said the divine creature . . . must thou have suppressed! What a dreadful, what a judicial hardness of heart must thine be; who canst be capable of such emotions as sometimes thou hast shown; and of such sentiments as sometimes have flowed from thy lips; yet canst have so far overcome them all, as to be able to act as thou hast acted. (iii. 152)

His is not that 'barbarous insensibility' which Clarissa condemns above all failings (ii. 466). Lovelace's presentation of himself to Clarissa as one who 'always *loved* virtue, although he had not followed its rules as he ought' is not mere hypocrisy (i. 180), not just a convenient self-deprecation. The really destructive villian must be shown to know what he destroys. It is this knowledge, this recognition of sensibility, that leads Lovelace to a final sub-jugation to the rule of virtue.

Lovelace may violate Clarissa's body, but not her 'will'; he may reduce her to physical 'insensibility' by a subterfuge which is 'but a thief to my own joys' (iii. 202), but the moral strength of her sensibility is retained. This is the point of what Richardson himself described as 'the supposed Tragical (tho' I think it *Triumphant)* Catastrophe'.[21] Sensibility, recognized in the self as the promptings of a *'feeling heart'*, is the privatized feminine principle of a virtue which the 'Catastrophe' is set to validate. In her denial of sensibility, Clarissa's sister denies value itself. Clarissa reflects that 'for ten times the pain that such a sensibility is attended with would I not part with the pleasure it brings with it' (i. 219). 'Pain' and 'pleasure' are linked by the sensibility which gives the heart access to both. The value of sensibility supports Clarissa's correspondence with Miss Howe, justifying a 'vivacity' on the part of the latter—a tendency to acid judgement and frank asperity—which is actually necessary to the narrative as a commentary not proper for the heroine herself to deliver. If 'pain' implies sensibility, the pain that a friend induces can be almost delicious too: 'who would not allow for the liveliness of a spirit which for one painful sensibililty gives an hundred pleasurable ones? And the *one* in consequence of the *other'* (i. 456).

Yet while Miss Howe's 'liveliness' is useful for exciting Clarissa's sensibility, it can also be a problem within the text. For Miss Howe takes the expression of sentiment to the verge of impropriety; her habits of ridicule and condemnation have to be contained. Clarissa describes her as *'friend-companion-sister-lover'* (iv. 340), but she also constantly reproaches her for the 'freedom' of her judgements. In her will she refers to her friend as *'the sister of her heart'*, to which Miss Howe replies 'Justly . . . does she call me so: for we had but one heart, but one soul, between us: and now my better half is torn from me' (iv. 404). But then it is a soul divided before death. Miss Howe

---

21 From a letter to Aaron Hill, Jan. 1747; Carroll, 83.

provides a commentary integral to the narrative, often explicating the limited options which define Clarissa's predicament, but her speculations must also be repudiated. Clarissa's paradoxically acute sense of duty precludes too bitter a reflection upon her family, and her saintly virtue rules out pragmatic calculation. Ironically in a novel of such unabashed didacticism, a novel dedicated to demonstrating the nature of virtuous judgement, it is Miss Howe's willingness to judge that has to be restrained: 'you *must* also know, that the freedoms you take with my friends, can have no other tendency, but to weaken the sense of my duty to them, without answering any good end to myself' (i. 133). Indeed, in the changes that Richardson made between the first and the third editions of *Clarissa*, he attempted to show more clearly how inverted commas might be placed around some of Miss Howe's comments (in one case literally—see i. 125-7). In passages that he added, he subjected Miss Howe's observations to a more piercing criticism (e.g. i. 132-5), emphasized her failures of feeling (e.g. in Hickman's letter, i. 335-6), or even toned down her expressions of resentment (e.g. ii. 171-2). No reader was to be allowed to sympathize too much with Miss Howe's more sardonic versions of events.

But, of course, there is another reason why Miss Howe's tougher diagnoses are there—why Richardson can work to point up, but cannot dissolve, her 'vivacity'. In taking 'liberties she should not take', this 'true modern wit, who thinks it not necessary, when it carries the keenest edge, to retain discretion in its service' allows Clarissa, in reply, to write but more naturally and more properly.[22] While the two friends are joined by their sensibility, the difference between their narrations is also structurally important. It is in reaction to Miss Howe's asseverations that Clarissa disavows such readiness to condemn, and can represent her narration as both discriminating and 'honest': 'As I ask for your approbation or disapprobation of my conduct, upon the facts I lay before you, I should think it the sign of a very bad cause, if I endeavoured to mislead my judge' (i. 212). The contrast between narrations within a heartfelt feminine correspondence may be difficult to contain— threatening, for instance, to produce an amenable alternative rather than a support to the heroine. It is necessary, however, to enable Clarissa's writing to aspire to a form in which, as William Beatty

[22] Letter to Isabella Sutton, Aug. 1750: ibid. 166.

Warner puts it, 'interpretation and judgement' are made to 'look as sure, as real, as nonproblematic as any person or object summoned into presence by language'.[23] It is this reconciliation of scrupulous propriety to immediate expressiveness that the language of sentiment is represented as enacting. The text labours to propose the natural articulacy, the impartial self-expression, of Clarissa's letters. Though virtuous feeling is thus further distanced from any means of application, it is necessary that Miss Howe should be a foil as well as a support.

So Miss Howe cannot be consistently adequate to the standards of sensibility. The means by which Richardson insists on those standards have become, in *Clarissa*, the means by which he also emphasizes their remoteness and their defensiveness. The maintainance of 'sensible' virtue has become a terminally private endeavour. Adam Smith classes Richardson as one of the 'poets and romance writers, who best paint the refinements and delicacies of love and friendship, and of all other private and domestic affections', and who 'are, in such cases, much better instructors than Zeno, Chrysippus, or Epictetus' (all Stoic philosophers).[24] In this formulation, the instructive capacities of the 'romance', even while it seems that they are celebrated, are, conventionally enough, limited to the realm of the 'private and domestic'; it is the paradox of Richardson's project that an ambition to produce a universally appropriate image of virtue—an absolute example—issues forth in 'refinements and delicacies' more privatized, and indeed desperate, than any to which Smith refers. Virtue and sentiment are exceptional. This novel is anything but a reflection of the putative confidence of a 'socially reformist bourgeoisie' in 'humanitarian benevolence'—'a sanguine trust in human goodness'.[25] 'Sweet is the pain which generous natures feel for the distresses of others' wrote Richardson in his *Collection of the Moral and Instructive Sentiments* from the novels.[26] But the commentary does not fit the narrative. Fellow-feeling in *Clarissa* has a vocabulary tragically divorced from

---

[23] *Reading* Clarissa: *The Struggles of Interpretation* (New Haven, Conn., 1979), 13. Warner describes well how Clarissa's narrative is made to seem natural: see 5–27.

[24] *Theory*, 143.

[25] Eagleton, *The Rape of Clarissa*, 15. This is Ian Watt's formula in *The Rise of the Novel* (1957; rpt. Harmondsworth, 1979); see Chs. 2 and 5.

[26] Richardson, *A Collection of Moral and Instructive Sentiments, Maxims, Cautions, and Reflexions, Contained in the Histories of Pamela, Clarissa, and Sir Charles Grandison* (London, 1755), 121.

application; there is no confidence in benevolent sociability here. Indeed, the novel's vision of social relations governed by internalized regimes of violence and desire has led some to read it as social critique.[27] But as its heroine is always fleeing to find only the solace of her sensibility, so the novel itself is on the retreat, away from analysis and into a last-ditch symbolism. Raymond Williams's description of what is at once the power and impotence of this text is a precise one: '*Clarissa* is an important sign of that separation of virtue from any practically available world which is a feature of the later phases of Puritanism . . . it is in the end not a criticism of a period or structure of society, but of what can be abstracted as 'the world'.[28]

Richardson's own anxiety about his extreme specialization of virtue, and of the language of sentiment, gave rise to the project of his third novel, *The History of Sir Charles Grandison*. Having, in *Pamela* and *Clarissa*, so insistently gendered sensibility, he attempts, in his final major work, to rescue instruction from his own mythology. This text attempts to answer what sounds like a classically approved question of moral philosophy: what is a 'Good Man'? But the question is displaced from the normal contexts of didacticism; for the novelist it has become a question about the representation of masculinity as much as one about 'goodness'. It is this question that is written into the abiding certainties of *Sir Charles Grandison*, unresolved in its flawless monopolies of propriety and righteousness. In *Pamela* and *Clarissa* Richardson had invested all moral value in paragons of the 'Fair Sex'—how then to redeem the 'Foul Sex'?[29]

Richardson's letters cannot get away from the improbability of an attempt to tell the story of a 'Good Man'. He writes in June 1750 to Susan Highmore of a visit from 'two very worthy ladies' who are 'both very intimate with one Clarissa Harlowe: and both extremely earnest with me to give them a *good man*. Can you help me to such a one as is demanded of me? He must be wonderfully polite; but no Hickman! How can we hope that ladies will not think a good man a tame man?'[30] Hickman, the butt of Miss Howe's 'wit' in *Clarissa*, is

---

[27] The best-known such reading is probably C. Hill, 'Clarissa Harlowe and her Times', *Essays in Criticism*, 5 (1955).

[28] R. Williams, *The Country and the City* (1973; rpt. St Albans, 1975), 84.

[29] For these descriptions see Richardson's letter to Sarah Chapone, 18 Apr. 1752: Carroll, 211.

[30] Carroll, 161.

no possible prototype. He represents what an exemplary and 'manly' virtue must be shown to transcend: he has been unable to effect action or consequence, unable to aspire to public virtue because powerless to govern the conduct of others. Yet what Richardson has previously offered as an image of virtuous and 'sensible' femininity has also been an image of an ultimately private devotion, an example in isolation. Now, as if perturbed by the implications of his own myth, he turns to the redemption of masculinity—of virtue as active, effective, public. And the pious banter of his correspondence never quite subsumes his worries about the feasibility of this project: 'The *good man*, alas! I knew not what the task was which I undertook . . . there are so many things that may be done, and said, and written by a common man that cannot by a good man, that delicacies arise on delicacies.'[31] A mock-avuncular resignation becomes Richardson's means of phrasing his sense of the project's unavoidable demands: 'I am teazed by a dozen ladies of note and virtue, to give them a good man, as they say I have been partial to their sex, and unkind to my own'.[32]

Richardson's circulation amongst his correspondents of early drafts of *Sir Charles Grandison* (as ever, the habit of his particular quest for approval) elicits a swell of enthusiasm—but then the enthusiasm seems, indeed, swollen; hyperbole perhaps signals something less than assurance. Writing to Hester Mulso, another of Richardson's favourites, Susan Highmore wishes into being a figment made the more unlikely by the relentless logic of *Clarissa*: 'Oh! my dear, Sir Charles will be all we wish him—I am sure he will—and is destined to show the world what the purest love should be, when inspired by an object irresistibly amiable, like Miss Biron!'[33] Throughout Richardson's letters of the early 1750s, an attention to the necessity for a masculine 'Example' bespeaks the very uncertainty of that example.[34] The novelist's claims for his creation on its final presentation 'to the Public' were for 'the Example of a Man acting uniformly well thro' a Variety of trying Scenes, because all his Actions are regulated by one steady Principle: A Man of Religion and Virtue; of Liveliness and Spirit; accomplished and

---

31 Letter to Mrs Dewes, 21 June 1752: Carroll, 218.
32 Letter to Mr Defreval, 21 Jan. 1750: Barbauld, v. 272–3.
33 Barbauld, ii. 259.
34 A useful narrative of the correspondence in which Richardson engaged while composing *Sir Charles Grandison* is given in Eaves and Kimpel, *Biography*, 365–86.

agreeable; happy in himself, and a Blessing to others' (*Sir Charles Grandison*, Preface, i. 4); but this was an ideal shadowed by the implications of his earlier novels.

The constitution of the 'Good Man' is certainly odd. Every different variety of literary criticism that has taken on Richardson's last novel has had occasion to remark that its hero is not really there at all. In the novel, as in the novelist's correspondence, he is produced by acclamation; in the end, he *is* that acclamation. Sir Charles remains, more than anything else, an effect of feminine awe. Before he appears in person, he is present in reputation, given form by a woman's praise: 'Once Miss Grandison, speaking of her brother, said, My brother is valued by those who know him best, not . . . for this or that single worthiness; as for being, in the great and yet comprehensive sense of the word, a *good man*' (i. 182). Throughout the book, this affirmation, this judgement, is echoed by every voice, for Grandison's goodness is guaranteed by the absolute uniformity of discourse which he produces and which produces him. It is only through that uniformity that he exists, utterly potent and utterly 'affecting'. As his sister says, 'He came over to us all at once so perfect . . . with so much power, and such a will, to do us good, that we were awed into a kind of reverence for him' (i. 444). Clarissa's particular powerlessness was the condition not only for the representation of her potent sensibility, but also for the development of a narrative in which vice acted out its dream of acquisition for the final, paradoxical, purpose of the confirmation of virtue. In *Sir Charles Grandison*, virtue and power are given the same name which is the name of a 'Man'.

Whereas Clarissa had only the inviolate will which was her resistance, Grandison can enact every purpose and gratification of will. In fact, this happens quite literally; while *Clarissa*, originally to have been entitled *The Lady's Legacy*, plays upon the problem of enacting any 'will', the hero of Richardson's last novel solves without difficulty the questions posed by his parents' failure to prescribe inheritance. He is 'an executor of a will, that *ought* to have been made, and perhaps *would*, had time been given' (i. 383). The faultless exercise of power meets with the tears and speechlessness of all—the inevitable responses of excited sensibility: 'Caroline found out her brother . . . but could only express her gratitude by her lifted-up hands and eyes'. With the perfection of this will and the matchlessness of this power comes a narrative which is condemned ever to repeat itself, constantly to reaffirm what should be least of all in doubt: Grandison's goodness. T.C.D. Eaves and B.D. Kimpel, Richardson's most recent biographers, criticize *Sir Charles Grandison* for the fact that certain 'characters' 'show signs of life, only to subside into ecstatic praises when exposed to the Good Man'.[35] But the adulatory, and largely female, chorus to which they refer must precisely absolve the text from any conflict, from the problems of shifts in viewpoint, for it is as the register of that unanimity that the 'Good Man' is represented.

In a sense, Sir Charles acts to forestall narrative development. Such is the effect of his necessary power. He intervenes in a plot which threatens another rape—which has the makings of another *Clarissa*. He comes between an angelic woman and a 'threatening Lover', defeating the strategies of 'bold men'. Everywhere, if he is to be a man of virtue, he must resolve conflicts. He is the remaker of broken conversation, he who brings 'agreement' in the place of the 'quarrels of married people' (ii. 278). He reforms social relations and becomes himself the function of social homogeneity; he 'but accommodates himself to the persons he has to deal with' (ii. 272). He is 'good upon principle, in every relation of life'. As if to include every eventuality, the relations are listed: 'could HE be otherwise than the best of HUSBANDS, who was the most dutiful of SONS; who is the most affectionate of BROTHERS; the most faithful of FRIENDS' (iii, 462). His vaunted 'goodness' ensures the ideal stability of these relations, and, by the text's tautology, this goodness is an effect of these relations. The 'Good Man' is the space where feminine desire, aspiration, opinion, and trust all meet and agree: 'So much goodness, so much sensibility, so much compassion (whence all his woes, I believe), never met together, in a heart so manly' (ii. 134). The text's compliant and obsessive feminine voices, whose constant theme he is, represent him as the nexus of all concern and deference: 'Lucy, Nancy, calls him THE man: and every one looks upon him as if there were not one soul in company but *he* and themselves' (iii. 50). 'THE man' is a proper husband for Harriet Byron, surrounded by less adequate suitors, and the absolute type of an abstraction. He is the only conceivable object of desire for Harriet, the woman with the 'countenance of an angel' (i. 35), and he is the steady and all-determining centre of any 'company'. 'Bless me,

---

[35] Eaves and Kimpel, *Biography*, 390.

madam! said Lucy to my aunt, on more occasions than one, this man is every-thing' (iii. 95).

But he is also nothing. He is a name whose resonance is as great when he is away on a journey as it is when he is in the company of the women who talk of him. In his absence, 'Every one referr'd to Sir Charles' (i. 413). He exists as a constant point of reference, a resolver of differences even at a distance; but he remains a strangely absent apparition, his desires ever 'secret'. Whilst the feelings of women in this novel are always legible, read in the blushes and hesitancies of affected sensibility, Sir Charles, his travels a minor mystery to all, is just a reputation, the man who 'might' break 'half a dozen hearts'. He is the focus of all feminine apprehension, but his desires remain hidden until, inevitably, they are revealed to correspond with the goal of marriage to Harriet. Desire as it featured in *Clarissa* was identified with the force of male destructiveness. In *Sir Charles Grandison* it has become a gap which a woman's voice attempts to fill: 'And have you been in love, Sir Charles Grandison? thought I to myself' (i. 414). For Sir Charles is a paragon of virtue and the locus of all feminine aspirations: 'We are *laudably* fond of distinguishing merit. But your brother's is so dazzling—Every woman is one's rival' (iii. 119). As the construction of male goodness can only come with the absolute equivalence and repetitiveness of the voices and letters which affirm its ubiquity, so the desires of women produce a rivalry which is represented as self-denying agreement rather than as conflict. In the necessity of its reference to the name of 'THE man', these desires are univocal.

The incantation of the (usually capitalized) name of male goodness is everywhere, insisting on the virtue that Richardson was so concerned to prove: 'But my guardian's goodness makes every-body good . . . What a blessing it is, to have a guardian that will second every good purpose of one's heart' (ii. 421). This goodness is the unifying preoccupation of feminine correspondence, an ultimate definition which is the sanction of writing and speech. It becomes the principle of coherence of the letters which Harriet writes, and of the scenes of 'society' described in those letters. 'Where is he, at this moment!', asks Emily during his visit to Italy (ii. 422); everywhere where there is correspondence could be the answer. The name of the 'Good Man' is a constant proximity, an unchallenged presence which, even in Sir Clarles' reported absence, metonymically defines the scope of association and validation. The many (many statements, many characters, many aspirations) must end in the one. This one is 'THE man'. His name, and his goodness, substitute for the presence of 'all other men'. As Harriet writes, 'Must not all other men appear little, and, less than little, nothing, in my eyes?' (ii. 423). It is in the impossible figure of Sir Charles Grandison that Richardson attempts his unreserved redemption of male power. It is the compulsion of this project, its introspective fascination with the reconciling of sensibility to power, which produces a text now scarcely readable, a text for which *aficionados* of Richardson often tend to apologize.

It requires an absolute fixation of correspondence and conversation upon the empty space of masculine virtue to assure social harmony. The organization of bonds and gestures within the embrace of conversation is fundamental to the representation of any such harmony; conversation has become the healing influence which it is one of the tasks of correspondence to celebrate. This enactment of polite sociability is, of course, a conventional enough ideal in the period; the cultivation of conversational style, of what Fielding called 'The Art of pleasing or doing Good to one another',[36] is the common requisite of social pleasures increasingly seen to depend on private affiliations.[37] But precisely because conversation is seen to belong to a private world, its usefulness as a model of social intercourse is elaborated with difficulty. Hume may have proposed conversation as the occasion on which 'feeling' can flow, but he had to abstract a polite privilege as a universal condition in order to argue that, as a fact of 'human nature', 'we' can always come, through 'company' and 'conversation', to know 'a rational and thinking Being like ourselves, who communicates to us all the actions of his mind; makes us privy to his inmost sentiments and affections; and lets us see, in the very instant of their production, all the emotions, which are caus'd by any object' (*Treatise*, p. 353). Conversation in *Sir Charles Grandison*, on the contrary, is strained because it must embrace gendered differences; it must redeem the conflicts of the earlier novels, and especially that complex struggle for value and self-possession in *Clarissa* which draws 'a few drops of

---

[36] Henry Fielding, 'An Essay on Conversation', in *Miscellanies by Henry Fielding, Esq; Volume One*, ed. H. K. Miller (Oxford, 1972), 123.

[37] See N. Phillipson, 'Hume as Moralist: A Social Historian's Perspective', in S. C. Brown (ed.), *Philosophers of the Enlightenment* (Brighton, 1979): in a 'private world . . . conversation meant learning to discuss one's ideas and observations not simply in order to inform one's friends but to be sure that one's own understanding was as free as possible of affectation, idiosyncrasy and personal prejudice' (p. 142).

blood after it' (*Clarissa*, iii. 319). Conversation must be made to bear arguments about the private duties and prerogatives of the sexes—arguments resolved into a solemn sportiveness reminiscent of much of Richardson's awkwardly intimate correspondence.

Of course, conversation in the Grandison household is peculiarly harmonious. Sir Charles's goodness oversees the confluence of all sentiments—it ensures that all opinions are eventually swallowed up in reverence and applause: 'it is surely one of the sweetest pleasures in the world, to hear a whole company join in applauding the absent person who stands high in our opinions' (i. 287). A 'topic' as potentially awkward as 'Man's usurpation, and woman's natural independency' (iii. 242) is brought before his gaze that it might be absorbed into a conversational protocol over which he rules. The most difficult of problems is adapted to the style of a conversation in which everyone is made familial. Jane Austen may have found in the text precedents for her comedies of manners, but the manners which the conversations of *Sir Charles Grandison* exemplify can comprehend none of the disparities upon which comedy might capitalize. The claustrophobic sense sustained by *Clarissa* is renowned, but the restrictions placed upon all correspondence in *Sir Charles Grandison* confine 'happiness' and 'virtue' within the narrowest of spaces. There is to be no escape from the circle of applause and compliant sensibility around Sir Charles's empty presence; only in this space of conversation can affections circulate, manners be learned. J.G.A. Pocock, amongst others, has described how, during the eighteenth century, 'manners' came to be seen more and more as providing the best basis for social relations in a world in which lofty ideals of civic virtue appeared increasingly inappropriate. If, in 'the new world of the social and sentimental, . . . virtue could be defined as the practice and refinement of manners',[38] then *Sir Charles Grandison*'s rehearsals of virtuous intercourse offer 'social and sentimental' standards restricted to the most limited of environments and guaranteed by the most abstracted of characters. It all works, but only in what Harriet describes as 'this happy asylum' (i. 310). The artificial family sheltered by Sir Charles's 'goodness' is a place for virtue's retreat as certainly as Clarissa's coffin. Richardson's final novel was to assure his readers that virtue could prevail, but such assurance could only be given by

---

[38] J. G. A. Pocock, *Virtue, Commerce, and History: Essays on Political Thought and History, Chiefly in the Eighteenth Century* (Cambridge, 1985), 50.

correspondence reduced to a kind of euphoria of repetition: 'SIR CHARLES has come at last! . . . Every word that passes now, seems to me worth repeating. There is no describing how the presence of this man animates every one in company.'

The politeness which Sir Charles sanctifies deadens with one touch. In the conversations of his household, contradiction exists to be suffocated. Each 'lively sally' of his sister Charlotte is turned to her eventually submissive sensibility, her 'sweet confusion' (see i. 397–413). When Lovelace has shown how conversation can be the scene of impropriety, deceit, and infatuation, all the more reason to record social intercourse brought round to unassailable consensus. Indeed, conversation with a designing or lovelorn man is replayed in *Sir Charles Grandison* as if in an act of exorcism. The conversation to which femininity must stop its ears (the resort of the disappointed lover, the desperate suitor) is brought to an end by the good man's intervention: 'since I have seen and known Sir Charles Grandison, I have not only (as before) an *indifference*, but a *dislike*, to all other men', writes Harriet (i. 218). In every way, she is secured from the attentions of 'all other men' by Sir Charles's ruling presence. Her conversations with him must be distinguished from those in which 'love' is a 'Prostituted name! made to cover all acts of violence, indiscretion, folly, in both sexes' (i. 269). Under Sir Charles's influence, conversation enacts a different, now almost holy, kind of infatuation: 'I think, if I know my own heart, I had rather converse but an hour in a week with him, and with Miss Grandison, than be the wife of any man I have ever seen or known' (i. 218). In his orbit, conversation is given the shape of virtuous obsession; it is where 'THE man' predominates, and where all references are finally to his name.

Sociability in *Sir Charles Grandison* does not, though, just mean conversational unanimity. The 'magnetism' of Sir Charles's goodness (ii. 45) produces and controls feminine sensibility, and its manifest 'expressiveness of meaning, tho' not of language' (iii. 213). Around him the women of the novel, all 'full of unmeaning meaningness', blush, tremble and weep. In the presence of male 'goodness', virtuous femininity is legible most when unable to speak: 'But what shall I do with my gratitude? O my dear, I am *overwhelmed* with my gratitude: I can only express it in silence before them. Every look, if it be honest to my heart, however, tells it' (i. 167). In a letter of 1746 to Sophia Westcomb, Richardson refers to the '*Air* and *Attention*' which 'will shew *Meaning* beyond what *Words* can, to the Observing'.[39] A capacity for such '*Air* and *Attention*' distinguishes the women who palpitate in the presence of Richardson's masculine paragon, and who are made to observe and record their own tremulous sensibilities. All attraction to Sir Charles has to be rendered in terms of excited sensibility, which means also a kind of serious and breathless sexlessness; to this task the correspondences of Harriet and Charlotte devote themselves. In the Grandison household, 'feelings' are sufficiently aligned that conversational procedures are often secondary: 'there was nothing so very extraordinary said; but the *manner* was the thing, which shewed a meaning, that left language behind it' (iii. 213). Attention to the meanings of looks and gestures binds the members of a social group turned inward—for the sake of virtue—on their 'lively sensibilities'. A feminine body is the private place in which the novel finds a responsive confirmation of masculine virtue.

Sir Charles Grandison, then, has to produce conversation as well as refined emotion, polite unanimity alongside pulsating sensibilites. Here we can turn back to *Clarissa* to see how the implications of that novel have apparently been revoked. For Clarissa's world is one in which feeling is set against speech—a world of threatening or irremediably broken conversation. The speech of others demands impossible sacrifices from her, and demands them with menaces. All she has is her writing. In *Clarissa*, correspondence is surrogate sociability, referring the reader to failures of communication even as it outlines an expressive ideal. Such communication as is possible between Clarissa and Miss Howe (and even this is typically incomplete, thwarted, in doubt) is shown to imply a peculiarly feminine faculty. Miss Howe's final testimony to 'the character of my beloved friend' emphasizes that 'the familiar style' is the proper specialism of educated women of sensibility—the articulation of 'the delicacy of their sentiments' through a 'natural ease and freedom' (iv. 495). By this account, 'MASCULINE' writers substitute 'bombast', 'wit' or pedantry for the truths of sentiment—'the *sublime*, with them, lying in *words* and not in *sentiment*, they fancy themselves most exalted when least understood'. However, the feminine excellence which expresses itself in 'sentiment' remains a model too good for the transactions of this world; indeed, Miss Howe, the

---

[39] Carroll, 68.

composer of this encomium, has herself been seen sometimes failing by these standards, and 'aiming at *wit*, that wicked misleader'.

In Richardson's own correspondence—his own diligent practice of sociability—the model has to be more playfully entertained because of the novelist's understanding of his own gender. He writes to Sophia Westcomb that the feminine familiarity conjured in correspondence is 'friendship avowed under hand and seal: friendship upon bond, as I may say: more pure, yet more ardent, and less broken in upon, than personal conversation can be even amongst the most pure, because of the deliberation it allows, from the very preparation to, and action of writing'.[40] But the correspondence which makes 'distance presence' belongs primarily to 'your sex' since 'ours . . . makes a correspondence dangerous'. So he must elucidate coyly a vicarious enjoyment of what he has supposed a feminine privilege: 'Who would not choose . . . to have a delight in retiring to her closet, and there, by pen and ink, continue, and, as I may say, perpetuate, the ever agreeable and innocent pleasures that flow from social love, from hearts united by the same laudable ties?' In the guise of a receptive amanuensis, and always professing admiration for those who were his admirers, Richardson cajoled many an expression of 'social love' from his female correspondents. The placing of masculinity within a 'social' world celebrated in supposedly feminine writing was to be a different kind of problem in *Sir Charles Grandison*.

Richardson's 'Angel of a man' is to be distinguished in the potency of his actions, the efficacy of his arrangements, from the privately virtuous females who endlessly discuss him. Yet the effect of his management of everybody's aspirations is constantly to return the narrative to privately familial patterns of 'society', and to the private confidences of the largely feminine correspondence which defines him. The strange status of virtuous masculinity in this novel is captured in Mrs Shirley's characterization of the book's substance-less hero: 'He, compared to us, is as the public to the private. I hope we are good people . . . But yet, to him, we are but as that private' (i. 307). The reduction to simile of a vocabulary devised for the apportioning of social responsibilities bespeaks the actual impossibility of showing 'public' action and 'public' virtue in this novel. Sir Charles is always off arranging something to somebody's

---

[40] Carroll, 65.

benefit ('*His* welfare is the concern of hundreds, perhaps') but women can only speculate about this. He does write letters, but they are literally enclosed within the correspondences of his female admirers, or read aloud by Dr Bartlett to the assembled company—the private society—in his own drawing room. Residually, the vocabulary that Richardson deploys may have referred the eighteenth-century reader to standards of disinterested public responsibility, but formally the novel is empowered only to produce a paragon defined by relations of private allegiance, relations consistently represented in metaphors of familial affiliation.

And these are often metaphors, in excess of ties of blood.[41] The Grandisons are 'a family of love . . . We are true brothers and sisters' (i. 133), and into this 'family', with the 'Good Man' at its centre, all deserving characters are admitted: 'call me' 'daughter', 'sister', 'brother', 'father', they demand of each other. Sir Charles is a former and reformer of families. 'Were every family so happy as to have Sir Charles Grandison for a mediator when misunderstandings happened, there would be a very few lasting differences among relations' (ii. 344); but, in this book, no family is untouched by his blessing or unreformed by his recommendations. This 'matrimony-promoter' (ii. 323) roams widely to perform his ministry, drawing even the previously blameworthy into the familial fold. Here, where the novel appears most secure and unrelenting in its establishment of moral value, it is, as ever, most vulnerable. For it is a text in which sociability is narrowed to an elysium of familial contentment, a domain where sentiments can be shared (eyes glisten and cheeks glow) because of the exclusion of any non-familial name for social relations. Indeed, this generates problems internal to the ideal, most notably in what Tony Tanner refers to as the text's 'pervading sense of incest'. The difficulty that Harriet has in naming her relationship with the male paragon ('*ought* there not to have been a relation between us' (ii. 264)) is the text's real problem. What kind of figure can Sir Charles be who is immaculate father to all—'virtuous, even . . . to chastity' (ii. 497); who is prospective husband, yet goes by the name of 'brother'? Even in the sentimental bliss of Colnebrooke, even in a world shrunk to the familial, identities can be protean, relations uncertain.

---

[41] For a succinct description of the novel's 'familialization' of relations, see Tony Tanner's note in *Adultery and the Novel*, 178.

Here again, Richardson's problems arise from the very consistency of his vocation as instructor. Everywhere are attempted redemptions of *Clarissa*'s harsh logic. Sir Charles is made some sort of anti-type of James Harlowe; he is the son who takes over paternal responsibility, but to save rather than to usurp. As if to convince the reader of the efficacy of the hero's benevolent machinations, he is even likened to the villainous male, the abiding example of Lovelace: 'Were he and I alone, he'd have me before I knew where I was. Had he been a wicked man, he would have been a *very* wicked one', writes his sister Charlotte (i. 297). The chorus of unified sentiments which is the odd, embracing family constructed around Richardson's virtuous man refers us back to the Harlowes, and to his earlier depiction of degraded social relations. For Clarissa's family have been 'all of a sentiment' only in their opposition to her personified virtue (i. 30). From the very beginning of '*Clarissa*', 'Our family has indeed been strangely discomposed.—*Discomposed!* —It has been in *tumults*' (i. 3). For Clarissa herself 'the world is but one great family', yet the 'narrow selfishness' which she sees opposed to this ideal derives from the presumptuous pursuit by her own family of what it sees as its interests. The family is the ideal of harmony and yet also the body of contradiction and conflict.

The Harlowe family is ruled by 'the great motive, *paternal authority*' (i. 61) whose 'loud voice' (i. 209) reverberates through the rooms of the house and the reports of whose dissatisfaction inform all its conversations. The family is ruled by the purposes of male violence and 'aggrandisement', by the son who acts out, but usurps, the angry strategies of '*my father's will*'. Such purposes manifest themselves in the 'language of the family' (i. 58) which stresses Clarissa's absolute dependence on this will. As a subordinate in this despotism, Clarissa's mother, too, is caught up in the effort to possess her heart. Like her daughter, Clarissa's mother, a 'gentle and sensible mind', envisages order in terms of familial harmony and 'dreads, for jealousy and heart-burnings in her own family, late so happy and so united' (i. 22). At the behest of male will she assails Clarissa with a 'language so condescendingly moving' (i. 209) as to confirm the irreversibility of her daughter's isolation. The supposed head of the Harlowe family, whose 'authority', says Clarissa, 'could have saved me from the effect of . . . deep machinations' (iii. 341), can realize that 'authority' only in the debased form of a paternal 'curse'. This family is a model of all responsibilities traduced.

Eventually, turned in upon itself in the silence of guilt and recrimination, removed from the particular society in whose regard Clarissa's marriage to Solmes should have elevated it, the Harlowes live out a fated peversion of the laws of sentiment. 'What an unhappy family was this family', in which all try to avoid 'the mutual reproaches of eyes that spoke when tongues were silent' (iv. 534). Now, too late, a communication beyond words is recognized; the 'loud voice' is silenced. But now the members of the family flee the meanings in each others' eyes, moving restlessly and blindly through the rooms and corridors of the family home.

For Richardson, to celebrate the possibilities (though we might think this is exactly the wrong word) of masculine virtue is necessarily to have to provide an alternative to *this*. But then *Clarissa* has elucidated all too graphically the predicament of sensibility. *Sir Charles Grandison*'s answer is refrain, insistence, compulsive unanimity; it has only a 'language of the family' made universal. At the heart of the family, and the novel, is an 'exemplar' who is to guarantee the operations of sentimental communication. Yet this 'Good Man' can only be a shadow of others' discourse. The problem may become apparent in Richardson's last novel, but it is implicit in his earlier fiction.

*   *   *

I am apt to add three pages for one I take away.

(Richardson to Edward Young, December 1744).[42]

Sir *Charles Grandison* is as it is because it is a supplement to, rather than a departure from, its author's earlier writing, and *Clarissa* in particular. In fact, it makes sense to see the composition of Richardson's last novel in terms of his renowned habits of addition and recapitulation—the production of texts out of the rereading of his own writings. The delineation of virtue involves, for this novelist more than any other of the eighteenth century, practices of revision and belated explanation. A professional organizer of others' texts for the press, Richardson was the most fastidious editor of his own works. To understand what it might have been to read 'for the sentiment', it is important to understand how, and why, his attempts to compose instructively affecting narratives necessitated rigorous

---

[42] Carroll, 61.

procedures of correction—how he attempted to control interpretation.

The novelist had to be an editor as well, because he had to ensure that his novels moved and instructed in the right proportions. He had to attend to how his stories were (or might be) read. The work of correction, control, censorship was a moral imperative. The irony is that Richardson's attempts to govern, for the sake of virtue, the interpretation of his narratives reveal exactly their capacity to generate ambiguities, to proliferate the most untoward of readings. Like others who turned to novel-writing, Richardson had to rescue his chosen 'vehicle' from the reputation of impropriety and moral equivocation. His minute and pietistic attention to the details of possible (mis)interpretation (an attention made insistent within the novels themselves) was one guarantee of instructive intent. It also was, and is, an intrusive anxiety, a practice testifying to the morally refractory tendencies of narrative. Everywhere claims to rectitude are shadowed by the possibility of hermeneutic error and fickle excitement.

Richardson was led to the writing of *Pamela* by the composition of his *Letters written to and for Particular Friends, on the Most Important Occasions*, which was begun in the late 1730s but not completed and published until 1741, after the first two volumes of *Pamela* had already appeared. In one sense it is a prototype for the novels, and gives us a glimpse of how Richardson developed his cameos of sentiment out of a fiction of letter-writing as the most poignant form of moral discourse. The exemplary epistles it contains show intimate enquiry touching off 'sensible' moral reflection. In another sense, the peremptory fragments of instructive correspondence that it provides are prescriptive in a way that, he was to discover, novels could not be. The *Letters* address themselves to problems which reappear in the novels: the selection of a spouse, the dangers of remarriage, the nature of correct conversation, the disastrous temptations of profligacy. Indeed, much of the editorial direction is also the same; the letters are written 'to *mend the heart and improve the understanding*', 'to inculcate the principles of virtue and benevolence';[43] the exemplary letter conflates stylistic propriety and moral exactitude, like the correspondence of the novels' heroines. Yet this edifying text is separated by a gulf from the powers and demands of those novels. In the latter, the writer attempted

---

[43] Richardson, *Letters written to and for Particular Friends, on the Most Important Occasions*, ed. B. W. Downs (London, 1928), xxvii.

something especially 'lively and affecting' (*Clarissa*, i, p. xiv)—a recruitment of sympathy, a sustained engagement of 'interest'. Even as he set his fiction to correct the habits of readers expecting only 'diversion', he also exploited the compulsion to read 'for the story'. While he worked to control the implications of his narratives, and to raise them above the level of 'mere' story, he was curiously highlighting the possibility of diverted readings.

The means by which Richardson strove to explicate his texts' moralisms, and to absolve them from any reputation of impropriety, are many and various. Most important is the process of rewriting by which, often through several editions, his novels were realigned to actual and imagined debates concerning their instructive potential. The length and density of the novels is the more remarkable given that they were minutely revised. (I will return later to the editorial processes by which *Clarissa*, which was amended with special care, was transformed.) But the novels were also supplemented by other, extraneous and sometimes querulously corrective, texts. There were pamphlets written by Richardson defending aspects of the fiction: his 'Answer to the Letter of a Very Reverend and Worthy Gentleman' justifying the fire scene in *Clarissa*; the 'ANSWER to a LETTER from a FRIEND, who had objected to Sir CHARLES GRANDISON'S Offer to allow his Daughters . . . to be educated Roman-Catholics'.[44] There were notes, prefaces, postscripts, and indexes, uneasily inhabiting a marginal territory made both possible and difficult by the very fiction of writing as editorship. There were the letters, many transcribed by Richardson for posterity, which constitute a moralistic commentary on the instructive novelist's career. There were the collections of Sentiments, Aphorisms, and 'Meditations' drawn from the novels—perpetuated beyond Richardson's death in anthologies of their 'beauties'.

Such supplementary texts testify to the problems Richardson faced in attempting what, without the residual irony to be detected in Fielding's use of a similar phrase, he called 'a New Species of Writing'.[45] Take *A Collection of the Moral and Instructive*

---

[44] *See* W. M. Sale, *Samuel Richardson: A Bibliographical Record of his Literary Career with Historical Notes* (1936; rpt. New York, 1969).

[45] Letter to Aaron Hill, Jan. 1747: Carroll, 78. For Fielding's description of his version of narrative as a 'Species of writing, which I have affirmed to be hitherto unattempted in our Language', see the Preface to *Joseph Andrews*, ed. M. Battestin (Oxford, 1967), 10.

Sentiments, Maxims, Cautions, and Reflexions, Contained in the Histories of Pamela, Clarissa, and Sir Charles Grandison, published in 1755. Originally the separate sections of this work were devised as indexes to the novels, guides to their educative potential. But the (literal) separation of these 'Sentiments' from the narratives, while it is a gesture which assures the novel-reader of its explanatory capacity, inadvertently draws attention to a possible discrepancy between moralism and novel. What Richardson referred to as the 'Pith and Marrow' of 'reading'[46] comprises a text which exists to justify the novels, but which is also completely divorced from them. The alphabeticized platitudes of the *Collection* have escaped the pressing requirements of the narrative 'moment'. Abstracted from the 'heart'-felt communications of the epistolary novels, evading the problematic claims of particular feeling, these 'sentiments' are all precept, and are strangely inapplicable to the narratives that they reconstitute. The 'Advice' directed at 'Young Women' with which the *Collection* abounds scarcely copes with the significance, and the irreversibility, of Clarissa's fate. The insufficiency of specific rules and the conflict between different impulses of propriety might be dramatized in the novels, but they are silenced in Richardson's remedial gloss. Avoiding the difficulties of making narrative instructive, the pure instruction of the *Collection* has no story to tell. It calls attention, therefore, to those very difficulties. The need to clarify and re-propose speaks of a doubt inherent in 'Instruction'.

Richardson's strategies to make his novels correct were not just the consequence of personal obsession. His elevation of sensibility had to be something 'new' because it had to be distinguished from the content of dangerously exciting 'romance'. His claims for the moral efficacy of his writings imply an intensification of the effects of reading (and many of his correspondents were keen to describe how they were brought to a 'passion of crying' or a complete euphoria by his products).[47] They must therefore work particularly hard to acquit themselves of the excitement and intoxication conventionally associated, at the time Richardson was writing, with too intense an experience of seductive narratives. Indeed, in the third edition of *Clarissa*, published in 1751, he adds to the Conclusion ('*Supposed to*

---

[46] Letter to Thomas Edwards, Aug. 1755, cited in Eaves and Kimpel, *Biography*, 421.
[47] See, for instance, letters from Colly Cibber (Barbauld, ii. 169) or Lady Bradshaigh (Barbauld, iv. 239–49).

be written by Mr Belford') a solemn demonstration of the fate awaiting those (women) whose terrible error is to be captivated by the wrong kind of book. For the purpose of 'answering the *good ends* designed by the publication of this work' (iv 536), he provides a description of how Polly Horton is brought to ruin by her fondness for 'that sort of reading which is but an earlier debauchery for young minds, preparative to the grosser at riper years, to wit romances and novels, songs and plays, and those without distinction, moral or immoral (iv. 543). Under the 'inflaming' influence of 'books so light and frothy' it is 'no wonder that, like early fruit, she was soon ripened to the hand of the insidious gatherer' (iv. 544).

Yet Richardson repeats those images which distinguish, if any are going to, the excitements of eighteenth-century 'romances': the abduction and imprisonment of a beautiful young heroine, the swoons and tremblings of afflicted feminine sensibility. As Alan McKillop writes of *Pamela*, 'If Richardson's story touches the apologues of the periodicals and the irresponsibility of pastoral romance on the one hand, it touches scandalous narratives of seduction and rape on the other'.[48] The remark could apply equally to Richardson's other two novels. There is a scandal internal to even the most 'instructive' of narratives; this is the possibility that it, too, might be 'inflaming'. The investment in feminine sensibility does not, in itself, produce a text which avoids such a possibility. Indeed, it can make matters more difficult, especially inasmuch as Richardson produces his feminine ideal as a guide for a notional female reader. For it is in an image of the relation of narrative to a construction of the feminine imagination that the myth of the disreputable text, a text which is always other than the one being written, looms so large.[49] Eighteenth-century novels worried over the reactions of their actual female readers, but they also made the female a metaphor of the mis-reader—gulled by narrative into improper excitements, released by the private experience of a text into a realm of otherwise prohibited fantasy. This image is famously supported by Dr Johnson in *The Rambler* of 31 March 1750, where he writes that what we call the novel and he calls 'the comedy of romance' remains dangerous as 'the entertainment of minds

---

[48] A. D. McKillop, *Samuel Richardson: Printer and Novelist* (1936; rpt. Hamden, Conn., 1960), 31.

[49] For an informative discussion of this see J. T. Taylor, *Early Opposition to the English Novel* (Morningside Heights, NY, 1943), especially 52–86.

unfurnished with ideas, and therefore easily susceptible of impressions; not fixed by principles, and therefore easily following the current of fancy; not informed by experience, and consequently open to every false suggestion and partial account.'[50] He credits narrative with a 'power of example' which is so great 'as to take possession of the memory by a kind of violence, and produce effects almost without the intervention of the will'.[51]

But then Johnson was one of Richardson's great admirers. In a brief introduction to the essay Richardson wrote for *The Rambler* of 19 February 1751, Johnson describes him as the author 'who has enlarged the knowledge of human nature, and taught the passions to move at the command of virtue'.[52] In fact, Johnson credits Richardson's writing with the same kind of power—the power to excite and direct passions—which he associates with the dangerous irresistibility of morally pernicious narratives. Richardson's achievement, for him, is not to neglect or suppress passions, but to bring them under the sway of virtue. The sensibility whose signs and gestures compose the picture of such virtue remains, even in the most self-consciously moral of all novels, ambiguous. It exists always alongside the possibility of its excess, and demands a reading which responds to the spectacle of the palpitating feminine body, a reading which can become excited. In his *Rambler* essay, Johnson finds it difficult to separate the topics and the construction of 'romance', the subjects which might not be 'most proper for imitation' and the possible promiscuity of the very form. The possibility of an inevitable conflation of form and content, whereby every novel becomes too exciting or ambiguous to be instructive, haunts Richardson's depictions of feeling.

Richardson's novelistic career is an important part of an as yet imperfectly written history; this is the history not of the self-confident 'rise of the novel', but of the self-consciousness of novels in the eighteenth century as they attempted to deal with the reputation of their impropriety or 'lowness'.[53] The reputation is typically preserved within the novels themselves; it is not uniquely in Richardson's writing that we discover a concern with the tendency of fiction to arouse inordinate passions, to evade moralistic control. A

---

[50] Samuel Johnson, *The Rambler*, No. 4 (Mar. 1750), *Yale Edition*, iii. 21.
[51] Ibid. 22.   [52] *The Rambler*, No. 97 (Feb. 1751), *Yale Edition*, iv. 153.
[53] See L. Davis, *Factual Fictions: The Origins of the English Novel* (New York, 1983).

nice example of how far this concern could be taken is Charlotte Lennox's *The Female Quixote*, first published in 1752; it is an example the more pointed because it was written in part in homage to Richardson, who was responsible for printing it. This novel represents, and finally corrects, the series of errors into which a young woman is led by 'supposing Romances were real Pictures of Life' and by drawing from them 'all her Notions and Expectations'.[54] Both Johnson and, more actively, Richardson advised and encouraged its author. With Johnson initially acting as an intermediary, Richardson received Lennox's manuscript of the novel, and through the correspondence which ensued we can be in no doubt as to his approbation of her project, or indeed as to her admiration for *Pamela* and *Clarissa*.[55] But this presents a problem, for *The Female Quixote* cannot simply be taken as a satire upon the fantastic extravagances of obscure French romances. At one stage in the book, its heroine, Arabella, asks a servant to construct for the men who are trying to rescue her from the delusions of romantic fantasy a narrative which will 'relate exactly every Change of my Countenance; number all my Smiles, Half-smiles, Blushes, Turnings pale, Glances, Pauses, Full-stops, Interruptions; the Rise and Falling of my Voice; every Motion of my Eyes; and every Gesture which I have used for these Ten Years past.'[56] Here is precisely that lexicon of gestures whose articulacy is so important to Richardson. It is a sign of the problem with which he was faced, that it is often difficult to distinguish the target of Lennox's satire from the sensitivities that he has celebrated, and the vocabulary that he has used. Biography tells us that Lennox was Richardson's admirer; the text tells us that criticism of the 'romance' can refer us to the most morally committed of novels. Arabella's fantasy, in *The Female Quixote*, is hardly removed from the facts of Clarissa's situation. The risks of abduction, improper communication, and dangerous contact with which Lennox's 'heroine' is obsessed, and which are the 'Mistakes' of her imagination, are the risks which all of Richardson's heroines actually run. And *The Female Quixote* itself establishes Arabella not as a gross parody or anti-type of feminity, but as one whose virtuous 'sensibility' and 'heart' are revealed in even the most ludicrous of her delusions. All it takes, after several hundred pages of her 'Mistakes',

[54] Charlotte Lennox, *The Female Quixote*, ed. Margaret Dalziel (London, 1970), 7.
[55] See Duncan Isles, Appendix, ibid. 418–27.
[56] Ibid. 121–2.

is a fairly perfunctory penultimate chapter to restore her to what was always her implicit condition, to 'every Virtue and laudable Affection of the Mind'.[57] Her sensibility may have been her weakness, but it was also the promise of her strength.

Most novels of the eighteenth century contain some warnings about the dangers of fiction, but it is rarely clear what the really disreputable texts are. The problem of Lennox's 'target' is an example of a more general problem. The debates and invective, the projects and imitations, which constitute the propriety of fiction as an issue during the eighteenth century have an almost perfect circularity. Richardson glorifies a self-intoxicating feminine sensibility yet warns of those books which turn sensibility into credulity and excess, citing Fielding as an example of one who has abused the powers of narrative.[58] Fielding suggests, in *Shamela*, the possibility of a sub-text to *Pamela* in which the virtuous heart and the appearance of vulnerability can be construed as the most hypocritical of invitations to the passion which they supposedly oppose. In turn, Fielding's novels are found accused by Lady Mary Wortley Montagu of 'being very mischievous. They place a merit in extravagant Passions, and encourrage young people to hope for impossible events to draw them out of the misery they chuse to plunge themselves into.'[59] The terms appropriated by all parties remain remarkably stable in the course of such arguments. Each monologue is on the side of virtue and condemns the tendency of certain writings to excite improper passions. All that changes is the identity of the critics and of the writers who are condemned. Even the imitations of pastiches of successful works interpret or reconstitute the works in question in a scurrilous manner for what they claim to be the cause of virtue. So, for instance, the anonymous *Anti-Pamela* of 1741 is no less moralistic a text than *Pamela* itself, and indeed surrounds its 'story' with a series of comments on the lessons to be drawn from the narrative in a way that is neither ironical nor actually incompatible with the specific moralism of Richardson's novel.

It is hardly surprising that the legend of indecency is one which

---

57 Isles, Appendix to *The Female Quixote*, ed. Dalziel, 383.
58 See, for example, R. Paulson and T. Lockwood (eds.), *Fielding: The Critical Heritage* (London, 1969), 174–7 and 334–6.
59 Lady Mary Wortley Montagu, *The Complete Letters of Lady Mary Wortley Montagu*, ed. R. Halsband and I. Grundy (3 vols., Oxford, 1977), iii. 66.

lacks an original example, a work to be held up as *the* dangerous and misleading romance. If we return to the popular novels of the early eighteenth century, to the writings of Eliza Haywood, for instance, or before that to Mrs Manley, we do not find the originally promiscuous narrative. Manley created a scandal by libelling Whig public figures, but (and the point is that it could be said about so many novelists of the eighteenth century) 'Assume a moral pose she did, as well as inveigh against the "vice" of reading romances'.[60] Equally, the work of perhaps the most popular novelist before Richardson, Eliza Haywood, might contain all those elements of the deluding romance identified in *The Female Quixote*, but cannot serve as the image of impropriety or indecency. If we take as an example *Love in Excess*, her first novel, published in 1719, we find the entanglement of male desire and feminine 'delicacy' which is recomposed in Richardson's novels: the intractable nuances and dangers of conversation and correspondence, the illicit rendezvous, the contravention of paternal edict, the tears 'which, unstudy'd and incoherent as they were, had a delicacy in 'em'.[61] If we wish, such figures can now be read as proleptic of *Clarissa*, or of later 'sentimental' novels like *The Man of the World* or even *The Vicar of Wakefield*. For the novel of sentiment, try as it might, is never completely to rid itself of the suspicion of romance. Indeed, the representation in Haywood's novel of a language describing pleasure in 'Excess', in the overflowing of the heart's yearning and impulses, might be said to find its redemption and refinement in the representation of sentimental articulacy.

What is more, it was not difficult for a writer like Haywood to adapt her novels to the expectations raised amongst prospective readers by Richardson's work. By the time of *The History of Miss Betsy Thoughtless*, written at the end of her career, his influence is registered by her in a narrative in which the defence of virtue in the form of virginity is paramount. But such defence is allowed to be dramatic only in the face of the perennial promptings of passion and excitability: 'Miss Betsy was now just entering into her fourteenth year,—a nice and delicate time, in persons of her sex . . . as she wanted nothing to render her liable to the greatest temptations, so

[60] R. Dobree, *English Literature in the Early Eighteenth Century 1700–1740* (1959; rpt. Oxford, 1968), 404.

[61] Eliza Haywood, *Love in Excess* (first published 1719; 4th edn., London, 1722), 53.

she stood in need of the surest arms for her defence against them.'[62] The temptations of mistaken alliance and ill-advised correspondence are central to the plot of this novel, and yet compose a narrative which moralizes upon the dilemmas and errors into which women of 'delicacy' might be led. It is not possible finally to separate romance from that which claims to be other than romance, the disreputable from the instructive text. Like Richardson himself, Eliza Haywood claims to write in the cause of 'Virtue'.[63]

We may think that the protestations of eighteenth-century novelists about their instructive designs, and about the pernicious tendencies of novels other than their own, are routine tokens. Even if they are just conventional concessions, though, the insistence of the convention is enough to suggest to us the formal and moral insecurities which novels of the period had to conquer. The cause of virtue had to be acknowledged somehow, and Richardson achieved the status that he enjoyed in his own day partly because of the scrupulous attention he appeared to devote to this cause. Nor was this a promotional illusion. Richardson dedicated himself to the moral intricacies of his texts. It was to assure himself and others of their perfectly instructive purposes that he constantly edited and supplemented them. Always there was the possibility of misinterpretation, and always there was the need to revise and restate. The clearest expression of this need is found in the passage from the first to the third edition of *Clarissa*.[64] Ironically, the very epistolary fiction which permitted misreading because it presented a variety of views and aspirations—sometimes complementary, sometimes contending—also left room for editorial intervention.

---

[62] Eliza Haywood, *The History of Miss Betsy Thoughtless* (4 vols, London, 1751), i. 19.

[63] For some discussion of Haywood's popularity and of the relation between her works and those of Richardson see J. C. Beasley, *Novels of the 1740s* (Athens, Ga., 1982), 36–7, and 162.

[64] In coming to grips with the changes that Richardson made, I have found invaluable S. Van Marter's two articles: 'Richardson's Revisions of *Clarissa* in the Second Edition', *Studies in Bibliography*, 26 (1973), and 'Richardson's Revisions of *Clarissa* in the Third and Fourth Editions', *Studies in Bibliography*, 28 (1975). See also M. Kinkead-Weekes, '*Clarissa* Restored?' *Review of English Studies*, 10 (1959). Though I have used originals of the 1st and 3rd editions of *Clarissa* for purposes of comparison, all references are given to either the Everyman version of the 3rd edition, or to *Clarissa; or, the History of a Young Lady*, ed. A. Ross (Harmondsworth, 1985), a recent and widely available version of the 1st edition of the novel.

In the passage through the second (1749) to the third (1751) edition, the novel became ever more dense with the editor's guidance and advice. The many minute changes that Richardson made to *Clarissa* in order to heighten its proprieties—'the massive refinement of thousands of details . . . designed to elevate the tone of his novel through greater formal clarity and disciplined restraint'[65]—are now hardly visible to us. But as he rewrote the book, he produced many amendments and directions which are anything but silent. He abandoned the voice of the pluralistic editor whom we are to suppose as the writer of the Preface to the first edition, the editor content to commit interpretation to the 'opinion' of 'several judicious friends';[66] in revised versions, he (overtly, sometimes clumsily) intervened to control the 'opinion' of the reader. Passages added to the second and third editions were actually drawn to the reader's attention by marks printed in the margin (not reproduced in twentieth-century editions of *Clarissa*). He went to the lengths of publishing in 1751 his *Letters and Passages Restored from the Original Manuscripts of the History of Clarissa*, which, clinging to the awkward fiction of 'restoration', provided for the purchasers of the first edition most of the more substantial passages added to later editions. Richardson's amendments were not self-effacing. The moral and instructive text, to be read 'for the sentiment', did not attempt to conceal the trace of its discriminations.

Even without some of the marks of reformulation available to the original readership, but since forgotten, many of these traces remain. There are, for example, the italicizations which emphasize in particular Lovelace's broken promises and Clarissa's moral sentiments, and whose number is greatly increased from the first to the third edition.[67] This increase alone is indicative of the novelist's concern to govern the interpretation of his characters' letters, but there are more cumbersome methods by which 'opinion' was to be organized. There is the long index-summary added to the beginning of the second edition of *Clarissa* and then placed at the end of each volume of the third edition. This is a special kind of index; it is a

---

[65] Van Marter, *Studies in Bibliography*, 28 (1975), 143.

[66] Richardson, *Clarissa*, 1st ed., edn. Ross, 35.

[67] Such recourse to internal differentiation and emphasis was repeated in the italicizations which distinguish the 1st from the 2nd editions of *Sir Charles Grandison*: see R. Pierson, 'The Revisions of Richardson's *Sir Charles Grandison*', *Studies in Bibliography*, 21 (1968), 163–89.

guide to reading, which recapitulates motives and attributes praise or blame. As Richardson himself explained to Aaron Hill, he chose 'to give a little Abstract of the Story, that it might be clearly seen what it was, and its Tendency, and to obviate as I went along, tho' covertly, such Objections as I had heard (as I have done by the Italicks)'.[68] And there are the directive footnotes which he added to his novel—didactic injuctions, compensating for the 'want of due attention' of his readers (i. 353), which have often been found embarrassing or hilarious by modern readers.

These notes are typically addressed to a 'reader' who is prone to misconstrue the implications of the narrative. Unsurprisingly, it is usually a female reader who is taken to be the habitual misinterpreter, the moralistic editor being especially liable to demand the 'particular attention of such of the fair sex as are more apt to read for the sake of amusement than instruction' (ii. 35). A feminine writing, the private record of sensibility, may be Richardson's model of virtuous discourse; a feminine reading, misguided into false excitements and empathies, is equally the model of mistaken identifications, of virtue forgotten. So when Lovelace boasts of being 'lord of the destiny of a Clarissa Harlowe', and warns Belford *Let not any of the sex know my exultation*', Richardson adds this footnote:

Mr Lovelace might have spared his caution on this occasion, since many of the sex (we mentioned it with regret) who on the first publication have read thus far, and even to the lady's first escape, have been readier to censure her for over-niceness, as we have observed in a former note . . . than him for artifices and exultations not less cruel and ungrateful, than ungenerous and unmanly. (ii. 33)

Such supplementary complaints are necessary to correct readers inclined to attribute to Lovelace 'a greater merit than was due to him' (i. 353), 'to remind the reader' (incessantly) of how 'artfully' he has contrived the trajectory of events (see i. 254 and 257).

The momentum of Clarissa's 'tragedy' cannot be allowed to be accidental, sweeping up Lovelace as well (though here the editor is straining against a consequence of the narrative's inflexible logic). A host of appended notes insists on Lovelace's manipulative capacities, his 'manner of working' (i. 463): 'She was mistaken in this. Mr Lovelace *did* foresee this consequence. All his contrivances led to it' (i. 425); 'It may not be amiss to observe in this place, that Mr

[68] Letter of July 1749: Carroll, 125.

Lovelace artfully contrived to drive the family on' (i. 441); 'Well he might be so sure, when he had the art to play them off . . . to make them all join to promote his views, unknown to themselves, as is shown in several of his preceding letters' (i. 453). Such notes were in addition to changes within the 'letters' themselves, many of these also seeming designed to amplify Lovelace's machinations. These corrections, like the exasperated footnotes, have the effect of high-lighting, rather than solving, the problem of Lovelace's qualities. In a series of elaborations of his attitude to any possible marriage to Clarissa, for instance, the text attempts to go further than it had previously done to show that he only genuinely thinks of marriage once his own actions have ruled it out—that all earlier protestations have been tactical. But as Richardson tinkered with the novel in order to emphasize this, he also showed Lovelace, at the far reaches of duplicity, even more appreciative of Clarissa's virtue. If he deceives her, she is 'A lady worth deceiving!' (ii 217); if he comes to state that marriage has not been a real prospect, it is via reflection on the attributes which would make Clarissa desirable as a wife—'that native dignity, and obvious purity of mind and manners, which fill every one with reverence' (iii. 473). The editorial effort is to demonstrate how disingenuous Lovelace's promises to Clarissa really are; the effect is to produce his correspondence as more than ever accurately introspective. To show him dissembling, the text must have him describing the truth. It is no wonder that Richardson needed the footnotes as well. The attempt was to show the extent of the villain's 'intriguing', for, indeed, all too intriguing was what he had become.

Richardson's problem with Lovelace is inherent in the novel's design. Having read the first four volumes of the earliest version of *Clarissa*, a 'Mrs Belfour' wrote to Richardson in October 1748 to draw attention to this fact: 'You have drawn a villain above nature; and you make that villain a sensible man, with many good qualities, and you have declared him not an unbeliever'.[69] 'Mrs Belfour' was, in fact, Lady Bradshaigh, who was to become Richardson's most important correspondent over the years that followed. Even this most enthusiastic of the novelist's admirers could not help but detect that Lovelace was a 'sensible man': 'you must know, (though I shall blush again,) that if I were to die for it, I cannot help being fond of Lovelace. A sad dog! why would you make him so wicked, and yet

[69] Barbauld, iv. 200.

so agreeable?[70] These are not just the (half-lamenting, half-rhapsodic) comments of one of those whom Richardson was to dismiss as 'Story-Lovers and Amusement-Seekers'[71] For Richardson, Lady Bradshaigh turned out to be the most gratifyingly responsive and moralistic of readers. The story of her protracted correspondence and near-flirtatious relationship with the novelist tells of a communication into which both entered with enthusiasm, and which always had Richardson's novels as its pretext.[72] Yet Richardson had to chide even her for misjudging his villain: 'I have told you in my first letter that he had some good qualities given him, in compliment to the eye and ear of Clarissa. But little did I think at the time that those qualities would have given women of virtue and honour such a liking to him, as I have found to be the case with many.'[73] With the most compliant of followers, he has to intervene to correct tendencies implicit in his own text.

Attempts to prescribe the proper interpretation of Lovelace's words and actions, though crucial, constitute only a part of Richardson's anxious editorial labour. Most significantly, he also worked to absolve Clarissa from various kinds of 'censure'. Footnotes apart (e.g. ii, 313–14), a perverse means was to introduce in succeeding editions more of his heroine's self-criticisms, as if in an attempt to foresee possible censure of her conduct and subsume it under the honesty of her self-examination.[74] Inasmuch as such elaborate amendment was prompted by specific evidence of readers' 'Inattention', that evidence was mainly gathered from those model readers admitted to the novelist's circle of virtuous correspondents. But then Richardson's editorial anxiety was in advance of, and in excess of, such evidence. From the first, he was in mind of misreading, and was organizing his novel to forestall objections. The first volumes of the first edition, for example, already contain some footnotes, referring the reader back to previous letters (or even forward to forthcoming ones) for proofs or explanations which might otherwise be missed. From the first, the 'editor' is stepping in

---

[70] Barbauld, iv. 180.
[71] Letter to Lady Bradshaigh, Dec. 1748: Carroll, 116.
[72] For the details of this story, see Eaves and Kimpel, *Biography*, 220–34.
[73] Letter of Oct. or Nov. 1748: Barbauld, iv. 233–4.
[74] Compare, for example, 1st edn., Letter 151 in the version edited by A. Ross (p. 517) and 3rd (Everyman) edn., Letter 52 (ii. 181); or 1st edn., Letter 176 (p. 576) and 3rd edn. Letter 77 (ii. 277); or 1st edn., Letter 200 (p. 643) and 3rd edn., Letter 101 (ii. 378–9).

to stitch together the text, to rid it of ambiguities. 'Clarissa as an example *to* the Reader: The Example not to be taken *from* the Reader', wrote Richardson in an early draft of the Preface to the third edition.[75] He became his own worried rereader, identifying the fissures in his narrative, the moments at which the instructive component of sentiment was liable to be forgotten. *Clarissa* comes to be massively supplemented. The space between precept and interpretation may be one in which literary criticism can now discover plural meanings and a conventionally valued freedom for the reader, but we should recognize that Richardson's endeavour was to make this space disappear.[76]

But there is another side to this. For Richardson, discussion of the implications of his novels was a necessary sign of their moral effectiveness. Though he seems rarely to have taken the advice that he solicited from his correspondents, he hungered after suggestions and reactions. As well as the anxiety of instructive intent, there was the (perhaps equally insecure) narcissism of instructive self-reference. In his correspondence, in his life as an author, Richardson strove to make *Clarissa* and *Sir Charles Grandison*, in particular, the topics of a moral debate: a debate about morality, and a debate in itself moral. To this effect he wrote to Hester Mulso in August 1754 about *Sir Charles Grandison*: 'the whole piece abounds, and was intended to abound, with situations that should give occasion for debate, or different ways of thinking. And it is but fair that every one should choose his or her party.[77] In the same month, Anne Dewes wrote to him enthusing over the pleasures to be gained from the novelist's very habit of supplementing his works: 'I am always glad to hear the few objections that have or can be made, or imagined, to Pamela, Clarissa, or Grandison, as it obliges the excellent author to give us more of his thoughts; and *more* and *more* we are wishing and desiring to have.'[78]

His testing of his last two novels on his friends before publication is not just insecurity; it looks more like a test of the readers than of

---

[75] R. F. Brissenden (ed.), *Samuel Richardson, Clarissa: Preface, Hints of Prefaces, and Postscript* (Los Angeles, 1964), 5.

[76] Warner (*Reading* Clarissa) and Eagleton (*The Rape of Clarissa*) both variously celebrate a freedom of interpretation that Richardson tried severely to limit. See also T. Castle, *Clarissa's Ciphers* (Ithaca, NY, 1982).

[77] Carroll, 311.

[78] Barbauld, iv. 93.

the texts.[79] Raised from 'the humble Guise of a *Novel*' (a form adopted 'only by way of Accomodation to the Manners and Taste of an Age overwhelmed with a Torrent of Luxury, and abandoned to Sound and Senselessness'[80]) each of Richardson's texts was to circulate as a devotional object, needing, like a catechism, to produce circumscribed inquiry. Editorial anxiety was never so far from authorial smugness:

> Many things are thrown out in the several characters, on purpose to provoke friendly debate; and perhaps as trials of the reader's judgement, manners, taste, and capacity. I have often sat by in company, and been silently pleased with the opportunity given me, by different arguers, of looking into the hearts of some of them, through the windows that at other times have been close shut up.[81]

When it comes to this business of discussing his fiction, the novelist's self-image is peculiarly uncensored: complacently patriach and voyeur. His was a social circle in which interpretation could be contained. The moral delicacies of the fiction were to arouse, in a small world of specialized discussion, the proper sentiments of the virtuous. So it was consistent with the eccentrically socialized context of Richardson's moralizing that Lady Bradshaigh should be introduced to Hester Mulso via the young woman's capacity to debate the intricacies of *Clarissa*:

> I am at present engaged with a most admirable young lady of little more than twenty, Miss Mulso, on the subject of paternal authority, and filial obedience, grounded on Clarissa's duty to her persecuting parents and on her dread of her gloomy father's curse. Miss Mulso is a charming writer . . . Your ladyship will be charmed with her part of the subject.[82]

No kind of discussion could be more congenial to Richardson; 'I have been voluminous in my part', he adds, 'When I love my correspondents, I write treatises.'

The attention that Richardson gave to his correspondence was hugely self-regarding, but it was not only that. By working to produce a circle of responsive female readers he was constituting a

---

[79] For an account of this process, see T. C. D. Eaves and B. D. Kimpel, 'The Composition of *Clarissa* and its Revision before Publication', *PMLA* 83 (1968), 416–28.

[80] Letter to Lady Bradshaigh, Dec. 1748: Carroll, 117.

[81] Richardson to Lady Echlin, Oct. 1754: Carroll, 315–16.

[82] Carroll, 184.

social ideal which was to be the proof of the moral efficacy of his writings. It was of the logic of this enterprise that the reverential writer of the 1749 *Remarks on Clarissa, Addressed to the Author* (probably Sarah Fielding) should frame her eulogy as a lengthy argument amongst a group of characters as to the merits of this novel. Such earnestly fixated conversation was the model for the attuned virtues of a text and its readers. In the way that he tried to live out this model, Richardson was looking for a social identity both for himself and for his writing.

*   *   *

My hand trembles, for I can scarce hold my pen. I am as mad as the poor injured Clarissa.

(Lady Bradshaigh to Richardson, October 1748)[83]

In 1748 and 1749, Lady Bradshaigh wrote to Richardson describing at some length her responses to *Clarissa*. Evidently, she was strongly affected: 'I verily believe I have shed a pint of tears, and my heart is still bursting, tho' they cease not to flow at this moment, nor will, I fear, for some time'.[84] If the accounts which she gave him of her responses seem hyperbolic, their hyperbole accords almost uncannily with the affected state which he and others imagined as the consequence of novel-reading. Here, apparently, are the confessions of one who has known 'the passions to move at the command of virtue'. Here, apparently, is a dutifully responsive reading which borders on the dangerously possessive excitements that Richardson saw as the property of irresponsible 'romance': 'When alone, in agonies would I lay down the book, take it up again, walk about the room, let fall a flood of tears, wipe my eyes, read again, perhaps not three lines, throw away the book, crying out, excuse me, good Mr. Richardson, I cannot go on.' In the letters that she wrote to *Clarissa's* evidently gratified author, the experience of reading is taken to have what now seems a strange, perhaps unbelievable, intensity. Lady Bradshaigh's descriptions of her susceptibility to fiction seem to replicate the sensibility of the virtuous heroine of whom she avidly read. The pathos of narrative is as upsetting as it is gripping: 'My spirits are strangely seized, my sleep is disturbed; waking in the night, I burst into a passion of

---

[83] Barbauld, iv. 201.   [84] Letter to Richardson, Jan. 1749: ibid. 240.

crying; so I did at breakfast this morning, and just now again.'
Indeed, this version of her experience of reading *Clarissa* goes
further; it follows the logic of Richardson's development of
sensibility to a conclusion discovered in the novels: to ailment,
affliction, disability—the final proofs of feeling.

In *Pamela*, Richardson attempted to reconcile the law of sentiment
(the principle of Pamela's natural and virtuous feelings) to a rigid
domestic regularity. The continuation of the novel beyond what
might have been its terminus (the marriage which conventionally
binds moral and material economies) led to the representation of a
'clockwork' world, in which benevolence is a necessary element in a
household's organization.[85] The ideal was one of sentiment serving
to organize social relations, to guarantee the proper postures of
submission, gratitude, and respectful unanimity. But sensibility in
Richardson's novels can be articulated as something other, and more
troubling, than this prim 'Virtue Rewarded'; the capacity for feeling
can also be excessive or self-destructive. When Lady Bradshaigh
declares herself struck down by the feelings aroused in reading
Clarissa, she seizes on an image to which that novel itself refers. As
long as sensibility, that capacity which escapes speech, is
represented as a set of bodily symptoms, the picture of exemplary
femininity can be one of sickness, of physical debility. The
palpitations of the 'sensible' woman can take on the appearance of an
ailment, the symptoms of a melancholy or hysteria which connote a
sensitivity become almost unsupportable. The body's collapse is the
sign of virtue *in extremis*. In Richardson's novels there is all that
trembling, fainting, constant application of hartshorn; sensibility
turns in on itself to illness because it is almost too good for this
world. Pursued by Mr B, Pamela stages the swoon which looks like
death—'they both, from the cold sweats I was in, thought me dying'
(i. 179); Clarissa, her delicacy apotheosized as the world's exemplary
exception, retreats into illness from which there is no return. What
could be more appropriate than that Lady Bradshaigh should
display her sensibility in this approved mode?

Clarissa's death is the inevitable end of her irremediable grief, her
physical decay represents a sickness of the heart. Dr H is the
exceptional practitioner who can recognize the body's eloquent
protest: 'Her heart's broken: she'll die, said he: there is no saving her'

[85] For the invocation of metaphors of 'machinery', see *Pamela* (i. 331; ii. 25; ii.
250).

(iv 177). He can recognize the wasting of her body as her heart's expression—the guise of a melancholy which is final proof of her embattled virtue. In this case, the physical frailty which has always been the sign of defensive sensibility is irreversible. Capitalizing on the Puritan injunction to meditate upon death, and working hard to persuade his readership that there is nothing suicidal in Clarissa's fate, Richardson lingers on his heroine's final illness, and makes her 'gratified rather than discomposed' at the contemplation of her demise: 'I must say I dwell on, I indulge (and, strictly speaking, I enjoy) the thoughts of death' (iv 258). Clarissa's ailing body is the symbol of virtuous sensibility; she is too good for the world, and feels too much.

This 'too much', this excess, is always a potential feature of femininity in Richardson's fiction. The heroine of *Sir Charles Grandison* may be rescued from distress, but in that novel we are still shown, with Clementina, a spectacle of admirably afflicted sensibility passing into sickness. Clementina's melancholy arouses the devoted tears of her family and of those who fascinatedly read of her in Sir Charles's correspondence. Her 'ramblings' bring together the novel's characters in the solidarity of a distressful affect: 'Thus rambled the poor lady! What, my dear Dr Bartlett can be more affecting than these absences, these reveries, of a mind once so sound and sensible?' (ii 489). Even though her conversation has become fragmented 'free talking' (ii 477), she is admitted to the community of affections which is the society of Sir Charles's friends and dependents. 'Gratitude, piety, sincerity, and every duty of the social life, are constitutional virtues in this lady. No disturbance of mind can weaken, much less efface them' (ii 490). As she reels and rambles, her every gesture a symptom of her distress, her 'malady', all are joined in the tears which testify to her virtue and to their sensibility.

'Delirium', amnesia, 'ramblings', do not, here, erase a 'delicacy' which affects as much through looks and gestures as through speech: 'In her unhappy delirium, she always preserved a high sense of that delicacy, which distinguishes the woman of true honour' (ii. 579). Indeed, looks and gestures, and the 'tears' which accompany them, speak beyond words. They speak of a 'distressed' saintliness which manifests itself as illness. 'Every good habit she preserves; yet, at other times, rambles much' (ii. 243). Her 'malady' does not truly disturb those around her and those who read of her back in England. Instead it confirms the power and value of a susceptibility to feeling.

The only complete cure for Clementina's affliction is envisaged as marriage. As in *Clarissa*, doctors accurately identify a sickness whose origin is more than physical: 'The physicians have absolutely given their opinion that she should marry' (iii. 301). Clementina herself accepts both diagnosis and prescription. She herself agrees with the vision of marriage as a perfect economy of pleasures: 'How happy . . . are those marriages which give as much joy to the relations on both sides as to the parties themselves' (iii. 345).But Sir Charles is spoken for, and illness is the recourse for one who cannot be accommodated in the order of things.

In Clementina's acceptance of her disordered condition is a necessary domestication of the dangers posed by an excessive sensibility. In a novel which proposes settlement and containment, the strength of feeling can pose a threat to controlling decorum. In fact, the possibility of real excess is enacted by Laurana in a sub-plot too histrionic to be cautionary: 'A deep melancholy first seized her; that was succeeded by raving fits; and it is suspected that the poor creature, eluding the care of her attendants, came to a miserable end' (iii. 447). This is the depiction of a capacity for feeling untethered from reticence and moral self-government. But it is Richardson's Italy where 'melancholy', by report, acts out such terminal desperation. The moral geography which produced the headings to the list of characters at the beginning of *Sir Charles Grandison* (grouped in the categories 'Men', 'Women', and 'Italians') may be laughable enough now, but it was influential enough then. 'Gothic' fiction of the later eighteenth century, for instance, was to alight upon Italy as the scene for many of its more extravagant fantasies. For Richardson (a man who never left England) Italy was, as it was to be for Anne Radcliffe, 'the other'. Italy is a convenient place of projection—a location for the excesses of feeling. It is where we find 'enthusiasm'—the overflowing of passions and affections beyond the bounds which in England, and in the gatherings around Sir Charles Grandison, are so properly established. Yet even if afflicted, even if 'Italian', virtue can rest secure in the tears of those who understand its integrity.

The object of the spectacle of 'melancholy' is the female body. It is through this body that the ennobling sensitivity of the feminine heart is revealed. The feminine body of Richardson's novels is given us in the representation of gesture, convulsion, irresolution, and involuntary movement; these are the signs of sentiment's purity.

Richardson constructs a, specifically feminine, body in terms of a system of symptoms, a set of indubitable correspondences between internal and external. The spectacle of the body, with its legible palpitations, evidences the movements of the heart. The body's visible fluctuations are symptomatic of the sensibility which cannot be disguised, but which is supposed not to be spoken. It is a corpus of irrepressible signs. At one point Sir Charles Grandison's sister reaches to her throat and declares that it is always possible to 'affix a proper meaning to those sudden throbs just here, puffing my neck; those half-suppressed but always involuntary sighs' (i. 421). She is reaching to her own body in an act of interpretation which the text itself is constantly performing. In a Richardson novel, the woman's body is the mediator of the truth of sentiment; it is beyond her control yet displays her virtue. It is, we are asked to believe, natural. The moral condition must have its physical embodiment; we are required to accept more than a metaphor when we learn that '[Clementina's] bosom heaved with the grandeur of her sentiments' (ii. 596). Such meaning cannot be challenged. Through *Sir Charles Grandison* can be read a list of the collapses, embraces, and blushes of women. They weep, and their bodies pulsate involuntarily, but all according to the rule of sentiment—Emily's eyes 'glistening . . . tho' she knew not for what, but sympathetically, as I may say' (ii. 133). Women are bound together—in Richardson's extraordinary version of femininity—in sighs, in tears, in postures and movements instantly understood. This is his version of essential sociability. It is a condition that he can only ever imagine.

3

The Availability of Virtue

IN 1779 there appeared through three consecutive issues of the Edinburgh periodical *The Mirror* a sentimental tale which became known, and much anthologized, as the 'Story of La Roche'. It was written by Henry Mackenzie, editor of *The Mirror*, and a man renowned chiefly for the success of his novel *The Man of Feeling*. It tells of how an atheistic philosopher living in France meets a clergyman (La Roche) and his daughter, how he comes to admire their simple virtue, and how, when the daughter dies, he learns to appreciate the combined sensibility and religiosity of the 'good old man's' reactions. The sceptical philosopher is made to acknowledge the worth of a religion which 'was that of sentiment, not theory'.[1] As he listens to La Roche preach, he is almost swayed: 'even the philosopher felt himself moved, and forgot, for a moment, to think why he should not'. As he sees 'The effects of religion on minds of sensibility' (Mackenzie's later title for the story), he almost succumbs to the effects himself:

Mr——'s heart was smitten;—and I have heard him, long after, confess that there were moments when the remembrance overcame him even to weakness; when, amidst all the pleasures of philosophical discovery, and the pride of literary fame, he recalled to his mind the venerable figure of the good La Roche, and wished that he had never doubted.[2]

In one way, the story is just a minor relic of sentimentalism, which would be noticed only because its author also wrote what was one of the most renowned and fashionable sentimental novels of the eighteenth century. But it is something slightly odder than most relics of this fashion. When Mackenzie showed it to Adam Smith, he immediately recognized its subject (or target) as David Hume, who

---

[1] Henry Mackenzie (ed.), *The Mirror* (first published 1779–80; 2 vols., London, 1794), No. 42, i. 190.

[2] Ibid., No. 44, i. 196.

had died three years earlier.[3] Many of Mackenzie's Edinburgh readership would have done likewise; no philosopher was as famous for 'scepticism' as Hume. And Mackenzie himself had Hume, whom he had known and admired as head of Edinburgh's life of letters, quite clearly in mind. He noted in the margins of his own copy of *The Mirror*: 'This story is purely a fiction founded only on the circumstances of Mr David Hume's living some time in France about the period of his first publications'. It is a fiction which, though it cannot quite make Hume into a Christian, is an attempt to exorcise the spirit of his philosophical reputation. The philosopher of social instincts is shown acknowledging that his scepticism severs him from the benefits of feeling, the virtues of responsive sensibility.

We might say that Mackenzie warns against what Hume has investigated in parts of the *Treatise*—the disparity between the demands of philosophical questioning and the habits of social existence. The ironies of choosing Hume's stay in France as an occasion for the fiction perhaps run deeper in this respect than Mackenzie realized. Mackenzie takes Hume's period abroad as that of the philosopher's retreat—the finally unhealthy seclusion of the intellectual self from the redeeming influences of society. In fact, Hume did not just distance himself from a known social world in order to compose the *Treatise*; in what now looks like a perversely calculated move, he retreated to the small French town of La Flèche, whose Jesuit college had been a European centre of the Counter-Reformation and the place where Descartes had been educated.[4] It was here that Hume chose to work on his own reformation of philosophical enquiry, pondering the incurable 'malady' of sceptical thought in a place famous for its associations with the maintenance of belief. But then Mackenzie's fantasy is never quite going to silence the more troubling repercussions of Hume's philosophy because it always has to remind us of some of the problems which it wishes away. It wants to reclaim Hume, rather than just reject him; he was, after all, the paragon of Scottish learning as well as an awkward unbeliever. As the story attempts to bring sentiment and philosophy together it begins to reveal how unsettling a figure Hume could be for those, like Mackenzie, who looked up to him in his lifetime as leader of the Edinburgh literati. It uncovers doubts about whether Hume's

---

[3] H.W. Thompson (ed.), *The Anecdotes and Egotisms of Henry Mackenzie* (London, 1927), 171.
[4] See E.C. Mossner, *The Life of David Hume* (Oxford, 1980), 92–105.

philosophical project could be reconciled to a desirable model of social life.

It is telling in another way that Mackenzie chose to make an instructive fiction out of an episode in Hume's career, for that career was something of an anomaly for the Enlightenment Scotsman. Hume may have been famously a man for 'Company' in a city whose ruling class was attentive to the expression of its own sociability. But though a pivotal figure in polite and progressive societies, he never achieved the professional advancement which distinguished his fellow members of those societies. Though he was an example of the literary prowess to which the Scots could aspire, he was also something of an exception amongst the successful lawyers, merchants, doctors, and academics with whom he mixed.[5] His failure to achieve the kind of preferment within the Academy attained by his friend Adam Smith was, of course, no accident; it was all of a piece with the sceptical habits implicitly criticized in Mackenzie's story. His writings were too destructive of customary beliefs for him to receive a university appointment.[6] In a city in which the self-improving intellectual typically aimed to be professionally as well as culturally active, Hume's philosophy turned out to be an impediment to one kind of social recognition.

And so he is commemorated in the 'Story of La Roche' as a solitary figure, melancholy at his separation from the pleasures of feeling and belief. The story is the product of a society, and a class, committed to discovering words as well as institutions for the expression of its social identity. It tells, therefore, of the subversive effects of philosophical doubt—indeed, of a certain kind of philosophy *per se*. A tale of 'sentiment'—of many glistening eyes and simple affections—is chosen as the appropriate vehicle for a parable about the uncorrupted powers of feeling; it is a sophisticated society's myth of natural virtue. Both the origins and the form of the periodical in which it appeared testify to the project of constructing sociability—the project in relation to which Hume's legacy was ambiguous.

The Mirror was produced by the Mirror Club, a group of young Edinburgh lawyers with Mackenzie as its eventual representative. In the periodical's very genesis it was a social production, an index of

---

[5] See D.D. McElroy, *Scotland's Age of Improvement: A Survey of Eighteenth-century Literary Clubs and Societies* (Washington, 1969).

[6] See Mossner, *Life*, 153–62.

the polite solidarity which the ruling class in Edinburgh was learning to substitute for political identity;[7] in its aims it was constitutive of shared cultural values, addressing readers who were to find social coherence via politeness. Mackenzie might be remembered now as the novelist who, in *The Man of Feeling*, took sentimentalism to its (popular) extreme; when Sir Walter Scott commemorated him in the Dedication to *Waverley*, however, it was as 'Our Scottish Addison'.[8] *The Mirror*, along with the later *Lounger*, was an attempt to find in an Addisonian model of polite discourse the basis for social being. The wishfulness of Scott's hyperbole signals how the attempt arose partly out of a patriotism which was also an inferiority complex, a sense of the province at the political margins whilst at the cultural centre. The fiction about Hume comes amongst all the talk of 'manners' and proprieties, of literary judgement and civilized taste, that runs through both the periodicals that Mackenzie edited. This talk (an appropriate metaphor for a discourse that claims the informality but propriety of a conversational style) is for the benefit of an ideal of social virtues that is still not quite confident—an ideal of 'the partriotism and civic virtue of a citizen class . . . released through non-political institutions'.[9] Despite his prominent role in Edinburgh's life of societies, and the adaptability of writings such as his *Essays* to the cultural needs of this self-conscious 'citizen class', Hume offered too equivocal an example to be a model. In the midst of his Addisonian undertaking, Mackenzie tried to put that example in its place.

Yet the sentimental fiction which was supposed to celebrate the benefits of sensibility, and wish from the sceptic a susceptibility that he never confessed, has its own limitations as an example. To read it now is to see the problem of sentimental narrative; it is to see how uncertain a vehicle for values and aspirations such a fiction has become. Its limitations are those of much sentimental fiction (and those which now make it slightly ludicrous): the model offered is of a simple virtue which has to be removed from the world in order to exist. La Roche is a variant on Harley, Mackenzie's original 'Man of Feeling'; he may have been there to be admired, but his inimitable

---

[7] For the processes of this substitution, see N. Phillipson, 'The Scottish Enlightenment', in R. Porter and M. Teich (eds.), *The Enlightenment in National Context* (Cambridge, 1981).

[8] Sir Walter Scott, *Waverley* (first published 1814; London, 1982), 478.

[9] Phillipson, 'The Scottish Enlightenment', 25.

simplicity was the fantasy, and not the practice, of a complex urban society. The cultural leaders of this society enjoyed their position because they were also typically practical professional men, as proud to be committed to the improvement of agriculture or manufactures as to literary learning. Mackenzie was as practical as any—a lawyer who disapproved of men of letters where they formed 'a caste separate from the ordinary professions and habits of common life'.[10] His description of this segregated class of writers was directed against the literati of London; in a progressive Scotland there was to be no such discrepancy. Yet the paragons of sensitive virtue that he created in his fiction were far removed from any 'common life'. The practical man produced the impractical model.

The gap between the social identity that Mackenzie styled for himself and the exemplary Man of Feeling that he created was recorded retrospectively by Henry Cockburn, a fellow Edinburgh lawyer: 'Strangers used to fancy that he must be a pensive sentimental Harley; whereas he was far better—a hard headed practical man, as full of worldly wisdom as most of his fictitious characters are devoid of it; and this without in the least impairing the affectionate softness of his heart'.[11] While involved in the composition of his first novel, and recently qualified as an advocate, Mackenzie recognized the gap himself, in a letter to his cousin about his different activities: 'The Ideas which are confined to those elegant volumes the Statute-Books of Great Britain, (as mine have been for this month past) are perhaps of all others the most distant from Sentiment or Fancy'.[12] The recognition, and perhaps the acceptance as conventional, of a gap between ideal and practice disturbs some received ideas about the functions that sentimental fiction might have served. Its pieties and platitudes cannot just be the resource of moralism; or if they are, it is a moralism that is floundering.[13] With the publication of Mackenzie's *Man of Feeling* in 1771, the sentimental novel has evolved into a terminal formula precisely because, with all its talk of virtue, it cannot reflect at

---

[10] Cited in D. Craig, *Scottish Literature and the Scottish People 1680–1830* (London, 1961), 41.

[11] Ibid. 45.

[12] Henry Mackenzie, *Letters to Elizabeth Rose of Kilravock* H.W. Drescher (Münster, 1967), 13.

[13] For a description of sentimental fiction as a 'reflection' of a discourse about 'conduct', see J.M.S. Tompkins, *The Popular Novel in England 1770–1800* (London, 1932).

all on the problems of conduct, the practices of any existing society.

Thus, paradoxically, the historical significance of this novel's vogue. A society (or the part of one that called itself such) self-consciously engaged in the transformation of virtue from political capacity to provincial politeness had produced for its own delectation a fantasy of virtue as private susceptibility. It is the logic of Richardson's fiction taken to an extreme which evades the actual contradictions of his didacticism. Like any of Richardson's heroines, of course, the Man of Feeling, Harley, displays a faith in the speechless sentiment whose power is greater than any words. In the 'pastoral' poem that he writes, he places value on that 'love' which

> . . . ne'er was apparell'd with art,
> On words it could never rely;
> It reign'd in the throb of my heart,
> It spoke in the glance of my eye.[14]

As in Richardson, true sentiment is of a poignancy that actually precludes speech: 'There were a thousand sentiments;—but they gushed so impetuously on his heart, that he could not utter a syllable'.[15] And, in a simplification of Clarissa's example to an easy specialization of pathos, the power of sentiment is made that which 'the world' chooses to ignore: as Harley says, as he dies a death 'replete with the genuine happiness attendant upon virtue', 'There are some feelings which are perhaps too tender to be suffered by the world. The world is in general selfish, interested, and unthinking, and throws the imputation of romance or melancholy on every temper more susceptible than its own.'[16]

To depict the feelings that connote virtue is, by Mackenzie's account of his fiction, to be allowed a certain indulgence which the private experience of novel-reading makes possible. As he writes in another of his letters, 'at bottom, we cannot write with too much Freedom; and the Reader will be Pleas'd in Proportion as these Qualities reside in himself'.[17] The 'Freedom' which 'Sentiment and Feeling' allow belongs to a type of writing which does not so much recommend correct conduct to its readers as assume virtue in their capacity to understand the sentimental text. Virtue, in this context, has come to consist not in a set of prescribed social or political practices, but in the recognition of a series of 'sentimental' images

---

[14] Henry Mackenzie, *The Man of Feeling* (London, 1771), 234.
[15] Ibid. 216.   [16] Ibid. 260.   [17] *Letters to Elizabeth Rose*, 17.

and conventions. The appeal of the sentimental text is held to reside in 'sentiment' rather than 'story'—as Johnson's dictum has it. *The Man of Feeling* is 'simple to Excess; for I would have it as different from the Entanglement of a Novel as can be'.[18] Mackenzie, like Richardson, rejects the idea that *he* might be writing a 'Novel'. Richardson, concerned to produce an 'instructive' text, wrestled with the problem of the gap between precept and interpretation, between writing and reading. Mackenzie writes books in which virtue is utterly stylized, specialized beyond the possibility of application.

In later decades, novels were to develop critiques of this celebration of 'feeling', by describing the discrepancy between sensibility and capacities for productive action or effective judgement. Mary Wollstonecraft's *Maria* and Jane Austen's *Sense and Sensibility* are two very different examples of such descriptions (though sensibility is not simply valueless or illusory in either of these novels). Yet the separation of ideal and precept in *The Man of Feeling* seems not to have made it less congenial to its eighteenth-century readers;[19] indeed, the appeal of Mackenzie's novel presumed this separation. It was a text in which sentimentalism had become genre, in which the cultivation of sensibility was limited to habits of reading. Gone are the strained tactics of exhortation employed by Richardson, to be replaced by a narrative tense of lament. Drained of the energies of struggle, the novel asks only that the reader recognize its cameos of feeling as demonstrations of a natural faculty which it has taken fiction to detect. The novel, in fact, rehearses the habits of a sentimental reading; its 'story' is not just told—it is presented as a fortuitously discovered manuscript to which Mackenzie's fictional narrator can react. We get not only the tale of Harley, but the stricken sensibility of one who has read the tale and is supposed to ponder its significance by Harley's grave: 'every beat of my heart awakens a virtue:—but 'twill make you hate the world—No: there is such an air of gentleness around, that I can hate nothing; but, as to the world—I pity the men of it.'[20] This affect itself belongs to a place outside 'the world', ending the book not with the lessons to be drawn from the story of Harley's demise but with a

18 Letters to Elizabeth Rose, 18.
19 The book was a popular success; for its many editions see H.W. Thompson, *A Scottish Man of Feeling* (London, 1931), Appendix I.
20 Mackenzie, *The Man of Feeling*, 268.

confirmation of the divide between the virtue of the sentimental hero and the purposes of that 'world'. The supposed editor of the papers which constitute the narrative claims that they contain 'something of nature, and little else'.[21] The abstracted distinction between world and sentiment enables the production of a myth of this 'nature', of a 'humanity' which is 'a feeling, not a principle'.[22] Whilst this 'nature', and virtue with it, must repudiate 'the world', it retreats to a location where it cannot be challenged. In the Conclusion, even the movements of the branches of the tree in the churchyard recall the 'predictive' gestures of the man of sentiment; the novel ends in its own perfect environment, in which all signs have their elegiac meaning, all feeling its natural reflections.

From beyond the opposition between world and feeling, though, the 'editor' occasionally comments on the divide between the two. Like many a wandering hero of an eighteenth-century novel, Harley, at one stage, meets a 'Misanthropist', and the supposed 'editor' intervenes in the presentation of this figure to observe that the person whose 'pen' is responsible for the 'performance' 'seems to have catched some portion of the snarling spirit of the man he personates'.[23] The intervention is necessary because misanthropy is all too close to sentimental affliction; it is but a different kind of rejection of the world's demands. Misanthropy is the *alter ego* of feeling. It is one of the contrary states in antagonism to which true feeling is typically defined, but it is also an alternative version of dissatisfaction which, somehow, has to be exorcised. The 'editor' of *The Man of Feeling* stands aloof from the contest between the two perceptions, but this editorial separation is ambiguous. It can enable the novel to warn its reader that misanthropy (that final scepticism concerning the value of social attachment) is a dangerously plausible habit of perception. It can also be read as an acknowledgement that sensibility, however desirable, is simply unattainable—unworldly in a way that misanthropy would never be. The text is either complacent about the superior capacities of sensibility, or fatalistic about the inapplicability of those capacities. It has become almost impossible to separate the ideal of sentimental susceptibility from a lament for the sheer unlikeliness of that resource. As sentimentalism passes into hyperbole in Mackenzie's fiction, we can see the defensive postures forced on such writing by its own contradictions.

[21] Ibid., p. viii.   [22] Ibid. 22.   [23] Ibid. 78.

The text is ever on the point of conceding that any belief in actual communities of 'affections' has to be abandoned.

In Richardson's fiction, the enemies to affection, however metaphorical, were clearly and cruelly specified. While Mackenzie obsessively reproduces the images of sentiment found in Richardson's novels, he sets feeling simply against an impervious 'world' which is the cause of every misery. Mackenzie was to underline this opposition by following the publication of *The Man of Feeling* in 1771 with that of *The Man of the World* in 1773. In this bizarre tale of a dissolute young aristocrat's destruction of the virtuous Annesly family, the opposition even takes the form of an attack by one of the agents of the 'man of the world' on 'sentimental' literature itself—his disdain of the 'set of opinions which they term sentimental', which 'are set forth with such parade of language in novels and romances, as consisting in sympathy of soul, and the mutual attraction of hearts destined for each other'.[24] The world which is inimical to this operation of sympathy, but which gives it scope and reason for its most grandiloquent gestures, is destructive of moral value and sympathetic solidarity. The world is not society; indeed, with respect to the attempts by philosophers and essayists in the eighteenth century to describe social relations, it is imagined as non-'society'. 'The World, I know, is selfish and looks for Virtues by which something may be gain'd to itself', wrote Mackenzie in a letter of 1771.[25] The formula of his novels can be seen as one by which 'the World' is distanced from any association with the actual society in which he lived and advanced himself.

The disparity between the life of a novelist and the ideals celebrated in his novels is not, perhaps, so rare. Yet, as has already been indicated, Mackenzie acted out the role of a Scottish man of letters with some seriousness, and self-consciousness. That role would have been spoiled if his novels had only been readable as flippant or disingenuous creations. The disparity, in fact, is of a significance beyond mere reference to Mackenzie and his marginal role in the development of the novel as a genre; it suggests something about the development of sentimentalism as a project for the depiction of virtue. For the virtue offered in novels such as Mackenzie's as synonymous with exquisite sensibility cannot be,

---

[24] Henry Mackenzie, *The Man of the World*, in *The Works of Henry Mackenzie*, vol. ii (Glasgow, 1818), 227.
[25] *Letters to Elizabeth Rose*, 103.

and is not proposed as, a practicable model. The *Monthly Review* may have declared of *The Man of Feeling* that 'the Reader, who weeps not over some of the scenes it describes, has no sensibility of mind',[26] but it was advocating a reaction which seems ludicrous now, and which was to seem odd by the 1790s, precisely because it was narrowed to the act of reading. Richardson had attempted to subjugate narrative to the solemn discipline of instruction, and the signs of his influence are present in a novel like *The Man of the World* in what have become the formulae of 'sympathetic' tears and ecstatic feeling. But these formulae are deployed in calculatedly 'simple' or 'rustic' tableaux designed to please rather than to correct polite readers. The novel of sentiment had come to offer the thrill of a private feeling to a private reader. The conventionality, and easiness, of the expected effect are caught in the *Critical Review*'s comment on *The Man of Feeling*: 'By those who have feeling hearts, and a true relish for simplicity in writing, many pages in this miscellaneous volume will be read with satisfaction'.[27] The experience of reading such a novel was to be itself proof of a 'feeling heart'.

The means to such a proof in novels that do homage to Richardson involve plots that depend on the subjection of sentimental virtue to the assaults of (typically male, typically aristocratic) vice. In *The Man of the World*, violence is visited upon a 'harmless family' by Sindall, the aristocrat's son, who, as a child, has received not the education in 'beneficence' which Annesly gives to his children but 'that instinctive affection which nature has bestowed on the lowest rank of creatures'.[28] His father is the type of landowner who employs a lawyer 'in carrying on some proceedings against his poor neighbours': a man who has spurned sociability.[29] The social 'felicity' which Annesly has fled into the country to find is not in the vocabulary of this aristocracy. The son has inherited some of the characteristics of the most renowned of all well-born rapists, Lovelace. He displays the same contempt for the ultimate sign of bourgeois self-validation, the marriage contract. 'The trammels of form are insupportable to that fineness of soul, to which restraint and happiness are terms of opposition. Let my mistress be my mistress still, with all the privileges of a wife, without a wife's

---

[26] Cited in Thompson, *Scottish Man of Feeling*, 126–7.
[27] Ibid. 127.
[28] Mackenzie, *The Man of the World*, 39.
[29] Ibid. 132.

indifference, or a wife's disquiet.'[30] And inevitably, Sindall's most destructive act is his abduction of a young woman, that act which figures prominently throughout Richardson's fiction. He follows Lovelace as far as drugging his virtuous female captive, and then performing the 'monstrous deed'.

The debt to *Clarissa* is clear here. But there is a reason beyond cynical calculation for this type of replication. Time and time again, after Richardson, abduction or the threat of abduction is crucial to the plots of novels of sentiment. Here is preserved one of the elements found often enough in the 'romances' of the earlier part of the eighteenth century, like those of Eliza Haywood; it is preserved because sensibility, and therefore virtue, is most excited, and therefore most manifest, when threatened. If sensibility tends to be a feminine prerogative—and even in Mackenzie's stories of lachrymose males the virtuous virgin has an important place—then it exists to be assailed. After *Pamela* and *Clarissa*, the story of assault became an almost inevitable part of a novel of sentiment. Texts like Hugh Kelly's *Memoirs of a Magdalen* of 1767 were happy to confess their attachment to Richardson. In this novel the moment of abduction is explicitly referred to *Clarissa*, as if such a reference is enough to establish the text as one which promotes virtue: the abduction of the heroine (Louisa) by 'the villain Hastings' comes as she is 'reading Clarissa Harlowe'; she 'had just got into that passage where the vile Lovelace attempts the sanctity of her chamber at midnight, in the house of that detestable monster Sinclair'.[31] Louisa's fate is kinder than Clarissa's. She flees her abductor (last shown reading a volume of *Tristram Shandy*!) to find temporary refuge in the Magdalen Hospital for reformed prostitutes (an institution of which Richardson was actually a benefactor). She is then returned to family, marriage, harmonious society. Her sensibility has been revealed in her defensive and reclusive responses to particularly masculine 'vice', and her capacity for tears which are both painful and delicious.

But then the influence of Richardson is marked, in the novels of the 1750s and 1760s, not simply by the habitual apotheosis of sensibility, but by the association of sensibility with a virtue under threat. It is a virtue which has to be *in extremis*. Frances Sheridan, the mother of the dramatist, acknowledged the provenance of this

---

[30] Mackenzie, *The Man of the World*, 128.
[31] Hugh Kelly, *Memoirs of a Magdalen* (2 vols., 2nd edn., London, 1767), ii. 129.

association by dedicating to Richardson her contribution to the fashion (and the market) for fictions of distressed virtue, *Memoirs of Miss Sidney Bidulph*. After all, the writer who had made the novel respectable had also made it potentially lucrative. Sheridan's relationship with Richardson was closer as well; like Charlotte Lennox before her, she had received advice and encouragement from the great patriarch of the novel: 'it was in consequence of the admiration he expressed upon the perusal of her manuscript novel, *Eugenia and Adelaide*, that she was first encouraged to try her powers in a work of higher importance and greater length'.[32] The dedication of *Sidney Bidulph*, of which three volumes were published in 1761 and two more in 1767, to 'The Author of Clarissa and Sir Charles Grandison' was the acknowledgement of an affiliation both personal and public.[33] In her 'Editor's Introduction' we are told that her heroine is one whose 'portion was affliction',[34] and Richardson is declared the presiding spirit of the tale of suffering sensibility. The articulation, in the heroine's letters, of 'the feelings of my heart', is to be produced out of this 'affliction'.[35] Sensibility, as in *Clarissa*, is oppositional or desperate. For writers like Sheridan, it cannot be anything else.

In an article, 'On Novel-writing', that he wrote for *The Lounger*, Mackenzie regretted the influence of many novels, and attacked the 'species called the Sentimental' for presenting, rather than 'duty', a 'war of duties'.[36] We can read this as retrospective recantation, but it is a commentary not necessarily at odds with Mackenzie's undertaking as a writer of fiction. For we do not get any 'war of duties' in his novels; in their pages, the representatives of sentiment are hounded by villians and libertines who simply threaten all social virtues. Moral choice is not an issue; the novel of sentiment has actually purified itself of any vestiges of debate. The villain makes virtue perfectly knowable (which also means completely reclusive). In his *Lounger* article, Mackenzie went on to reject the 'refinement' of representation through which 'virtues' manifest themselves in 'competition', and thus in obscurity. He made clear that virtue must

---

[32] Alicia Lefanu, *Memoirs of the Life and Writings of Mrs Frances Sheridan* (London, 1824), 86–7.

[33] Frances Sheridan, *Memoirs of Miss Sidney Bidulph* (5 vols., 5th edn., London, 1796), vol. i.

[34] Ibid. 7.   [35] Ibid. 100.

[36] Henry Mackenzie, 'On Novel-writing', *The Lounger* (1785–6; 2nd edn., Edinburgh, 1787), 181–8.

be transparent, knowable. Such a narrative as *The Man of the World*, or for that matter *The Man of Feeling*, may not show faith in the availability of such virtue, but it does construct the myth of such knowledge. But then this knowledge is bought at the cost of the isolation of feeling and its stylization in defeat. Upon Annesly's grief-induced death, the narrator of *The Man of the World* addresses himself to the agent of a doom which must be relished as much as regretted: 'Sindall: and ye like Sindall—but I cannot speak: speak for me their consciences'.[37] But Sindall is absolutely necessary to feeling's expression; he must hound sentiment to its grandest, and most silent, gestures. Not that the hopelessly dissolute and destructive landowner is Mackenzie's only representative of the 'world'. In his novels there is a clear separation between 'trade' and 'land', most marked in *The Man of the World*, but it is a separation which does not permit conflict or class antagonism. Those who wield economic power come into conflict with feeling, but not with each other. The profit which comes from trade, from 'the drudgery of the world', is also antipathetic to the man of sentiment—another form of the negation of sensibility. It is from the unacceptable promise of 'profit' that Annesly turns to rural anonymity, rejecting the gains of his 'wealthy tradesman' father:

Annesly looked on happiness as confined to the sphere of sequestered life. The pomp of greatness, the pleasures of the affluent, he considered only as productive of turbulence, disquiet, and remorse; and thanked Heaven for having placed him in his own little shed, which, in his opinion, was the residence of pure and lasting felicity.[38]

This movement of retreat, which becomes a common property of novels of this period, bespeaks, as Raymond Williams says of *Clarissa*, 'not a criticism of a period or structure of society, but of what can be abstracted as "the world" '.[39] Such abstraction marks the distance of these literary texts from any politics of criticism and analysis.

The association of virtue and retirement is scarcely unique to Mackenzie's fiction, but it is suitably fantastic there. From the centre of an urban culture usually taken to be, in the latter half of the eighteenth century, a nexus of progressive intellectual and commercial developments, is produced a type of fiction which finds

---

[37] Mackenzie, *The Man of the World*, 156.   [38] Ibid. 8.
[39] Raymond Williams, *The Country and the City* (1973; St Albans, 1975), 84.

value in reclusiveness. Richardson had seized on the novel as the refractory but necessary form for a depiction of threatened values; if Mackenzie was, like others, capitalizing on Richardson's example, are we to believe that he was showing sociability and moral consistency as estranged, bucolic exceptions? The simple answer is no—an answer for which we can find documentation if we return to the polite journalism to which Mackenzie was committed. For *The Mirror* and *The Lounger* are full of narratives of retirement which insist that this is not a proper response to the occasional corruptions encountered in an urban society. Through several numbers of *The Mirror*, for example, Mackenzie narrates the exploits of Mr Umphraville, a man of natural taste who retreats with disgust from a world motivated by 'luxury, and the love of vain expense' in which 'the sentiments of public virtue are extinguished'.[40] This figure is mobilized to articulate criticisms of the fashionable excesses of polite society (politeness has to be a more secure basis for social being than mere fashion), so his perceptions have to be reliable enough for the criticisms to be credible. But then a narrator has to step in to assure his audience that the figment of Umphraville is not a paragon, but exists to sound out its own values—that he is 'a spectator of . . . manners', and not properly involved in the social relations which those manners should regulate: 'in his apprehension of facts he is often mistaken, and the conclusions he draws from those facts are often erroneous'. 'When I introduced Mr Umphraville to my readers, I never meant to recommend that seclusion from the world, and that abstraction from the duties of life, which, with all the dignity of mind he is possessed of, have given occasion to his little oddities, and disqualified him for every active purpose.'[41]

To forsake 'manners'—'those little attentions without which no man can be agreeable in society'—is to forsake social being itself.[42] The narrative involution by which the periodical essay tells us that the recluse is not to be imitated brings us back problematically to the sentimental novel. For the recluse only features in such an essay because the journals that Mackenzie edited are concerned to expose abused or subverted forms of sociability. Where the periodical essays propose themselves as practical guides in a way that the novels do not, their very worries about the levels of

---

[40] *The Mirror*, No. 28, 126.   [41] Ibid., No. 94, ii. 188.
[42] Ibid., No. 104, ii. 250.

sophistication and collective virtue achieved in a provincial commercial society can give us a clue to the appeal of the novel. By idealizing individual human value away from any specifically social realization, novels like Mackenzie's avoided the problem faced in the Addisonian essay. This problem is the possibility that instincts and faculties educated for social purposes might defeat their own object. As William Craig, one of Mackenzie's collaborators, put it in *The Mirror*:

Refinement, and delicacy of taste, are the productions of advanced society. They open to the mind of persons possessed of them a field of elegant enjoyment; but they may be pushed to a dangerous extreme. By that excess of sensibility to which they lead . . . they may unfit their possessor for the common and ordinary enjoyments of life.[43]

So it is that *The Mirror* and *The Lounger* warn about the dangers of excessive 'delicacy', and embrace in their strictures novels which exalt rare sensibility. Both periodicals are full of the kind of warnings to be found in the Mackenzie article ('On Novel-writing') to which I have already referred. The danger of novels is taken to lie in their habitual 'entanglements of delicacy'. 'In the enthusiasm of sentiment there is much the same danger as in the enthusiasm of religion'—the forgetting of 'real practical duties'.[44] Mackenzie declares that he wants to rescue novels for respectability and that he is not 'disposed to carry the idea of the dangerous tendency of all Novels quite so far as some moralists have done.'[45] He asserts that the novel 'merits a higher station in the world of letters than is generally assigned it', and that it is—in theory at least—a form as well adapted as the polite essay to 'the necessary refinement in manners of highly-polished nations'. But this does not completely defuse his attack on fiction that glorifies 'the intricacies of Sentiment, or the dreams of Sensibility'—his castigation of novelists who convince their readers of the merits of a 'sickly sort of refinement', a 'superior delicacy' far removed from 'ordinary but useful occupations'.[46] Yet his own works were prized for just such 'refinement'. One contemporary celebration of them might be enough to make the point. In *Sensibility: A Poetical Essay* of 1782, that sternest of moralists Hannah More idealizes a cultivated susceptibility to ennobling affliction:

[43] The Mirror, No. 10, i. 40.   [44] *The Lounger*, i. 185–6.
[45] Ibid. i. 183.   [46] Ibid. i. 187.

Where glow exalted sense and taste refin'd,
There keener anguish rankles in the mind:
There feeling is diffus'd thro' every part,
Thrills in each nerve, and lives in all the heart:
And those, whose gen'rous souls each tear would keep
From others eyes, are born themselves to weep.[47]

Alongside Richardson (from whom 'I first caught that flame' of the 'love of virtue') who is it but Mackenzie (proclaimed, with odd geography, 'the tender moralist of Tweed') who is taken to have popularized what is nothing if not a 'superior delicacy'.

Perhaps Mackenzie had indeed become uncertain of the consequences of his own fictions. Or perhaps the conventional trick of representing those fictions as the moralizing exception to a rule of beguiling illusions was enough to absolve them from their author's critique. Whatever the case, the hostility of his essay towards perceived novelistic fashion is evidence of doubts as to whether novels as such could educate or improve. 'Instructive' writing should socialize its readers—should teach them the values that were the manners and refinements of a polite, commercial, increasingly meritocratic, society. *The Mirror* and *The Lounger* are impelled by this criterion to provide stories of those who are not so much morally corrupted by the indulgence of sensibility which reading novels is supposed to encourage, as simply rendered incapable of proper social intercourse by it. And this is the problem of the novel of sentiment. Inherited from Richardson was a scheme in which virtue was equivalent to an intense, private sensitivity. It was a scheme for the virtue of the protagonists of a novel, and for the moral integrity of the form itself. Yet in the improving commercial world of Mackenzie and his friends virtue was not to be the guarantee of social identity. The language of virtue had long since faltered as a validation of status and relationship. The unavailability of virtue is implicit in the novels themselves; it should not be surprising that the polite essay, the kind of text *par excellence* committed to the sociability of its readers, should recognize such a failing. In literary histories 'the novel' is described as the form which grows to dominance in the second half of the eighteenth century; so it does, but it preserves an atavism in many of its most popular shapes. The

[47] Hannah More, *Sacred Dramas; Chiefly Intended for Young Persons: The Subjects Taken from the Bible. To which is Added, Sensibility, a Poem* (Dublin, 1784), 254.

novel of sentiment is constituted as a vehicle for virtue, but virtue is the main element of a superceded vocabulary of social identity. After the idea of the virtue of the singular, uncorrupted individual has been abandoned as a mainstay of moral and political discourse, the novel of sentiment continues to reproduce its own version of this figment. Inevitably, it has to do so in an elegiac strain.

So though novelists like Mackenzie, Goldsmith, and Sarah Fielding move virtue to the countryside, they do so with less of the apparent confidence in an ideal of settlement than can be construed from, say, the resolution of moral and material economies in Fielding's *Tom Jones*, or even the fatalistic turning from the world that concludes Smollett's *Humphry Clinker*. The country becomes a place of retreat which can never be quiet for long. The city, meanwhile, is not a place for sentiment. Mackenzie's *The Man of the World* is explicit about the loss of fellow-feeling with which it is associated. In this book, Annesly, disinherited when his father leaves his wealth to a 'haberdasher' nephew distinguished only by 'that patient dulness which qualifies for getting rich', finds himself also socially disconnected. Tears fresh in his eyes, he wanders among the 'buzzing sons of industry' in a crowded London street: 'In the faces of those he met, he saw no acknowledgement of connection, and felt himself like Cain after his brother's murder, an unsheltered, unfriended outcast'.[48] The new vision of society, the vision of his father which recalls the imagery of Mandeville, is of 'a hive' in which the worst sin is to be a mere 'drone'. Mackenzie has no doubts of the purposefulness of this society. In place of it, his sentimental characters look for 'that cordial friendship, that warm attachment which is only to be found in the smaller circles of private life, which is lost in the bustle and extended connection of larger societies'.[49] The solution to this version of alienation is typically given as a limited domestic cordiality which, in Mackenzie's novels, exists to be destroyed. The 'felicity' of a 'little circle' ('too perfect to be lasting') is offered to the privately responsive reader as a mirror of the best social inclinations.[50]

But, as ever, the novel of sentiment finds it difficult to imagine how this sociability could be projected on to a wider society. Novels after Richardson therefore tend to restrict themselves to a fatalistic statement of its value. This statement is the testimony of the virtuous

[48] *Man of the World*, 10.
[49] Ibid. 198.   [50] Ibid. 14–15.

in many novels of the mid-eighteenth century, and lingers on in the definitions of affection given by, for example, Anne Radcliffe's heroines. It is caught in the self-explanation of a worthy recluse, retired to his family and his garden, in Richard Graves's novel *The Spiritual Quixote:* Mr Rivers (a character who declares this book's allegiance by claiming the friendship of Richardson's Grandison family) tells Graves's wandering protagonist,

However unsociable I may appear, or however I may renounce the common friendship, or rather impertinence of the world, yet I think the chief happiness of this life was intended by Providence to arise from the exercise of the social affections . . . The pride, malice, and perverseness of too great a part of mankind, arising from the opposition of their several interests, may make it prudent to restrain our connexions to a few friends, and almost within one's own family.[51]

The Man of the World tries out a reconciling representation of 'felicity' in which domesticity is substantiated by an almost feudal ideal of tenantry, an ideal later denied in Mackenzie's last novel, *Julia de Roubigne*. In *The Man of the World*, after the deaths of both Annesly and his daughter, we are given the image of a rural order which resists the assaults and temptations of the world because it is founded on an older (and for eighteenth-century readers no longer feasible) disposition of wealth. Settlement comes with the passing on to Bolton—possessor of 'an exquisite sensibility of heart'[52]—and Annesly's granddaughter of their friend Rawlinson's estate. Rawlinson, 'the friend of mankind', has managed this estate in the proper, but unusual, manner: '[he] lowered the rents, which had been raised to an extravagant height, and recalled the ancient tenants of the manor; most of whom had been driven from the unfriendly soil, to make room for desperate adventurers, who undertook for rents they could never be able to pay'.[53] On taking up his inheritence, Bolton confirms this order, against the trend of contemporaneous agrarian developments, by rejecting 'the usual mode of *improving* estates' in favour of increasing 'the love of my people'. As he and his new wife settle into this inheritance, 'the country smiles around them with the effects of their goodness. This indeed is the only real superiority which wealth has to bestow.'[54] The benevolence of a

---

[51] Richard Graves, *The Spiritual Quixote, or the Summer's Ramble of Mr Geoffry Wildgoose* (first published 1773), ed. C. Whibley (2 vols., London, 1926), i. 236.
[52] *The Man of the World*, 181.
[53] Ibid. 217.   [54] Ibid. 295.

rural economy depends upon such as Rawlinson or Bolton achieving the ownership of the land, an eventuality which the narrative concedes as unlikely. Such virtue makes sense because it is maintained against the current of 'improvement'. In Mackenzie's last novel, *Julia de Roubigne*, the melancholy Montauban declares his desire for such an economy of wealth and 'sentiment' by rejecting 'the language of those devourers of land, who wish to make a wilderness around them, provided they are lords of it. For my part, I find much less pleasure in being the master of acres, than the friend of man.'[55] But Montauban's fate, in the last frenzied chapters of the book, is to commit murder and then suicide, as the narrative gives itself over to the histrionic form of a 'mistaken passion' which can only be called melodrama. The mania of revenge, finally the word that dominates Montauban's every sentence, overpowers any possibility of the enactment of the part of 'friend' which the 'pensive' landowner might have styled for himself. A certain excess of feeling, that excess called passion, has defeated any promise of beneficence. Even a nostalgia for a kind of feudal community has been revoked.

The unlikely appearance of land-ownership in Mackenzie's novels as a basis for the operation of fellow-feeling is a literary device eschewing political projection. As a general fact, it is not possible to identify the virtue of feeling as represented in the novel of sentiment with any particular social class, nor yet with antagonism to any class. Indeed, in different but contemporary narratives one can find both a landed neo-feudal order and an enriched commercial plutocracy as bearers of the distinguishing features of sentiment. In Frances Brooke's *Lady Julia Mandeville*, published in 1763, the aristocrat, Lord Belmont, is represented as a benevolent patriach, affirming against the tide of new money and the power of 'exchange brokers' an order which harks back to the feudal in its indulgence of a mythology of timeless bucolic ritual. The patriach surveys the ancient dances and festivities of his retainers, and makes them a mark of that order: 'Lord Belmont is extremely fond of all these old customs, and will suffer none of them to be left off on his estate'.[56] His belief that 'the independent country gentlemen' are 'the strength and glory of this kingdom', and his resistance to 'the greedy Leviathans of our days', is at one with his benevolence, a term which

55 Mackenzie, *Julia de Roubigne*, 27.
56 Frances Brooke, *The History of Lady Julia Mandeville*, ed. E. Phillips Poole (London, 1930), 152.

is constantly used with reference to him: 'I have a fund, which I call "the bank of friendship", on which it is my rule to take no interest,' he boasts.[57] 'Friendship' is the proper establishment of a stability of social and material relations through an economy of feeling and power. Money, for Frances Brooke, is both the curse of the *nouveaux riches*, the 'cit' and his daughter, and the blessing of the 'beneficent father' whose wealth comes from the inheritance of an estate: 'Lord Belmont enjoys the most unmixed and lively of all human pleasures, that of making others happy'.[58] In Henry Brooke's *The Fool of Quality*, published between 1765 and 1770, in contrast, we find an education in sentiment clearly identified with an individual who has accumulated his wealth from being a merchant. This miraculous proponent of sensibility abducts the young son of a land-owning lord in order to remove him from the pernicious lures of 'luxury' and teach him the signs and values of 'feeling'. Needless to say, this education is entirely successful, enabling him to be returned to his station in life. This text depicts a clear debate between the merchant and the earl, between the 'industry and commerce' which sees itself as 'the natural, the living, the never-failing fountain, from whence the wealth of the world can alone be taught to flow' and an aristocratic belief in the permanence 'of the degrees of men to their respective departments' and the pre-eminence of 'the steadfast extent' of 'landed possessions'.[59] This argument is between two brothers, and it is into familial harmony that it is finally resolved. By one of the 'miracles' of such a narrative, the abductor finally reveals himself as the child's uncle, the very long-lost brother with whom the earl has previously argued. The aristocrat concedes his errors and commends the education in sentiment which his son has received, and the narrative unreservedly endorses both the virtue and the economic probity of the merchant.

Though *Lady Julia Mandeville* and *The Fool of Quality* might seem to provide different readings of a reconciliation between wealth and feeling, a reconciliation which Mackenzie does not attempt, the signs by which such feeling makes itself known in the two novels are absolutely compatible, reproductions of a silent language of tears and gestures, of blushes and involuntary palpitations. This reiterated claim to expression beyond words

---

[57] Ibid. 68.   [58] Ibid. 47.
[59] Henry Brooke, *The Fool of Quality*, first published 1764–70 (London, 1906), 24–7.

distinguishes the investment in sentiment. In *Lady Julia Mandeville*, the formula is reminiscent of Richardson: 'her conscious blushes, her downcast eyes, her heaving bosom, her sweet confusion, have told me what her tongue could not utter'.[60] Congruently, in *The Fool of Quality*, 'blushing' 'demonstrates . . . sensibility'. Here too it is characterized as a 'sweet confusion', for it is 'from the fountain of virtue alone that this flush of shamefacedness can possibly flow'.[61] Lady Julia claims 'every sentiment of my soul is in my eyes: I have not learnt, I will never learn to disguise their expressive language'.[62] Mr. Clinton, the benevolent abductor of *The Fool of Quality*, mirrors this remark with 'I am persuaded that there is not a single sentiment . . . that has not its distinct and respective interpreter in the glance of the eye, and in the muscling of the countenance'.[63] These signs, and a full list of comparisons would be endless, compose what has evidently become a conventional iconography of sympathetic relations.

These two texts, deploying the same conventional signs of feeling and virtue, are distinguished not only by their different constructions of various forms of wealth. For their endings lead in very different directions not to be separated from their different resolutions of wealth and goodness. *Lady Julia Mandeville* cannot see fulfilled a sociability founded on sympathy. It ends with the melodrama of the deaths of hero and heroine, a conclusion similar to that of *Julia de Roubigne*. *The Fool of Quality*, on the other hand, envisages a perfectly sympathetic sociability, and perfectly wordless communication: 'While Mr Fenton spoke, the muscles of Harry's expressive countenance, like an equally tuned instrument, uttered unisons to every word he heard.'[64] In the place of the atavistic idealization of Frances Brooke's novel, is the identification, in *The Fool of Quality*, of sentimental virtue with a rising, trading class. But even in this novel, the merchant, his wealth successfully accumulated, has to retire from the world to enjoy and communicate the full benefits of feeling. Even here, where a tryst is represented between sentiment and wealth got through commerce, it is necessary to locate this correspondence at a remove from the city. The text does not provide an analysis of society, but it does envisage a society which is 'a happy interchange of kind offices and affections', a

60 *Lady Julia Mandeville*, 117.   61 *The Fool of Quality*, 125.
62 *Lady Julia Mandeville*, 121.   63 *The Fool of Quality*, 129.
64 Ibid. 54.

society which can best be established outside the city. As the virtuous Mr Fielding says, 'I love society, but yet a society that is founded on friendship; and people in great cities are so divided and dissipated by the multitude of soliciting objects and acquaintance, that they are rendered incapable of a particular attachment.'[65]

This kind of lament is hardly a unique reflex of sentimental fiction. If the ideal of such 'particular attachment' is not Utopian, it is perhaps always elegiac—the community which is lost or exceptional. But it is difficult in the case of Henry Brooke's novel, as in the case of most of the sentimental fiction of the mid-eighteenth century, to explain how the lament for 'particular attachment' can be even a refined, or sublimated response to specific social or economic changes. Indeed, if we were to try to isolate the ideological traits of *The Fool of Quality*, we would derive not reactionary elegy but muscular optimism: belief in the effects of a kind of 'natural' education drawn from Rousseau; final confidence in the progressive influence of the 'commercial' classes; missionary Christianity. (It was the odd mixture of these elements that made Brooke's novel one of Charles Kingsley's favourite books.)[66] The strain of regret for the rarity of sympathy remains, however. The peculiarity of novels of sentiment like Brooke's was that they offered the 'happy interchange of affections' as an example which had to be exceptional, had to be rooted to the pages of a fiction, to be entertained at all. Such a text could flatter the private sensibility of its reader—a reader presumed to understand the special pleasures of finer feeling and social affection. But such a text also depended on the realization that the examples it proposed could not be followed amidst any practical business of social life. The paradox of sentimental fashion was that the celebration of sociable instincts was also a move away from the depiction of a particular society. It was by the restriction of sociability to a private space, the curbing of any ambition to generalize society, that sentimentalism achieved its fashionable status.

We might speculate, then, that through the establishment of a special relationship with a complicit, private reader (the reader whose susceptibilities were a worry to Richardson) the novel of sentiment was able to make a virtue of what was such a problem for moral philosophy—the incompatibility of, on the one hand, society

---

[65] Ibid. 148.

[66] See F.R. Karl, *A Reader's Guide to the Development of the English Novel in the Eighteenth Century* (London, 1975), 226.

as a special experience and, on the other hand, society as an inclusive totality. We get further clues about this kind of relationship from the reception of one of the most perennially popular of the novels written in the period, Oliver Goldsmith's *The Vicar of Wakefield*, first published in 1766. For the habit of reading 'for the sentiment', transformed into fashion from the difficulty of Richardson's precedent, embraced this text in a peculiar way. In recent years there has been some debate between those who have argued that 'The sentimental view of life . . . has never been more subtly satirized than in this novel',[67] and those willing to take Goldsmith's book as a 'basic text' of 'the sentimental movement'.[68] The debate is of the novel's own making: its subtitle is '*a tale supposed to be written by himself*', and the argument about whether it is sentimental or a parody of sentimentalism, is largely an argument about the nature of this narrator. The analysis that has probably been most influential—even upon those who utterly disagree with it—is provided by Robert Hopkins in *The True Genius of Oliver Goldsmith*, a book which fixed upon the capacities for conceit and self-deception of Goldsmith's narrator in order to provide a polemical corrective to 'the whole sad history of criticism of *The Vicar* that refused to see any ambivalence in it at all and that *did* read it as a sentimental novel'.[69] Certainly Dr Primrose is something less than a paragon of either humility or percipience, and an attention to the errors or the smugness of his reasonings can lead us to the conclusion that Goldsmith's prefatory Advertisement is part of a satirical game, protesting just too much on behalf of his narrator:

The hero of this piece unites in himself the three greatest characters upon earth; he is a priest, an husbandman, and the father of a family. He is drawn as ready to teach, and ready to obey; as simple in affluence, and majestic in adversity. In this age of opulence and refinement whom can such a character please?[70]

---

[67] R. Hopkins, *The True Genius of Oliver Goldsmith* (Baltimore Md, 1969), 224.

[68] Karl, *A Reader's Guide*, 222. For a guide to recent criticism see S. Woods, *Oliver Goldsmith: A Reference Guide* (Boston, Mass., 1982), and id.,'The Vicar of Wakefield and Recent Goldsmith Scholarship', *Eighteenth-Century Studies* (1976), 429–43. See also R. Quintana, 'The Vicar of Wakefield: The Problem of Critical Approach', *Modern Philology*, 71 (1973), 59–65.

[69] Hopkins, *The True Genius*, 171.

[70] Oliver Goldsmith, *The Vicar of Wakefield, a Tale Supposed to be Written by Himself* (London, 1766), Advertisement. Unfortunately, this Advertisement is omitted from the Everyman edition to which I have otherwise referred. It is invariably reprinted, however, in 18th- and early 19th-cent. editions.

'Goldsmith offers us the vicar in the same spirit of commendation as the Advertisement would suggest', writes D. W. Jefferson[71]—but at the least the 'commendation' is only really rhetorically apprehensive: the sentimental vogue was testimony enough that nothing could be more acceptable in an 'age of opulence and refinement' than images of simplicity and voices of innocence. Why should we not go further, then, and find a deflating irony in this, strictly speaking, redundant protest?

If, like Hopkins, we scrutinize the apparent inconsistencies of the novel, and especially Primrose's confusions of self-interest and virtue, the preface does look mock-ingenuous.[72] Goldsmith's 'hero' may be 'simple' but in his innocence he is prone enough to mingle the calculation of advantage with the profession of benevolence. Indeed, the words of the Advertisement perturb because they echo the vicar's own, all too easy, conflation of the moral and the material in the last chapter of the novel, where he describes his family 'as merry as affluence and innocence could make them' and concludes with the memorably satisfied, or self-satisfied, statement, 'It now only remained, that my gratitude in good fortune should exceed my former submission in adversity'.[73] But then perhaps this is just one of those conventional endings, a resolving device used most famously by Fielding. It is true that, amongst his journalism, Goldsmith was dismissive not just of novels in general, but of the contrivance of happy endings in particular. In *The Monthly Review* in 1757, for example, he ridiculed the conventionally fortunate conclusion of a novel newly translated from French, *True Merit true Happiness*: 'Reader, if thou hast ever known such perfect happiness as these romance-writers can so liberally dispense, thou hast enjoyed greater pleasure than has ever fallen to our lot. How deceitful are these imaginary pictures of felicity! and, we may add, how mischievous too![74]

However, most of the best-known novelists of the period —Richardson and Mackenzie being examples—inveighed against

---

[71] D.W. Jefferson, 'The Vicar of Wakefield' and Other Prose Writings: A Reconsideration', in A. Swarbrick (ed.), *The Art of Oliver Goldsmith* (London, 1984), 24.

[72] For another useful chart of inconsistencies see J.A. Dussinger, *The Discourse of the Mind in Eighteenth-century Fiction* (The Hague, 1974), 148–72.

[73] Goldsmith, *The Vicar of Wakefield* (1908; rpt. London, 1979), 222.

[74] *Collected Works of Oliver Goldsmith*, ed. Arthur Friedman (5 vols., Oxford, 1966), i. 17.

novel-writing. It is possible that Goldsmith was merely following such customary practice, and that his advice to the author of a
novel called *The Fair Citizen* ('one good Pudding is worth fifty
modern Romances') stemmed from a routine prejudice which could
be presumed to exclude his own novel.[75] Goldsmith's disdain for 'the
flowery paths of novel and romance' was not in itself unusual for a
novelist of the period, whose own writings were always the
exception to such a pejorative description.[76] It is true that wherever
we find Goldsmith writing about novels we find unreserved
condemnation, as in the letter that he wrote to his brother in 1759 on
the education of his son:

> Above all things let him never touch a romance, or novel, those paint beauty
> in colours more charming than nature, and describe happiness that man
> never tastes. How delusive, how destructive therefore are those pictures of
> consummate bliss, they teach the youthful mind to sigh after beauty and
> happiness which never existed, to despise the little good which fortune has
> mixed in our cup, by expecting more than she ever gave.[77]

But this is too conventional to be proof that Goldsmith must have
undertaken *The Vicar of Wakefield* as a parody.

The most persuasive evidence that Goldsmith's novel is a kind of
parody is, in the end, to be taken from the text itself; it is the evidence
of Primrose's own judgements and justifications, set in motion in the
novel's first paragraph where he talks of his marriage as at once an
unselfish moral 'service' and a self-interested result of pragmatic
calculation (his wife chosen for 'qualities as would wear well'). It is
the influence of such calculation, an influence marked even when
Primrose is busy coming to mistaken conclusions, on which Hopkins
concentrates, contending that 'It is ludicrous how Dr. Primrose's
benevolence has been praised in the past . . . Under the subterfuge of
Christian humility he exercises a *petty* practicality.'[78] The kind of
close reading that produces this assertion is, in its own way,
irrefutable, but it does avoid a central issue. For if the novel is indeed
a parody, why is it that, until fairly recently, it has so rarely been
received as such? A careful critical attention to Primrose's version of

[75] *Collected Works*, i. 17. 82.

[76] See Goldsmith's article 'A True History for the Ladies', from the *British
Magazine* of July 1760, in *Collected Works*, iii. 120.

[77] *The Collected Letters of Oliver Goldsmith*, ed. K.C. Balderston (Cambridge,
1928), 60.

[78] Hopkins, *The True Genius*, 188.

his and his family's virtues may lead to scepticism regarding his reliability or his probity, but that leaves us with a history of 'misreadings' of the novel. Particularly disconcerting are the few records that we have of the reception of *The Vicar of Wakefield* in the decades following its publication—the reception by readers still close to the fashion of sentimentalism. We look in vain for perceptions of the novel as satirical. The judgement made in an anonymous preface in a volume of collected novels published in 1796 can stand as a summation of what had been the reactions to *The Vicar* since its first appearance:

The diction is chaste, correct, and elegant. The characters are drawn to the life, and the scenes it exhibits are ingeniously variegated with humour and sentiment. The hero of the piece displays the most shining virtues that can adorn relative and social life; sincere in his profession, humane and generous in his disposition, he is himself a pattern of the character he represents, enforcing that excellent maxim, that example is more powerful then precept . . . [the novel] inculcates the purest lessons of morality and virtue, free from the rigid law of stoicism.[79]

If *The Vicar of Wakefield* was a parody, it was, and is, difficult to distinguish it from the type that it might have parodied. It is not because eighteenth-century readers were unsophisticated that Goldsmith's novel failed to trouble them; on the contrary, it is because they were practised novel readers that the book was absorbable into established habits of reading. So from the first reviews of the novel to the praise lavished on it by Scott and Goethe, the fact that, as a reviewer put it in 1766, its narrator is possessed of 'some vanity and more credulity' was not supposed to subvert the same character's 'Piety and fortitude, a glowing benevolence, an uncommon share of parental fondness'.[80] 'Simplicity'—proclaimed by Primrose as the characteristic of his family—justified, even necessitated, those failings, and 'simplicity' or 'innocence' was what readers had been taught to expect from the virtuous protagonist of a novel of sentiment. The expectation made it possible that, when 'Beauties' of Goldsmith were compiled, the more sententious of Primrose's observations could be included, along with extracts from Goldsmith's poetry and essays, as if the Vicar's maxims were

[79] *The Vicar of Wakefield*, in Henshall's Ornamented Library of Classic Novels, vol. iv (Dublin, 1796), 'Memoirs of the Author', 6.

[80] *Critical Review*, June 1766, in G.S. Rousseau (ed.), *Goldsmith: The Critical Heritage* (London, 1974), 46.

unambiguously admirable, marking 'in a striking manner, the unbounded benevolence of his temper, or the elegant simplicity of his mind'.[81] The normal platitudes about the elevating effects of images of innocent virtue were fitted to the novel:

We find nothing in this performance to turn the attention upon the writer, or to inflame the passions of the reader; as we see daily practised by the common herd of novelists. Genuine touches of nature, easy strokes of humour, pathetic pictures of domestic happiness and domestic distress, (a happiness proceeding from innocence and obscurity, and a distress supported with resignation and chearfulness) are some of the methods here made use of to interest and move us.[82]

Whatever the problems or defects of the vicar's story, there could be no doubt about 'its moral tendency', 'the exemplary manner in which it recommends and enforces the great obligations of universal BENEVOLENCE: the most amiable quality that can possibly distinguish and adorn the WORTHY MAN and the GOOD CHRISTIAN!'[83]

Later critics and biographers preserved and enhanced this reputation of *The Vicar of Wakefield*, acknowledging Primrose's faults but going on to celebrate his capacities for fellow-feeling and rectitude. Sir Walter Scott saw in the vicar 'just so much of pedantry and literary vanity as serves to show that he is made of mortal mould, and subject to human failings' but did not doubt his 'worth and excellency'; Goldsmith's novel was one in which 'we find the best and truest sentiments enforced in the most beautiful language; and perhaps there are few characters of purer dignity have been described than that of the excellent pastor, rising above sorrow and oppression'.[84] James Prior, the author of the first systematic biography of Goldsmith, described the popularity of the book amongst eighteenth-century readers in the same terms, regarding 'the little foibles and weaknesses common to the best specimens of humanity' as an integral part of its 'picture of warm-hearted simplicity': 'The Vicar of Wakefield secured friends among every description of readers; with the old by the purity of its moral lessons, and with the young by the interest of the story.' He obviously

---

[81] *The Life of Dr Oliver Goldsmith: Written from Personal Knowledge, Authentic Papers, and other Indubitable Authorities* (London, 1774), 15.

[82] *Critical Review* (June 1766), in *Goldsmith: The Critical Heritage*, 46.

[83] *Monthly Review* (May 1766), ibid. 44.

[84] Sir Walter Scott, *The Lives of the Novelists* (London, 1910).

thought his own reading continuous with the novel's initial reception when he accepted unconditionally 'The unwearied benevolence and submission to the will of Providence under all his distress of the good pastor'.[85] The vicar could be taken to be not so much an untrustworthy narrator as an innocent one. Where there had been an audience willing to accept Pamela's account of her own modesty, it is hardly surprising that there were readers for whom Primrose's celebration of his own humility did not look like Goldsmith's satire.

If *The Vicar of Wakefield* was a parody, it was one that was just too accurate; it could be read, comfortably enough, 'for the sentiment'—as a morally edifying and emotionally delectable text. Fanny Burney was subjecting Goldsmith's novel to such a dominant habit of reading when she confessed 'in the second volume, I really sobb'd'.[86] Much that was 'affecting' was found in a plot which heaped one misfortune or 'distress' upon another, and which, in that respect, was close enough to being typical of novels of the period. The sequence of 'Fresh Calamities' visited upon the Primrose family may now look like calculated excess, but it was the characteristic mode of the novel of sentiment. Misfortunes scarcely come thicker in *The Vicar of Wakefield* than they do in novels before and after Goldsmith's. Sensibility is best excited in distress, and poignancy is often insisted on by narratives which themselves rehearse the effects of a tale of pathetic suffering. The hunger of readers for touching tales of misfortune was to be vindicated as well as satisfied. Sarah Fielding's *Adventures of David Simple*, for example, depicts a sensitive hero who is not only always ready to weep at a story of suffering, but also energetic in seeking out any who might have such a story to tell. He looks and listens for its signs: tears, sighs, the sound of 'lamentation' from the next room. 'David, according to his usual Method, could not be easy without enquiring what could be the Cause of this Complaint'—and the 'Cause' is always given to us as somebody's tale of affliction, which is also the occasion for the 'sensible' responses of those who listen.[87] Herbert in Mackenzie's *Julia de Roubigne*, having failed in commercial ventures through ill fortune, 'enjoys also that privilege which misfortune

[85] James Prior, *The Life of Oliver Goldsmith* (2 vols., London, 1837), ii. 110–11.

[86] *Goldsmith: The Critical Heritage*, 53.

[87] Sarah Fielding, *The Adventures of David Simple*, ed. M. Kelsall (London, 1969), 253.

bestows on the virtuous';[88] the 'privilege' is 'a delicacy and fineness of sentiment', a 'privilege' which can pass to those who respond readily to the account of his ordeals. Modelled in such novels was a connoisseurship of (vicarious) suffering which Goldsmith did not unsettle.

The Vicar of Wakefield would have been hard-pressed to outdo the extraordinary sequences of 'distress' that feature in novels like *David Simple* or Mackenzie's *The Man of the World*. The man of feeling in the latter literally dies of the undeserved sufferings forced upon him, collapsing in a gesture beyond which parody could hardly go: 'Annesly had stretched his fortitude to the utmost—this last blow overcame it, and he fell senseless to the floor'.[89] The collapse is a sign learned from Richardson, though the strange, inexorable logic to suffering that Richardson elaborated in *Clarissa* is missing. Affliction had become no more than what readers expected to find in novels—not reforming critique, not social description, just self-sufficient, private sensitivity exceptionally enhanced. Goldsmith was hardly in a position to mock the implausibility of narratives which gratified the taste for pathos; the implausibility was written into the formula. Indeed, by making the susceptibility to a moving tale part of the narrative, a text like Brooke's *Fool of Quality* emphasizes the conventionality of sympathetic response: 'I gave him my story in parts from time to time, and he had plentifully watered the several passages with his tears'.[90] Responding properly to a story is here the truest sign of sensibility—enough in itself. When a virtuous character in *The Fool of Quality* begs to hear of another's afflictions, one is reminded of Adam Smith's explanation of how sympathy with pain could produce pleasure for a 'spectator': 'go on—I insist upon it: I love to weep—I joy to grieve—it is my happiness, my delight, to have perfect sympathy in your sorrows'.[91] Of course, this is effusive where Smith's description had to be calmly judicious; but then Brooke's novel is not attempting to make sympathy the basis of social and moral being. Sympathy here is focused to a special intimacy, an exceptional indulgence. It is to be enjoyed as an effect of narrative: 'Here Harry closed his narration, and all the company gathered about him, and nearly smothered him with their caresses'.[92] As a tribute to itself, the novel of sentiment can

---

[88] *Julia de Roubigne*, 141.   [89] *The Man of the World*, 148.
[90] *The Fool of Quality*, 109.   [91] Ibid. 198.   [92] Ibid. 257.

depict a narrator's arousal of speechless emotion as the rare, essential manifestation of sympathy.

Such illustrations of the possible effects of a story should alert us to the workings of benevolence in these novels, and therefore perhaps to the conventions which allowed Dr Primrose's impulses to charity—now seemingly suspect—to be taken as simply admirable. We understand a good deal about the habit of reading for sentiment if we understand the surprising obscurity (it is, after all, a 'simple' story) of Goldsmith's novel. For, offering narrative as the theatre for sympathy, novels of sentiment (which Goldsmith might have been satirizing, if only readers had known) take fellow-feeling as visceral instinct rather than practical model. The point can be made by applying the formula usually cited in the eighteenth century in any attempt to establish the moralistic potential and obligation of novels—namely that they substitute enlivening 'example' for arid 'precept'. It is the formula that Clara Reeve attempts to use in her summary of the history of the novel, *The Progress of Romance*, published in 1785: discussing novels such as *The Fool of Quality* as texts written to correct 'the passion for desultory reading' engendered by circulating libraries, she writes that they 'endeavoured to stem the torrent by making entertaining stories their *vehicle* to convey to the young and flexible heart, wholesome truths, that it refused to receive under the form of moral precepts and instructions'.[93] Or, as a contributor to *The Sentimental Magazine* put it, 'Moralists . . . must be sensible that precept will never prevail against sentiment; writing that edifies should arouse 'the tear of compassion'.[94] If Richardson struggled to reconcile precept to example, later imitations left precept (the rule that had to be applied, the code for living) well behind. What remained was the example of a benevolence experienced in its purity in attending to a story—sympathy condensed to the pleasures of reading. A representative essay in *The Sentimental Magazine* puts it clearly enough when it uses a vocabulary descriptive of social relations in order to idealize a reader's experience of the best kind of novel as one

---

[93] Clara Reeve, *The Progress of Romance* (2 vols., London, 1785), ii. 41.

[94] *The Sentimental Magazine; or, General Assemblage of Science, Taste, and Entertainment* (Feb. 1774), 61. The title of this journal, which ran from 1773 to 1777, might alone signify the triumph of a 'sentimental' vocabulary in the idealization of social virtues; it was subtitled, 'to Improve the Understanding and to Amend the Heart'.

interspersed with liberal and generous sentiments, perfect in the delineation of characters, representing virtue in the most engaging dress, and vice in the most odious colours, tending to ennoble the passions, to awaken tenderness, sympathy and love (I mean virtuous love) to soften the finer feelings of the mind, and having for object some important moral . . . Novels of this kind insensibly operate on the mind.[95]

For the writer of this kind of paean, it was the relationship of touching narrative and sensitive reader which was true society.

The most influential histories of sentimentalism have usually, in some measure, accounted for this literary fashion as symptomatic of developing beliefs in human capacities for benevolence.[96] R. S. Crane has described sentimentalism as the 'expression' of a 'philosophy' most influentially taught by a latitudinarian clergy, a philosophy distinguished by 'The identification of virtue with acts of benevolence and still more with the feelings of universal goodwill which inspire and accompany these acts; the assumption that such "good Affections" are the natural and spontaneous growth of the heart of man uncorrupted by habits of vice; the antistoical praise of sensibility.'[97] In two particular ways, however, the benevolence depicted in novels of sentiment fails to live up to this model of a 'universal' capacity, a general bond. In the first place, where novels do show benevolence as an operative, reforming influence it is typically like the benevolence of Pamela to the poor of the neighbourhood: rewarding the obedience of the socially inferior, affirming hierarchy, differentiating the deserving from the undeserving. The period of sentimentalism is also the period in which the institutionalizing of benevolence becomes a fashion and 'charity' comes to refer to an organization or establishment as well as an inclination or duty.[98] It is hardly surprising that the practice of philanthropy in the eighteenth century should have been notably tough-minded—dedicated as much to the disciplining as to the relief of the poor. Perhaps, in *The Vicar of Wakefield*, when Primrose

---

[95] *The Sentimental Magazine*, 31.

[96] See, for example, R.F. Brissenden, *Virtue in Distress* (London, 1974); L.I. Bredvold, *The Natural History of Sensibility* (Detroit, 1962); A.R. Humphreys, ' "The Friend of Mankind" (1700–60)—An Aspect of Eighteenth Century Sensibility', *Review of English Studies*, 24 (1948).

[97] R.S. Crane, 'Suggestions Toward a Genealogy of the "Man of Feeling" ', in *The Idea of the Humanities* (Chicago, 1967), 189.

[98] For the history behind the etymology, see D. Owen, *English Philanthropy* 1660–1960 (London, 1965), 11–88.

describes himself 'giving sensibility' to the 'wretches' in the prison, organizing their labour and their moral welfare, instituting 'fines for the punishment of immorality, and rewards for peculiar industry', we should detect satire upon a ludicrous self-righteousness: 'Thus in less than a fortnight I had formed them into something social and humane, and had the pleasure of regarding myself as a legislator, who had brought men from their native ferocity in to friendship and obedience'.[99] But this was too close to a current ideology to look very odd to its polite readers. It would have looked no odder than the boast of Savillon in Mackenzie's *Julia de Roubigne*, when he tells of how he has brought 'liberty' to the slaves on a West Indian plantation:

I have had the satisfaction of observing these men, under the feeling of good treatment, and the idea of liberty, do more than almost double their number subject to the whip of an overseer. I am under no apprehension of desertion or mutiny; they work with the willingness of freedom, yet are mine with more than the obligation of slavery.[1]

It is not obviously more smug than the declaration in *The Fool of Quality* that the 'relative differences of rich and poor, strong and weak' are ordained 'to exercise us in the offices of that charity and those affections, which, reflecting and reflected, like mutual light and warmth, can alone make our good to all eternity'.[2] 'Surely relieving a heart-felt distress is an entertainment of no mean kind', says the hero of Charles Jenner's *The Placid Man*.[3] In one way the novel of sentiment duplicates the 'entertainment' which the polite classes derived from charity, and the social regulation which such benevolence was supposed to effect.

The second, and more fundamental, problem about the novels is that their representatives of 'feeling'—the dispensers of charity to artisans down on their luck and gentlefolk temporarily dispossessed of their proper privileges—are characterized as anomalous, and the sympathy of which they are capable is unusual and fleeting. It is appropriate that Henry Brooke made a child the benevolent hero of *The Fool of Quality*, for the sentimental paragon was supposed to possess an innocence which 'the world' had lost. The instinct to benevolence celebrated in such novels was not being put forward as

[99] *The Vicar of Wakefield*, 172–3.
[1] *Julia de Roubigne*, 136.   [2] *The Fool of Quality*, 221.
[3] Charles Jenner, *The Placid Man* (1770; 2 vols., rpt. London, 1773), i. 93.

a universal phenomenon or a possible influence on social reform. Sympathy was shown as a rare and delicious moment. 'It began to be too much for me; I squeezed his hand that was clasped in mine; his wife's I pressed to my lips, and burst from the place to give vent to the feelings that laboured within me':[4] thus Harley's account, in *The Man of Feeling*, of his pleasure as he rescues a deserving couple from debt and prison and restores them to a life of 'industry'. The righteous hyperbole of this is ludicrous now, but was a necessary element of sentimentalism; the intensity of a special experience of feeling was a substitute for common and prevailing sympathies. To read novels 'for the sentiment' was to discover the capacity for fine feeling as its own justification, a condition cultivated by the reader who appreciated that true 'delicacy' was always an exception. In the novels themselves, benevolence belongs to the 'simple', the 'innocent', the 'sensible'—those who have had to retreat from a world which maligns or abuses their feelings. (Thus the celebration of the domestic unit in many of these texts as the only true society, and the singularity of *Clarissa* in its identification of the family as the very realm of violence and conflict.) The novel of sentiment makes its predictable drama out of the limitations as well as the powers of fellow-feeling. In *The Vicar of Wakefield*, Burchill warns against a 'sickly sensibility of the miseries of others', a benevolence unable to distinguish between 'real' and 'fictitious' ills;[5] if this was directed against the effects of sentimental narratives, it was redundant. For the novels discussed in this chapter did not propose a generosity to be put into practice, a scheme of virtue founded in the social lives of their readers. They represented the protagonist who relies on feeling, indulges benevolence, and yearns for sociability as one who is a species only by being an exception—a simple soul in an unsentimental world.

---

[4] *The Man of Feeling*, 254.   [5] *The Vicar of Wakefield*, 16.

4

Laurence Sterne and the 'Sociality' of the Novel

Tristram is the Fashion.

(Sterne to Catherine Fourmantel, March 1760)[1]

THE anonymous pamphlet *A Funeral Discourse, Occasioned by the Much Lamented Death of Mr Yorick*, published in 1761, was but one of the many spoofs and rejoinders which attached themselves to Laurence Sterne's *Tristram Shandy* throughout the 1760s and 1770s. It imagines Dodsley, Sterne's publisher, telling the novelist that *Tristram Shandy* 'is wonderfully suited to the taste of the age; it will tickle the wanton, amuse the unthinking, countenance the profane, and carry-on to perfection that spirit of trifling, that makes such a rapid progress among us'.[2] This scores some kind of point by imagining a conspiracy between the bookseller and the novelist—an exploitation of popular taste which is, from the first, a marketing exercise. Not that it reveals a relationship which Sterne attempted to hide: in the first volume of *Tristram Shandy* he had wryly exaggerated his subordination to Dodsley, requesting any aristocrat willing to pay for 'a tight, genteel dedication' (a form which he was in the process of mocking) to give the money to the right person—'Be pleased, my good Lord, to order the sum to be paid into the hands of Mr *Dodsley*, for the benefit of the author'(*Tristram Shandy*, p. 16). Sterne's joke is about the power of the bookseller, a power which the *Funeral Discourse* sees controlling the success of his novel. This pamphlet represents *Tristram Shandy* as a symptom of the triumph of the booksellers—men pandering to debased tastes, circulating texts which were to be only marketable commodities. Novels were conceived of as the bookseller's typical wares (detached from

[1] *Letters of Laurence Sterne*, ed. L. P. Curtis (Oxford, 1935), 102.

[2] *A Funeral Discourse, Occasioned by the Much Lamented Death of Mr Yorick* (London, 1761), 24–5.

patronage, collusive with vulgar enjoyments, immorally titillating); *Tristram Shandy* could be represented as the most opportunistic of all such creations of these entrepreneurs.

Whatever the questionable moralisms of this pamphlet, it recognized that *Tristram Shandy* (which at the time had only reached Volume iv) was a publishing phenomenon as well as a text—that it was a fashionable object, a triumph of self-promotion. If we are to recover Sterne's 'sentimentalism', we should look at the reception and circulation of his writings, and if we do this we can follow the lead of the pamphleteer. For *Tristram Shandy* was not just an ingenious book; it became a reputation, an object of debate, a proliferation of texts.[3] In fact, the writer of the *Funeral Discourse* was fuelling the notoriety of *Tristram Shandy* even while he was condemning it—thus Sterne's famous reflection on reading 'a shilling pamphlet wrote against Tristram': 'I wish they would write a hundred such'.[4] Sterne boasted that he wrote 'not to be *fed*, but to be *famous*', and for his novel he initially sought publicity before praise.[5] Of course, while often claiming, with a disingenuous shrug, to abandon itself to opinion and prejudice, *Tristram Shandy* worked to embrace and deflate criticism, making it but a symptom of the novel's success. The 'dear Anti-Shandeans, and thrice able critics' (III. xx. 193) become shadowy personages in *Tristram Shandy*, the butt of every fake apostrophe to the nobility or erudition of the text. Even as Sterne's writing generated criticism it exploited it, presuming a reader who would not be a critic.

Ironically, while the *Funeral Discourse* identified *Tristram Shandy* as the type of a new, and disreputable, literary commodity, bending only to the currents of the market-place, Sterne's first move as an author was to procure a surreptitious kind of patronage by priming David Garrick with the merits of his novel.[6] The book itself, whilst flattering Garrick, debases patronage. Its dedications are either opportunistic ('To the Right Honourable Mr PITT') or parodic ('My Lord, "I Maintain this to be a dedication, notwith-

---

[3] Any account of Sterne's use at the hands of critics and imitators would owe much, as mine does, to A. Howes's *Yorick and the Critics: Sterne's Reputation in England 1760–1868* (New Haven, Conn., 1958). I have also exploited J.C.T. Oates, *Shandyism and Sentiment* (Cambridge, 1968).

[4] Letter to Stephen Croft, May 1760 (*Letters*, 107).

[5] Letter [to Dr Noah Thomas?], Jan. 1760 (*Letters*, 90).

[6] See W.D. Cross, *The Life and Times of Laurence Sterne* (3rd edn., New Haven, Conn., 1929), Ch. 8; and *Letters*, 83–8.

standing its singularity in the three great essentials of matter, form and place" ', I. viii. 15). Sterne was delighted by the attention of aristocrats, but he did not need their imprints upon his text. Lords, like critics, were addressed only to be circumvented. The novel was let loose in the world—subject to no official control. Sterne was happy to pretend that his bookseller was in charge. While Richardson had attempted to exercise strict moralistic control over the interpretation of his novels, distrusting the very literary form that he was using, Sterne was willing to accept fashion as a virtue, trusting to the capacities of the private reader, and making his very life as an author (in the personae of Tristram or Yorick) a fiction to flaunt in the face of his critics.

From the first, some of these critics recognized the truth that *Tristram Shandy*, from volume to volume over five years, gleefully implied: readers were willing to accept and enjoy what the critics disdained. *Tristram Shandy's Bon Mots, Repartees, Odd Adventures and Humourous Stories* (1760) makes its gesture of resignation by having the spirits of Swift and Fielding express disgruntlement at the vogue of Sterne's novel. Fielding is made to state the incontrovertible fact of its popularity:

TRISTRAM Shandy I guess you mean—I have been just hearing of it, from a soul which arrived about two hours ago—he tells me that the author is caressed by people of the first fashion—who strive one with each other, for the honour of filling his belly and his pockets—and, withal, that his works are preferr'd beyond any thing which either you or I have written.[7]

Other pamplets resorted to a moralistic hyperbole that was either incongruous or fatalistically ironic. *The Clockmakers Outcry Against the Author of the Life and Opinions of Tristram Shandy* (1760) was driven to describing Sterne as 'the forerunner of *Antichrist* (pray heaven that he may not be the real one, of which there is not a little room to suspect when we contemplate his figure, and penetrate into his real sentiments)' (p. 10). It is as if, with *Tristram Shandy*, the ritual of condemnation found itself becoming part of the fashion which it attacked. This left only the defensive irony we find in a pamphlet which we can set against the passage above, resorting to the parody of stern strictures on the effects of novels even as it attacked *Tristram Shandy*. *A Genuine Letter from a*

[7] *Tristram Shandy's Bon Mots, Repartees, odd Adventures, and Humorous Stories; All Warranted Originals* (London, 1760), 67.

Methodist Preacher, also published as *A Letter from the Rev. George Whitefield, B.A. to the Rev. Laurence Sterne*, makes Sterne's critic a Methodist fanatic. As Alan Howes says, 'the attack on Sterne is used as an ironic device for attacking the Methodist as well'.[8] The exercise is not far from the rhetoric of the *Clockmaker's Outcry*:

> I cannot conceive how it was possible for a divine of the church of England to write so prophane a book;—a book penned by the Devil himself; and calculated, above all other books, to advance the interests of the Prince of Darkness, to lead mankind astray from the paths of righteousness, and conduct them towards the bottomless pit.[9]

We get the same tactic in the *Funeral Discourse* to which I have already referred. The title-page of this declares it to be 'Preached before a very mixed Society of Jemmies, Jessamies, Methodists and Christians at a Nocturnal Meeting': even as it sets out to satirize Sterne's achievement, it tries a dig at the most solemn moralizers about the dangers of fiction.

Tristram Shandy provoked more parodies and denunciations than any other novel of the eighteenth century, yet its antagonists were also parasitic upon the fashionable literary phenomenon of its day. Texts purporting to demonstrate its degeneracy attempted to do so by amplifying or explicating the 'obscenity' of its innuendo—by being more bawdy than the original. Some of what Howes refers to as the 'bantering attacks' on Sterne's novel merely tried to exploit, and not refute, its appeal, recognizing that if it was obscene, obscenity had become a popular mode. John Carr's *The Life and Opinions of Tristram Shandy* (1760) exemplifies this opportunism: in the feigned apology which is supposed to target Sterne, he concedes to a trend condemned in the paradoxical act of imitation: 'Whenever then there has been, or may hereafter be found any thing in *Tristram Shandy*, that gives the feeblest squint towards obscenity; be assured, once for all, that I was drawn into it by a certain oily conformity of temper' (p. 74). No doubt Sterne did tire of 'These strokes in the Dark, with the many Kicks, Cuffs & Bastinados I openly get on all sides of me',[10] but these were the sure signs, as well as the price, of fame.

---

    [8] Howes, *Yorick and the Critics*, 29.

    [9] *A Genuine Letter from a Methodist Preacher in the Country, to Laurence Sterne* (London, 1760), p. vii.

    [10] Letter to the Bishop of Gloucester, June 1760: *Letters*, 116.

Alongside rebukes and travesties, of course, were praise and admiring imitation. When, in 1798, the Manchester physician John Ferriar initiated Sterne scholarship with his *Illustrations of Sterne*, he prefaced his study with a tribute now no longer paid to the novelist—a tribute which recalled the favoured version of Sterne's appeal in the eighteenth century:

> But the quick tear, that checks our wond'ring smile,
> In sudden pause, or unexpected story,
> Owns thy true mast'ry; and *Le Fevre's* woes,
> *Maria's* wand'rings, and the *Pris'ners* throes
> Fix thee conspicuous on the shrine of glory.[11]

Ferriar, half uneasy with the borrowings from other writers that he was discovering in *Tristram Shandy*, needed to show that he was writing as an admirer, and this was the conventional way to do it—deference paid to the pathos of Sterne's texts. Indeed, Ferriar went on to suggest that the novelist's penchant for plagiarism had diverted 'his own force'—the power of sentimental representation: 'It may even be suspected, that by this influence he was drawn aside from his natural bias to the pathetic'.[12] He was hanging on to the Sterne who was celebrated and preserved in the decades after his death: Sterne the man of sentiment; the writer referred to in *The Sentimental Magazine* as 'Laurence Sterne, commonly known by the name of Yorick, and who introduced the present mode of sentimental writing'.[13] This comes from the introduction to what the magazine called a 'Sentimental Biography. The Life of Mr Sterne', a conflation of his life and his writings which is purely celebratory. This is Sterne not as the merchant of innuendo but as the man of feeling, writing with 'nerves too fine, that wound e'en while they bless'.[14] Fine feeling is to be considered as a characteristic of the texts and their writer: the crowning virtue of both. As the anonymous *Yorick's Skull* of 1777 puts it, 'The writings of YORICK bear visible marks of a great natural genius, seasoned with uncommon humour, and adorned with the most exquisite sensibility'.[15]

Though it was posthumously that this reputation became most secure, even from the beginning some hostile critics were struggling to discover in *Tristram Shandy* sentimental nuggets. *The*

---

[11] John Ferriar, *Illustrations of Sterne* (London, 1798), Preface.
[12] Ibid. 6.   [13] *The Sentimental Magazine* (Jan. 1774), 4.
[14] Ibid. 7.   [15] *Yorick's Skull; or, College Oscitations* (London, 1777), 34.

Clockmakers Outcry, for instance, pauses from the anatomizing of indecencies to praise one passage from the first volume of the book: 'The account of *Yorick* and his *Exit* . . . is well imagined and pathetically written. It has not a little contributed to provoke our indignation against the author, for mispending his time on ridiculous and immoral bagatelles, who seems to be possessed of talents, that, properly employed, cannot fail of penetrating the heart' (p. 27). While Sterne's putative sentimentalism is rarely more than a parenthesis in modern critical treatments of his writing, in the decades during and after their publication it was seized on as their distinctive merit. A series of lengthy articles in *The Monthly Review* can serve as an initial guide to the means by which *Tristram Shandy* was aligned to the image of a dominant literary fashion. It is a guide which is appropriate because *The Monthly Review*, like its rival *Critical Review*, was explicitly addressing a novel-buying readership, and could not simply fall back on that high-minded disdain of narrative fiction which was a settled rhetoric in the period.[16]

The reviewers for the *Monthly* emphasized both the 'indelicacies' of *Tristram Shandy* and its triumphantly 'pathetic' cameos. Two types of reaction to the novel are caught in the ambivalence of these reviews, objecting to volumes 'interlarded with obscenity' but declaring that 'Mr Shandy shows himself a master in the science of *human feelings*, and the art of describing them'.[17] The inconsistency of these readings is not a difference of opinion between the different reviewers writing for the *Monthly*; it is there in each single review. 'The fifth and sixth volumes of this work . . . are not without their stars and dashes, their hints and whiskers', complained Langhorne in the article that he wrote for the *Monthly* of January 1762; a few pages later, puzzled by what he saw as the text's moral unevenness, he was writing, 'Since Mr Sterne published his Sermons, we have been of opinion, that his excellence lay not so much in the humorous as in the pathetic; and in this opinion we have been confirmed by the above story of Le Fever'.[18] Ralph Griffiths, reviewing Volumes vii and viii of *Tristram Shandy*, threw up his hands at its 'bawdyisms': 'Why you might as well write *broad Rochester* as set down all these obscene asterisms!—setting the reader's imagination to work, and

---

16 See R.D. Mayo, *The English Novel in the Magazines* (Oxford, 1962), 190–208.
17 *The Monthly Review*, 26 (Jan. 1762), and 32 (Feb. 1765).
18 Ibid. 26, pp. 32 and 41.

officiating as pimp to every lewd idea excited by your own creative and abominable ambiguity.'[19] In the same article, commenting on Toby's courtship of Widow Wadman, he was adjusting his exclamations to a different end:

Never was any thing more beautifully simple, more natural, more *touching!* O Tristram! that ever any grosser colours should daub and defile that pencil of thine, so admirably fitted for the production of the most delicate as well as the most masterly pictures of men, manners, and situations!—*Richardson*—the delicate, the circumstantial RICHARDSON himself, never produced any thing equal to the amours of Uncle Toby and the Widow Wadman.

The puzzlement or exasperation recorded in such articles was provoked not so much by the formal audacity of *Tristram Shandy* as by what was perceived to be its moral unreliability. The novel itself was able to reflect wryly on the official concern of critical readers with the possibility of improper intimations—and to imply in the process their clumsiness as interpreters. One who dresses 'like a gentleman' will write like one, suggests Tristram. Therefore, 'when your honours and reverences would know whether I writ clean and fit to be read, you will be able to judge full as well by looking into my Laundress's bill, as my book' (*Tristram Shandy*, IX. xiii. 617). Here, as elsewhere, advantage has been taken of the serial publication of the novel to swipe at those by whom it has been 'abus'd, curs'd, criticis'd and confounded', and we might infer that this also enabled Sterne to respond to the critics by providing the sentimental interludes which they craved. Certainly there is something knowing in the way that some such passages are produced—as if they are too heavily marked off for special delectation, too retractable. Griffiths's sense that, even when *Tristram Shandy* delivers the 'pathetic', it can give way to bathos, gave rise, in his review of the final volume of the novel, to a judgement in which the *Monthly's* ambivalence is summed up. Discussing Tristram's meeting with Maria in Chapter 24, he wrote:

What a pretty, whimsical, affecting kind of episode has he introduced in his chapter entitled INVOCATION! . . . our readers shall have the chapter entire, except the abrupt transition in the last two lines, which, in our opinion, serve but to *spoil all*, by an ill-tim'd stroke of levity; like a ludicrous

---

[19] *Ibid.* 32, pp. 125–6.

epilogue, or ridiculous farce, unnaturally tagged to the end of a deep tragedy, only as it were, to efface every elevated, generous, or tender sentiment that might before have been excited.[20]

The sentence censored ('—What an excellent inn at *Moulins!*') is the device by which the text parenthesizes the sentimental encounter, returning us to the 'mirth' and frivolity of Tristram's travels. It is a device too ambiguous for Griffiths to approve.

Sterne's writings did, though, lend themselves to the processes of selection and citation by which he was eventually construed as the arch-sentimentalist. R.D. Mayo has described how Richardson and Sterne were the novelists most often quoted and imitated in the magazines of the time: 'the most important reason for their whole-hearted reception in the miscellanies was their sentimental philosophy, for in popular magazines from 1760 or 1765 the spirit of sensibility was completely in the ascendant'.[21] Sterne's fragmentary texts became famous for a certain kind of fragment. *The Monthly Review* foreshadowed a trend when, with some relief, it singled out the story of Le Fever for special praise: 'In the story of *Le Fever* the old Captain appears in the most amiable light; and as this little episode does greater honour to the abilities and disposition of the Author, than any other part of his work, we shall quote it at large . . .'.[22]. In the same month, the tale ('altogether a master-piece in its kind, and does the Writer great credit') was included in the *Gentleman's Magazine*.[23] It came to be taken as the epitome of, not the exception to, Sterne's style. As *The Sentimental Magazine* put it, 'the story of Le Fevre is one of the most highly finished, and masterly examples of true pathos to be found in any language, and would have made its author immortal, though he had never written any thing else'.[24] In John Ireland's account of the formation in Bath of a 'Shandean society' by the fashionable actor John Henderson, it is this extract from *Tristram Shandy* that is given as the best example of the readings by which the 'society' entertained itself, drawing 'tears from every eye': 'Never shall I forget the effect he gave to the story of Le Fevre. It kindled a flame of admiration, and promoted a proposal to devote a day to the memory of the author, pour a libation over his

20 *The Monthly Review*, 36 (Feb. 1767), 99.
21 Mayo, *The English Novel*, 325.
22 *The Monthly Review*, 26, p. 32.
23 *The Gentleman's Magazine*, 32 (Jan. 1762), 28–32.
24 *The Sentimental Magazine* (Jan. 1774), 6.

grave, and speak a requiem to his departed spirit.'[25] It was taken as a paradigm of sentimental eloquence. By 1787, in the Preface to her *Story of Le Fevre*, Jane Timbury could be confident that she was versifying a fragment accepted as being of exemplary pathos: 'Mr Sterne's affecting Story of LE FEVRE has been so much admired by the sentimental part of the literary world'.[26]

This Story became one of the main elements in the laudatory version of Sterne's writings that was constructed in the eighteenth century. Along with 'The History of Yorick' and 'Maria' it was the most popular of the extracts reprinted or imitated in magazines 'groaning under the deluge of sentimental fragments'.[27] These extracts were there in *The Beauties of Sterne*, first published in 1782 and appearing in another dozen editions by the early 1790s. Though later editions of the *Beauties* were to make some attempt to reconcile the 'morality' and the 'humour' of *Tristram Shandy* in particular, the Preface to the first edition admits to the censorship to which Sterne's texts have had to be subjected in order to provide unadulterated 'pleasure and instruction'. Subtitled 'Selected for the Heart of Sensibility', it provides the '*chaste* part of the world'—those who have 'with some reason' complained of 'the obscenity which taints the writings of *Sterne*'—with a text suited to 'their rising offspring'.[28] This immensely popular compilation perpetuated Sterne-the-sentimentalist, avowing, indeed, that 'the stories of *Le Fever*, the *Monk* [*from* A Sentimental Journey], and *Maria*' would be so poignant for 'the *feeling reader*' that they could not be placed too close together for fear that they might 'wound the bosom of *sensibility* too deeply'.[29]

The sentimental Sterne came to be used as a model of moralizing excellence by natural enemies of the novel. William Enfield, Rector and 'Lecturer on the Belles Lettres' at the Warrington Academy for Dissenters, included only Sterne amongst novelists in *The Speaker; or, Miscellaneous Pieces, Selected from the Best English Writers* (1774). This anthology, produced 'with a view to facilitate the

[25] John Ireland, *Letters and Poems of the Late Mr John Henderson: With Anecdotes of his Life* (London, 1786), 30.

[26] Jane Timbury, *The Story of Le Fevre* (London, 1787), 5.

[27] Mayo, *The English Novel*, 339; for the importance of Sterne in the magazines, see pp. 336–46.

[28] *The Beauties of Sterne* (London, 1782), p. vii.

[29] Ibid., p. viii.

Improvement of Youth in Reading and Speaking', set extracts from Sterne alongside conventional examples of elegance and pathos: Shakespeare, Milton, Pope, Thomson, Gray, and *The Spectator*. Enfield, more usually a writer of sermons, hymns, and prayers, recruited the 'pathetic' elements of Sterne (Toby's reflections on the plight of 'Negroes', 'Yorick's Death', 'The Story of Le Fever') as patterns of moral and stylistic achievement—good fodder for the young.[30] Vicesimus Knox did the same thing in his *Elegant Extracts*, first published in 1783. Knox (schoolmaster, priest, and conduct-book writer) made explicit in his Advertisement the desirable conflation of style and virtue to be taught by his collection, devised so that 'young persons' would acquire 'ideas on many pleasing subjects of Taste and Literature; and, which is of much higher importance, they will imbibe with an encrease [*sic*] of knowledge, the purest principles of Virtue and Religion.[31] Again, Sterne was the only novelist whose works were cited, in company with extracts from the *Spectator, Guardian*, and *Rambler*, and from the conduct-books of Watts, Gregory, and Chapone. It is strange enough to find the more lachrymose passages from Sterne's fiction in amongst a host of sober Protestant moralisms, and stranger still given that Knox elsewhere set aside 'the exquisite touches of nature and sensibility' he found in Sterne's novels to fulminate against him at full throttle:

the poison he conveys is subtle, and the more dangerous as it is palatable. I believe no young mind ever perused his books without finding those passions roused and inflamed, which, after all that the novelist can advance in their favour, are the copious sources of all human misery. Many a connection, begun with the fine sentimentality which Sterne has recommended and increased, has terminated in disease, infamy, want, madness, suicide, and a gibbet.[32]

Knox, at least, was not going to forget that only rigorous censorship could produce the instructive, pathetic Sterne.

Sterne's novels were shaken free of a reputation for low innuendo by their reconstitution as 'elegant extracts'. But *aficionados* kept

---

[30] William Enfield (ed.), *The Speaker; or, Miscellaneous Pieces, Selected from the Best English Writers* (London, 1774).

[31] Vicesimus Knox (ed.), *Elegant Extracts* (2nd edn., London, 1784), p. iii.

[32] From *Essays Moral and Literary*; cited in Howes, *Sterne: The Critical Heritage*, 251.

having to defend him against accusations that, as John Henderson's (eulogistic) ode to Sterne put it,

> . . . he, with all these powers fraught,
> Was loose in language, and impure in thought.[33]

Sterne's role as a literary personality had, thanks to his own efforts, become entangled with his writings, and attacks on the latter were always liable to be *ad hominem*. The famous objections to his publication of his *Sermons* as *By Mr Yorick* were objections to this calculated manipulation of a fictional identity—the use of suspect fame to sell a serious moral text. After his death, Sterne's personality lived on as an issue, given new prominence when the fragments by which he was known came, in the 1770s, to include volumes of letters, some genuine and some forged. Discoverable in these were the usual alternative aspects of his reputation: indecent suggestiveness or sentimental delicacy. The reviewer of *Letters from Yorick to Eliza* (1775) in the *Gentleman's Magazine* had to equivocate over Sterne's record of his friendship (or was it flirtation?) with Eliza Draper: '[the letters] are expressive of the most tender and (we trust) sentimental friendship. But, between married persons, such cicesbeism is always unsafe, and generally suspicious; and, to virtue, prudence, and even sensibility, must give abundantly more pain than pleasure.'[34] The author of *Letters from Eliza to Yorick*, published in the same year, had to secure Sterne's status as a laudably sentimental writer by showing the relationship to have been one of perfect sympathy based on 'sentiment alone'.[35] It offered to prove that 'Platonism, so much ridiculed, so long thought a chimera, may exist, and even with the strongest sensibility, and warmest imagination'.[36] This act of homage showed Eliza weeping and sighing over Sterne's novels, and describing her intimacy with him—for some a scandalous confirmation of the indecency of his writings—as an exemplum of sentimental understanding:

The sympathy of Sentiments bestows the most inexpressible pleasures—such sorrows are sorrows to be coveted—when your page compels the tears from my eyes, and makes my heart throb—I will say, Here my Bramin wept—when he penn'd this passage, he wept—let me catch the

---

[33] Ireland, *Letters and Poems of the Late Mr John Henderson*, 36.
[34] Cited in Howes, *Sterne: The Critical Heritage*, 221.
[35] *Letters from Eliza to Yorick* (London, 1775), 39.
[36] Ibid., p. xi.

pleasing contagion from each heart-felt sentence, and bedew the leaf with mutual streaming sorrows.[37]

This making of Sterne into a Man of Feeling was never completely assured, though—as I shall describe—the publication of *A Sentimental Journey* was taken to make the task easier. There was always the problem of the suggestiveness of his texts—not just their bawdy, but the half-concealment of that bawdy. No doubt many of the avid readers of *Tristram Shandy* were less worried than the critics about the novel's supposed improprieties—and *Tristram Shandy* was adept at holding up the stiff, critical pronouncement for the amusement of a reader always more knowing, more adaptable, than any critic. While the coexistence of sentimentalism and suggestiveness may have been a problem for the critics, it was no accident. The workings of both depended upon that relationship which Sterne elevated above any duty to literature or criticism—the relationship between a text and a private reader flattered to be segregated from 'the *herd* of the *world*'. This reader was capable of a private act of inference which would discover the 'humour', the insinuations, of the text, but which would also enliven its pathos into an intense, because visceral, experience: 'a true feeler always brings half the entertainment along with him. His own ideas are only call'd forth by what he reads, and the vibrations within, so entirely correspond with those excited, 'tis like reading *himself* and not the *book*.'[38]

*   *   *

There is so little true feeling in the *herd* of the *world*, that I wish I could have got an act of parliament, when the books first appear'd, 'that none but wise men should look into them.

(Sterne to John Eustace, February 1768)[39]

For Yorick in the *Sentimental Journey* perfectly intelligible conversation depends on gestures rather than words, on sensitivity to the non-verbal rather than confidence in what can be said:

There is not a secret so aiding to the progress of sociality, as to get master of this *short hand*, and be quick in rendering the several turns of looks and limbs, with all their inflections and delineations, into plain words. For my own part, by long habitude, I do it so mechanically, that when I walk the

---

[37] *Letters from Eliza to Yorick*, 34–5.
[38] Letter from Sterne to Dr John Eustace, Feb. 1768 (*Letters*, 411).   [39] Ibid.

streets of London, I go translating all the way; and have more than once stood behind in the circle, where not three words have been said, and have brought off twenty different dialogues with me, which I could have fairly wrote down and sworn to. (p. 172)

In the end all becomes 'plain words'—the transcriptions and inferences of a narrative. The 'progress of sociality' is the progress of this narrative: 'sociality' stands not so much for the relationship between the narrator and those whose 'looks and limbs' he describes (he is a distanced connoisseur, an amused translator), as for the relationship between the narrator and those who read, those who are to benefit by the habit and art of his translation. Yorick stands 'behind in the circle', not participant but transcriber. Out of his observations of gesture comes 'sociality': the sociality of the text. Sterne's coinage refines social understanding to the pact between a knowing narrator and a knowing consumer of novels. 'Sociality' is what we are to enter into when we read Sterne's text.

Sterne's fiction is notoriously self-conscious about the modes of a novel's coherence—about the powers of a narrator to convince, to beguile, and to satisfy. It is attentive to its 'sociality'. Sterne may have made new capital, and a new kind of instant literary fame, out of this self-consciousness, but he was exploiting conventional expectations. In an age in which narrative fiction was suspected by many, even of its more enthusiastic consumers, of being suggestive, improper, promiscuous, novels were thick with descriptions of how narratives should be attended to and interpreted. They constantly concerned themselves, technically and moralistically, with the effects of telling stories. As we have seen, novels of sentiment keenly rehearsed the art of comprehending the pathos of narratives; the capacity to respond with tremulous sensibility to a tale of misfortune was represented as a sufficient sign of virtue. The use of 'the story of Le Fever' in Volume vi of *Tristram Shandy* is a clear enough indication of Sterne's awareness of this genre of the internalized tale, included to demonstrate the sympathies of its auditors. It is a story that comes to us freighted with the responsiveness of Toby and Trim to another's misfortunes; its point is the sympathy of which they are capable. But then sympathy is most graphic when it is not spoken, Toby and Trim not being the most competent handlers of words. It takes Tristram's narrative to describe 'the several turns of looks and limbs' that accompany the telling and reception of Le Fever's story: 'fool that I was! nor can I recollect, (nor perhaps you) without turning back to the place, what it was that hindered me from letting the corporal tell it in his own words;—but the occasion is lost,—I must tell it now in my own' VI. v. 415–16). Narrative has to translate, has to make 'plain words' mediate the natural articulacy of feeling. And translation (a metaphor invoked throughout *Tristram Shandy*) is a matter of inference and induction—a freedom that comes with the acceptance of error. There is the understanding of which the likes of Toby and Trim are capable, signified in their gestures, their sighs, their looks, and there is the sociality of the text—the relationship between narrator and reader—through which that understanding is represented. Richardson attempted to produce the poignancy of sentiment in 'writing to the moment', which became writing which threatened to evade moralistic control. Sterne concedes that sentiment can only be glimpsed across the distance between a translator and an 'original'; that while feeling is supposed to transcend words, it takes words (at once judicious and inaccurate) to translate sentiment. *Tristram Shandy* is writing away from the moment.

There have grown up literary-critical versions of *Tristram Shandy* as an anachronism, a modern novel before its time. To represent it as such, however, is to ignore the ways in which the novel's field of play and manoeuvre might have been fitted to the competence of its admiring eighteenth-century readers. 'I know there are readers in the world, as well as many other good people in it, who are no readers at all,—who find themselves ill at ease, unless they are let into the whole secret from first to last, of every thing which concerns you' (*Tristram Shandy*, I. iv. 7): *Tristram Shandy* is always admonishing incompetent or intemperate readers, but that does not mean that it is not colluding with those who are more deft. All those moralisms about the dangers of novels which get repeated through the eighteenth century take reading only for the 'story' as the trap into which the unwary fall. Sterne's satire on story-lovers exploits such rhetoric, and presumes a reader who will know better. It is this implied reader with whom *Tristram Shandy* establishes its sociality, a reader privileged to look down on the possibilities of misinterpretation which the novel invokes. So the misunderstandings and non-communications shown in *Tristram Shandy* are only apparent. Walter and Toby Shandy shake their heads over the behaviour of women in pregnancy,

but certainly since shaking of heads came into fashion, never did two heads
shake together, in concert, from two such different springs.

God bless   }   'em all—said my uncle *Toby* and my
Duce take   }   father, each to himself. (IV. xii. 285)

Unknowing disagreement is resolved into intelligible gesture.
Eccentric differences of perception are only eccentric—the accidental crossings of Walter's and Toby's reasonings are comic
because the novel can trace the different paths by which they appear
to arrive at the same point: 'He was a very great man! added my
uncle *Toby*; (meaning *Stevinus*)—He was so, brother *Toby*, said my
father, (meaning *Piereskius*)' (VI. ii. 410). Difference is referred to
from a vantage-point from which it can be perfectly comprehended.
'There is nothing shews the characters of my father and my uncle
Toby, in a more entertaining light, than their different manner of
deportment, under the same accident' (VIII. xxvi. 578). Helene
Moglen is typical of many modern critics in seeing in this play of
differences, this entertainment, an admirable pluralism: 'there is
never an absolute truth (only a number of possible points of view
which must be balanced against one another)'.[40] But although the
novel does offer 'opinions' rather than truths, most of these come
from Toby, Trim, and Walter and are the products of obsession.
They are not offered to the reader as if they were adoptable
perceptions. What is offered as exemplary, in the usual manner of
sentimentalism, is the sympathy that can bridge the gulf between
perceptions.

'The truest respect which you can pay to the reader's
understanding, is to halve this matter amicably, and leave him
something to imagine' (*Tristram Shandy*, II. xi. 109): whatever its
promises of pluralism, Sterne's novel can only propose a sympathy
which overrides monomania because it is authoritative enough to
trace obsessions like Walter's and Toby's through their bizarre and
specific involutions. The certainty of this legibility allows the
narrator of *Tristram Shandy* ironically to project precisely the
promise of pluralism to which I have just referred. For 'so long as a
man rides his HOBBY-HORSE peaceably and quietly along the
Kings highway, and neither compels you or me to get up behind

[40] H. Moglen, *The Philosophical Irony of Laurence Sterne* (Gainesville, Fla.,
1975), 5.

him,—pray, Sir, what have either you or I to do with it?' (I. vii. 13). The text makes much of accepting privatized fixation as an inevitable condition, but the reader of this is safe in the knowledge that obsessions are just private. They are self-containing ('there is no disputing against HOBBY-HORSES'), and, in this novel, they are brought into the light of day by a narrative which sees them, follows them, socializes them. Sterne pilfered the singular vocabularies which possess members of the Shandy household from encyclopedias and reference books;[41] they were intended to be recondite, deracinated, impractical. 'It is the nature of an hypothesis, when once a man has conceived it, that it assimilates every thing to itself as a proper nourishment; and, from the first moment of your begetting it, it generally grows the stronger by every thing you see, hear, read, or understand. This is of great use' (II. xix. 151). The naturalization of monomania here involves the shift from 'a man' to 'you', a claim for the universality, and thus intelligibility, of obsession. Yet the 'great use' to which this form is put in *Tristram Shandy* necessarily involves the assurance of a distance between reading and the blindness of such obsession. For reading must be allowed to make sense of the differences and limited conflicts which are represented, and those in recent years who have detected the spectre of madness in this novel have failed to recognize how obsession is only introduced with a narrative which absolutely comprehends it, which plays upon it.[42] The Hobby-Horse is an impediment to identification: we are to understand, not to share, the odd commitments of characters in *Tristram Shandy*. And we are to understand, too, that these characters are not quite the slaves of their vocabularies because they are bound together by more than words.

Tristram declares that he believes that

the hand of the supreme Maker and first Designer of all things, never made or put a family together . . . where the characters of it were cast or contrasted with so dramatic a felicity as ours was, for this end; or in which the capacities of affording such exquisite scenes, and the powers of shifting

---

[41] See New's Introduction in Laurence Sterne, *The Life and Opinions of Tristram Shandy, Gentleman*, ed. M. New, R.A. Davies, and W.G. Day (3 vols., Gainesville, Fla., 1984), vol. iii, 'the Notes', 24–9. This edition is henceforth referred to as *Florida Edition*.

[42] Max Byrd, *Visits to Bedlam: Madness and Literature in the Eighteenth Century* (Columbia, SC, 1974), 114, and Michael DePorte, *Nightmares and Hobby-horses: Swift, Sterne, and Augustan Ideas of Madness* (San Marino, Calif., 1974), 116.

them perpetually from morning to night, were lodged and intrusted with so unlimited a confidence, as in the SHANDY FAMILY. (III. xxxix. 236)

In this family is found the 'felicity' of contrast, of comprehensible difference. Scenes in this 'whimsical theatre of ours' are 'exquisite', a word meaning, in the eighteenth century, esoteric or finely wrought or sensibly felt. Sterne means all these: we are given, as if spectators, the fastidiously drawn drama of inclinations at once ludicrously eccentric and keenly felt. Walter has 'exquisite feelings' about noses and names; while these prompt him to reasonings incomprehensible except to him and the reader, they also provoke (with his son's name and nose both botched) the benign sympathy of Uncle Toby for his distress. In this world of obsessions, intense feeling is both ludicrous and admirable.

This is the trick of Sterne's sentimentalism. As the writer of *Yorick's Skull* (1777) had it, *Tristram Shandy* should be considered 'rather as an admirable caricature of history, than an exact portrait of private life'—as a text which works by 'alluring mankind with flattering deceptions, beyond the bounds of probability'.[43] The fellow-feeling of which Walter, Toby, and Trim are capable does redeem the influence of obsession, leading R.F. Brissenden to write that against 'the isolating and socially disruptive force of the hobby-horse and the ruling passion Sterne sets the power of sympathy'[44] But then monomania and sympathy are also inextricable; as exercised in *Tristram Shandy*, they are equally 'beyond the bounds of probability'. As *Yorick's Skull* goes on to say, the bonds of sympathy, like the influences of each hobby-horse, are extrapolated past the 'usual': 'By carrying us beyond our usual feelings, he has taught us, that the human heart is capable of the greatest improvement; and that nature never feels herself more noble and exalted, than in the exercise of benevolence and humanity'.[45] The finer feelings illustrated in *Tristram Shandy*—the tears of Toby or Trim; Walter at his most eloquent when words are not enough—are as whimsical as what passes for conversation or argument in Shandy Hall. Sterne privileges the truths of gesture over those of words, but it is wryly done; characters reveal their better instincts, their 'benevolence and humanity', in moments of innocence which are to be approved by a reader who is anything but innocent—a reader

---

[43] *Yorick's Skull*, 34–5.   [44] Brissenden, *Virtue in Distress*, 194.
[45] *Yorick's Skull*, 35–6.

tutored enough in the ways of narrative to recognize the untutored 'human heart'.

Thus the use of Locke in *Tristram Shandy*—referring us to the mingled misunderstandings and sympathies of the Shandy household, but also to the understanding, the contract, between reader and narrator. The 'sagacious Locke' is mobilized to draw attention to that 'fertile source of obscurity' in Shandy Hall: 'the unsteady uses of words which have perplexed the clearest and most exalted understandings' (II. ii. 86). But Locke's concern with the ways in which words can fail, communication go awry, is appropriated by a narrative which can reveal obscurities, explain misunderstandings, show the sympathy that is supposed to transcend speech. References to Lockian epistemology are provided as only sham explanations of the eccentric preoccupations which Sterne describes. It is not necessary to possess a great deal of scholarly knowledge to have doubts about the seriousness with which Sterne does exploit Locke; the very tag 'sagacious' should be enough to arouse suspicions when it appears in a text which so satirizes deference to learning and literary precedent. The resources of scholarship can, however, confirm such suspicions. Melvyn New sees the question of the relation between 'philosophy and literature' as particularly problematic: 'That we cannot even settle the most basic problem of whether Sterne agrees or disagrees with Locke is perhaps a strong indication that the question has not yet been asked in a manner that could produce a satisfying answer'.[46] As he and Geoff Day have argued, there is little reason to believe that Sterne read Locke diligently; the evidence of specific borrowings suggests that Sterne might have arrived at his knowledge of the philosopher's writings through second-hand sources.[47] Tristram, indeed, warns us of the easy availability of Locke's *Essay concerning Human Understanding* (misnaming the title in the process): 'many, I know, quote the book, who have not read it' (*Tristram Shandy*, II. ii. 85). Perhaps too few modern commentators have attended to Ferriar's dry remark of the 1790s: 'It was not the business of Sterne to undeceive those, who considered his Tristram a work of unfathomable knowledge'.[48] As Ferriar began to show, *Tristram*

---

[46] *Florida Edition*, Introduction, iii. 17.
[47] Ibid. iii. 16–17, and see W. G. Day, '*Tristram Shandy*: Locke May Not Be the Key', in V. G. Myer (ed.), *Laurence Sterne: Riddles and Mysteries* (London, 1984), 75–83.
[48] Ferriar, *Illustrations*, 5.

Shandy is full of mangled erudition—plagiarisms calculated to make a virtue of the fragmentation of that 'literature' defined by Johnson in his *Dictionary* as 'learning; skill in letters'. If *Tristram Shandy* was a newly opportunistic kind of literary commodity whose ideal was fashion, it was appropriate that it should play fast and loose with literary precedents, and improbable that Locke could ever be absolved from this process. Locke is not Sterne's intellectual mentor. His writings are invoked in order to show the superiority to such specialized philosophy of the descriptions that narrative can provide. And Locke is a particularly useful measure of the capacities of Sterne's narrative because, while he theorized the inconsistencies of thought and language, *Tristram Shandy* sets out to demonstrate how understanding can surmount private fixation and misapplied vocabulary.

   Tristram Shandy first refers us to Locke for the description of 'an unhappy association of ideas which have no connection in nature' (I. iv. 9); in this case it is Mrs Shandy's association of the winding of the clock with 'some other little family concernments'. Any editor of the novel will direct the reader to Locke's discussion of the 'wrong Connexion in our Minds of *Ideas* in themselves, loose and independent one of another'.[49] Locke seems to describe exactly the fixating form of association to which Toby, Walter, and the rest are prey:

Some of our *Ideas* have a natural Correspondence . . . Besides this there is another Connexion of *Ideas* wholly owing to Chance or Custom; *Ideas* that in themselves are not at all of kin, come to be so united in some Mens Minds, that 'tis very hard to separate them, they always keep in company, and the one no sooner at any time comes into the Understanding but its Associate appears with it.[50]

Yet Locke characterizes the resultant 'Unreasonableness' as a 'Madness' which always threatens discourse, and which, if it prevails, will make 'a Man . . . fitter for *Bedlam*, than Civil Conversation'. There is some kind of distance between this and the hobby-horses harmlessly ridden through the pages of Sterne's novel. What an editorial direction to the relevant passage from Locke's *Essay* can actually obscure is the bathos of the allusion.

   This famous joke about the winding of the clock and the

---

[49] John Locke, *An Essay concerning Human Understanding*, ed. P.H. Nidditch (1975; rpt. Oxford, 1979), II. xxx. 397.

[50] Ibid. II. xxxiii. 395.

associated sex life of Tristram's parents is less at the expense of Mrs Shandy, who after a while cannot dissociate the one from the other, than of her husband, whose 'extreme exactness . . . to which he was in truth a slave' leads to the connection of the two incongruous activities. And what is Walter Shandy but the book's very own 'philosopher'? Always desiring 'exactness', he had 'an itch in common with all philosophers, of reasoning upon every thing which happened, and accounting for it too' (III. xviii. 189). It is into his mouth that Sterne puts the book's 'most extensive borrowing from Locke',[51] the discussion of *duration and its simple modes* begun in Volume iii, Chapter 18. But we can scarcely take too seriously any explanation that *he* would repeat so religiously. And the narrative does not allow us to follow it seriously: his argument terminates only in Toby's complete failure to understand him. Though Walter is 'in one of his best explanatory moods', nothing is explained. He is brought up short in his 'eager pursuit of a metaphysic point into the very regions where clouds and thick darkness would soon have encompassed it about'; Toby associates his brother's words with the military terminology on which he so often relies. The very process of habitual association on which Locke has commented has been set in motion to interrupt the paraphrase of Locke which Walter is producing. Not just bathos, but the matter of philosophical explanation made to frustrate its style. But then the authority of the philosophical text is constantly undermined by being tested against the special propensities of the members of the Shandy household. Locke's analysis of 'the great and principal act of ratiocination in man' is brought forward to explain Toby's strange 'deportment' as he listens to Walter's lecture on 'his systems of noses' (III. xl. 237–8). In fact, it can explain no such thing. Toby's 'fancy' is in excess of any thesis offered by the 'great reasoner'. In a parody of Locke's warnings about the dangers of metaphorical language, Toby is shown transforming Walter's figures of speech according to the dictates of his own obsessions. The customary errors against which Locke so seriously warned intervene to upset the application of his analysis of measurement and judgement. Examples of how parts of Locke's *Essay* are deflated by their introduction into *Tristram Shandy* are many and various, and almost all of them (as above) refer the reader to the explanation of misunderstanding and miscom-

---

[51] See Day, 'Locke May Not Be the Key'.

munication. The *Essay concerning Human Understanding* is used as if it will clarify failed acts of speech or interpretation; in fact, it falters before them.

There is one point at which the rejection of Locke as a proper guide to thought and language is made quite explicit. The 'Author's Preface' which appears half-way through Volume iii of *Tristram Shandy* promises that the book will provide 'all the wit and judgment (be it more or less) which the great author and bestower of them had thought it fit originally to give me' (III. xx. 193): 'wit and judgment in this world never go together; inasmuch as they are two operations differing from each other as wide as east is from west.—So, says *Locke*,—so are farting and hickuping, say I.' Locke had argued that 'judgment', which involved the careful discrimination of ideas, was incompatible with 'wit', which was defined as 'lying most in the assemblage of *Ideas*, and putting those together with quickness and variety, wherein can be found any resemblance or congruity, thereby to make up pleasant Pictures, and agreeable Visions in the Fancy'.[52] 'Wit' should be dissociated from 'judgment' because the former involved 'Metaphor and Allusion' which might provide 'entertainment and pleasantry' but which were not 'conformable' to the 'Rules of Truth, and good Reason'.[53] Locke characterized 'Figurative Speech' as 'an Abuse of Language',[54] a succumbing to opportunistic association which could only corrupt proper communication. In order to assert that 'wit and judgment' are 'indubitably both made and fitted to go together', *Tristram Shandy* contradicts Locke in the manner of its explanation, reflecting at inordinate length on an improbable analogy between these faculties and the 'curious' but symmetrical 'ornaments' on the back of the chair 'I am this moment sitting upon' (III. xx. 200–1). As it pursues the metaphor over several paragraphs, the text does not just contradict Locke, it also refuses to obey the Lockian stipulations for a reasonable discourse. This over-insistent pursuit, like most of the text's engagements with Locke, directs us to an anxiety which runs through Book III of the *Essay concerning Human Understanding*. Whimsically applied metaphor is one example of the unreasonable or eccentric association of ideas against which Locke wished to guard. For him, words should be tethered to the

---

[52] Locke, *Essay*, II. xi. 156.   [53] Ibid. 156–7.   [54] Ibid. III. x. 508.

privately conceived ideas that they were to recreate in the mind of another:

> To make Words serviceable to the end of Communication, it is necessary . . . that they excite, in the Hearer, exactly the same *Idea*, they stand for in the Mind of the Speaker. Without this, Men fill one another's Heads with noise and sounds; but convey not thereby their Thoughts, and lay not before one another their *Ideas*, which is the end of Discourse and Language.[55]

Of course, inappropriate ideas are always being excited in each other's minds by the inhabitants of Shandy Hall. But this is demonstrated not to confirm but to relieve Locke's worries about the inconsistencies of words. Sterne's characters can rely on bonds of unspeakable sympathy; the reader of *Tristram Shandy* can rely on the ability of the narrative to reveal the pressures of fixation and the paths of misunderstanding which are special to the enclosed world of 'Shandyism'.

Walter, Toby, and Trim are not inhabiting some Lockian nightmare of unmeaning 'noise and sounds'. In their odd, but intelligibly consistent, customs of conversation they point up the incapacities of Locke's theory of language. A contemporary philosopher puts the obvious objection to Locke like this:

> Since thoughts cannot be formulated whether inwardly or outwardly unless there are ways of formulating them, that is, unless a language is already presupposed, it follows that Locke's epistemological units must already be functioning as crypto-linguistic units before he comes formally to consider language at all. His official account of language is thus in a way redundant.[56]

Sterne's characters are indeed incapable of thoughts which are not fixed to particular, if strange, vocabularies. They are attached to the world by the metaphors and allusions on which they rely, and which protect them against death, discord, and disaster. They are not mad, first because they are attached to each other by sympathy, and second because they are innocents whose limited ways with words are displayed to a reader who has to be sophisticated to comprehend their transparent instincts.

The reader is constituted as knowledgeable not by any deep familiarity with learned texts, but simply by complicity with the

---

[55] Locke, *Essay*, III. ix. 478.
[56] R.F. Holland, 'Epistemology and Education', in *Against Empiricism: On Education, Epistemology and Value* (Oxford, 1980), 15.

narrative's confidences—by the sociality of the novel. One of the effects, in fact, of the rhetoric of the narrative is to subvert pretensions to the knowledge that is erudition:

> You see as plain as can be, that I write as a man of erudition;—that even my similes, my allusions, my illustrations, my metaphors, are erudite,—and that I must sustain my character properly, and contrast it properly too,—else what would become of me? Why, Sir, I should be undone;—at this very moment that I am going here to fill up one place against a critick,—I should have made an opening for a couple. (*Tristram Shandy*, II. ii. 85)

The irony is signalled by having this addressed to 'Sir Critick', for the understanding reader is anybody but one of the pedants whom the text treats with mock deference: 'Gentlemen, I kiss your hands' (p. 84). It is the 'Critick' who is invited to consider the relevance of Locke's *Essay*, and given enough to compose a pretence of erudition: 'It is a history-book, Sir, (which may possibly recommend it to the world) of what passes in a man's own mind; and if you will say so much of the book, and no more, believe me, you will cut no contemptible figure in a metaphysic circle.' It is the 'Gentle critick' who is told of Locke in order to be shown what 'the confusion in my uncle *Toby*'s discourse . . . did *not* arise from' (p. 86):

> THERE is nothing so foolish, when you are at the expence of making an entertainment of this kind, as to order things so badly, as to let your criticks and gentry of refined taste run it down: Nor is there any thing so likely to make them do it, as that of leaving them out of the party, or, what is full as offensive, of bestowing your attention upon the rest of your guests in so particular a way, as if there was no such thing as a critick (by occupation) at table. (p. 84)

The 'critick' is the representative of pedantic (and probably scanty) learning, and the moralizer on narrative impropriety; in later volumes 'he' is also to be quite specifically the hostile reviewer or lampooner of *Tristram Shandy*. The knowledgeable reader has to be somebody else.

Locke put into the hands of the 'critick' is never going to reveal much. But then it takes the critick to believe that Locke could be a sufficient guide. The reader who is not the critick will trust more to Tristram's ability to demonstrate the commitment to saving metaphors which qualifies the inhabitants of Shandy Hall as innocents. This narrator tells us of a world in which confusion reigns but is also contained. Locke's scheme is implied when we are told of Uncle Toby's problem—"Twas not by ideas,—by heaven! his life was put in jeopardy by words' (II. ii. 87)—but the hyperbole of this signals the reader's innoculation against the same confusions. The cadence of mock-concern defuses Lockian regrets because it is a reminder of the distance between Toby's simple, ingenuous 'perplexities' and the knowing confidences and nudges which pass from narrator to reader. It is this distance which allows another rebuff to Locke, the production of feeling, sentiment, that which can hardly be spoken, as a criterion of unanimity. For it is unworldliness, artlessness, that gives rise to overflowing sentiments, eloquent gestures, fraternal sympathy. Walter scorns Toby's hobby-horse, his innocent obsession, only to succumb to fellow feeling:

[Uncle Toby] look'd up into my father's face, with a countenance spread over with so much good nature;—so placid;—so fraternal;—so in-expressibly tender towards him;—it penetrated my father to his heart: He rose up hastily from his chair, and seizing hold of both my uncle *Toby's* hands as he spoke:—brother *Toby*, said he,—I beg thy pardon;—forgive, I pray thee, this rash humour which my mother gave me. (II. xii. 115)

Walter's association of his 'rash humour' with his mother is not arbitrary: fellow-feeling is largely a male prerogative in this novel. *Tristram Shandy* is punctuated by these rushes of sentiment, restoring a harmony which words have supposedly unsettled; the harmony is of a rather special kind—men neutered, segregated from women, the door closed behind them.

They depend on words, of course, but also on the meaningful look or the eloquent tear: the currency of sentimentalism. It is when they are silent that they best communicate. Trim, in his attempt to read out a sermon, is drawn into the story of his brother's fate at the hands of the Inquisition: '—The tears trickled down *Trim's* cheeks faster than he could well wipe them away.—A dead silence in the room ensued for some minutes.—Certain proof of pity!' (II. xvii. 125). Stricken by the disaster of the crushing of his son's nose, which is also an irony at the expense of his 'philosophy' of noses, Walter eventually looks up from the bed where he has lain 'as if the hand of death had pushed him down', to see the silent Toby: 'My father, in turning his eyes, was struck with such a gleam of sun-shine in his face, as melted down the sullenness of his grief in a moment' (IV. ii. 274). Toby's vocabulary may be restricted, but he does not have to rely on words:

There was a frankness in my uncle *Toby*,—not the *effect* of familiarity,—but the *cause* of it,—which let you at once into his soul, and
shewed you the goodness of his nature; to this, there was something in his
looks, and voice, and manner, superadded, which eternally beckoned to the
unfortunate to come and take shelter under him. (VI. x. 426)

The very impediments to speech, Toby's lack of talents 'that way',
allow, so the story goes, for a more fundamental communication.
And that communication is ever-visible: 'My uncle *Toby* stole his
hand unperceived behind his chair, to give my fathers a squeeze' (VII.
xxxiii. 586). The benevolent gaze, the clasping hand, the moistening
eye: these are not just ready defences when words fail; they are more
poignant communications than words can possibly manage.

But then there is an irony in this, which can be stated with
reference to Yorick's characterization, in *A Sentimental Journey*, of
a communication deeper than can be accomplished by speech:

There are certain combined looks of simple subtlety—where whim, and
sense, and seriousness, and nonsense, are so blended, that all the language
of Babel set loose together could not express them—they are communicated and caught so instantaneously, that you can scarce say which party
is the infecter. I leave it to your men of words to swell pages about it.
(p. 168)

The rhetorical suggestion is that the signifier (the look, the gesture)
can exist in all innocence, detached, for a special moment, from the
words which hamper expression. An irony of *Tristram Shandy* is
that Tristram is one of these 'men of words' (though the words are
often jolted from other contexts, other commentators). Much in
Tristram Shandy, like the uncomprehending gesture which Toby
offers Mrs Wadman when she asks about the location of his wound,
'requires a second translation', showing 'what little knowledge is got
by mere words—we must go up to the first springs' (IX. xx. 624).
Sterne's narrator provides translations, decoding obsessions and
gestures. His narrative, his garrulous commentary, lets the reader
into the secret of expressions which defy words, and can do so
because these expressions are the prerogative of those who are
(admirably and ludicrously) innocent. The text eludes questions
about whether its sentimentalism is 'sincere' or not by exploiting
(and not, like Richardson, agonizing over) the distance between the
reader it presumes and the paragons of feeling it describes. This
means that Sterne has shrugged off the usual duty of sentimentalism:

the teaching of virtue. 'Nasty trifling', F.R. Leavis called it;[57] given his belief in the moral duties of literature, the description is not so far from the mark.

Those who feel most strongly, and weep most readily, are Toby and Trim: 'The heart, both of the master and the man, were alike subject to sudden overflowings' (VIII xix. 568). Such overflowings mean that the 'story of the king of Bohemia', which they interrupt, gives way unfinished to the account of Trim's war wound, but, as they disrupt the anecdote, they seal the consanguinity of reciprocal 'feeling'. More than a preoccupation with the stories of regiments and sieges, 'the master and the man' have in common the willingness to shed a sentimental tear. The thought that they might provide for 'poor *Le Fever*'s son' finds in them the same unrestrained instinct: 'A tear of joy of the first water sparkled in my uncle *Toby*'s eye,—and another, the fellow to it, in the corporal's' (VI. v. 415). This sets up the story of Le Fever, Sterne's celebrated 'beauty', which illuminates the shared feeling of Toby and Trim:

> I never in the longest march, said the corporal, had so great a mind to my dinner, as I had to cry with him for company:—What could be the matter with me, an please your honour? Nothing in the world, Trim, said my uncle *Toby*, blowing his nose,—but that thou art a good natured fellow. (VI. vii. 420)

There is something staged about this, but then Sterne was happy to take credit for a description of artlessness which testified to his artful abilities. He wrote, early in 1762, to a 'Lady D—':

> 'Le Fever's story has beguiled your ladyship of your tears', and the thought of the accusing spirit flying up heaven's chancery with the oath, you are kind enough to say is sublime—my friend, Mr Garrick, thinks so too, and I am most vain of his approbation—your ladyship's opinion adds not a little to my vanity.[58]

The ascription of meaning to innocent experiences of feeling is a matter for the sophisticated, not the ingenuous, novelist.

Complimented warmly by Toby in the midst of his story of his brother Tom, Trim's speech falters:

> The Corporal blush'd down to his fingers ends—a tear of sentimental bashfulness—another of gratitude to my uncle *Toby*—and a tear of sorrow

---

[57] F.R. Leavis, *The Great Tradition* (1948; rpt. Harmondsworth, 1977), 10.
[58] *Letters*, 150.

for his brother's misfortunes, started into his eye and ran sweetly down his cheek together; my uncle *Toby*'s kindled as one lamp does at another; and taking hold of the breast of *Trim*'s coat (which had been that of *Le Fevre*'s) as if to ease his lame leg, but in reality to gratify a finer feeling—he stood silent for a minute and a half. (IX. v. 605)

The narrative here ascribes impossibly precise significance to each tear, making what is not spoken attain an articulacy beyond Trim's powers of speech. It makes it plain that it is telling us what Trim could not tell us himself. But this excess of interpretation can hardly be taken as a satire upon sentimentalism. Trim's tears accompany the story of his brother's imprisonment by the Inquisition, a story that he has been struggling to tell throughout the novel, and that has been reliably reducing him to tears each time. On the first occasion, much to the chagrin of Dr Slop, it prepares Trim's audience for his oration of a sermon which attacks the '*Romish* church', and which is punctuated by Trim's expressions of anguish at his brother's fate: 'My father's and my uncle *Toby*'s hearts yearn'd with sympathy for the poor fellow's distress, —even *Slop* himself acknowledged pity for him' (II. xvii. 138). Biography tells us not only that the anti-Catholic implications of Trim's emotional reading are at one with Sterne's own politics, but also that the sermon which triggers Trim's tearful story of his brother was one which Sterne himself delivered to a large congregation in York Minster.[59] The story of Trim's brother, and the servant's tears, are allowed to make more affecting one of Sterne's own sermons: 'I should have read it ten times better, Sir, answered *Trim*, but that my heart was so full.—That was the very reason, *Trim*, replied my father, which has made thee read the sermon as well as thou hast done' (II. xvii. 140–1). As one critic puts it, 'Trim does not get anything out of the text that was not put there by Sterne. His sentimental reaction emphasizes the sentimental aspect of what he reads.'[60]

To read is not necessarily to cry with Trim. The ability to weep that he demonstrates is praised by Toby—'Tears are no proof of cowardice, *Trim*.—I drop them oft-times myself, cried my uncle *Toby*' (IV. iv. 275)—but the readiness proceeds from an innocence

---

[59] See Cross, *The Life and Times of Laurence Sterne*, 87, and *Florida Edition*, ii. 946: 'all the materials for Trim's passionate response to the torments of the Inquisition are in the original version'.

[60] M. Loveridge, *Laurence Sterne and the Argument About Design* (London, 1982), 162.

which the text exploits rather than shares. The delivery of the sermon, republished in *The Sermons of Mr Yorick* of 1766, is a nice illustration. Trim is permitted reactions sparked by Sterne's serious, didactic composition, but reactions which could never have been part of the original delivery of that sermon. This does not mean that either Trim's reading or the content of the sermon is degraded; Trim's is a proper response, but an untutored one. Significantly, *The Monthly Review* praised the strategy whereby the sermon and the response were incorporated into *Tristram Shandy*: 'The address with which he has introduced an excellent moral sermon, into a work of this nature (by which expedient, it will probably be read by many who would peruse a sermon in no other form) is masterly.'[61] It is of Sterne's design that Trim and Toby should be foolish and yet capable of sentimental articulacy. Certainly, eighteenth-century readers found it easy enough to admire them—not as models of attainable virtue, but as examples of how an elegant text could reach to the heart of simple and unpolished feeling.

Sterne is cannier than any other sentimentalist about acknowledging the gap between the artlessness of his protaganists and the sophistication that he presumes in his reader. He looks to gesture as an instinctually communicative act, but he surrounds it with allusions to theories of gestural representation. In *Tristram Shandy*, the body's eloquence, in which the novel of sentiment always puts its trust, comes wrapped in references to other writings on painting, oratory, or drama. Some of these secondary discourses come in for satire—in particular the criticism that would reduce communication to a grammatical system. So one of the roles played by the 'Excellent critic' sardonically invoked throughout the novel is that of the obtusely attentive analyst who is insensitive to eloquence. Flattering his sponsor and newly acquired friend into the bargain, Sterne gives the reader this version of a criticism incapable of the act of interpretation:

—And how did *Garrick* speak the soliloquy last night?—Oh, against all rule, my Lord,—most ungrammatically! betwixt the substantive and the adjective, which should agree together in *number, case* and *gender*, he made a breach thus,—stopping, as if the point wanted settling;—and betwixt the nominative case, which your lordship knows should govern the verb, he suspended his voice in the epilogue a dozen times, three seconds and three fifths by a stop-watch, my Lord, each time. —Admirable grammarian! —But in suspending his voice—was the sense suspended likewise? Did no expression of attitude or countenance fill up the chasm?—Was the eye silent? Did you narrowly look?—I look'd only at the stop-watch, my Lord. —Excellent observer! (*Tristram Shandy*, III. xii. 180).

Sterne credited Garrick with 'some magick, irresisted power' released 'feelingly' on stage with the vibrations of 'every Fibre about your heart';[62] he is the standard for the gesture which touches 'the nerves',[63] the meaning that the critic cannot perceive.

He is also, however, the standard for the elusiveness of gesture. When Walter Shandy strikes an explanatory posture for the benefit of Toby, the first reference is to painting: 'My father instantly exchanged the attitude he was in, for that in which *Socrates* is so finely painted by *Raffael* in his school of *Athens*; which your connoisseurship knows is so exquisitely imagined, that even the particular manner of the reasoning of *Socrates* is expressed by it' (IV. vii. 278). The excessively grand comparison (Walter Shandy is, after all, reflecting on the importance of noses) leads to an invocation which is not just flattery: '—O *Garrick*! what a rich scene of this would thy exquisite powers make!' The novel can make a 'rich scene' only by bathetic analogy. '*Nature* . . . by an instantaneous impulse, in all *provoking cases*, determines us to a sally of this or that member—or else she thrusts us into this or that place, or posture of body, we know not why' (IV. xvii. 293): the 'impulse' which possesses Walter is given as allusive parody—a moment at which the text undermines the ideal of that meaning which is immediate, artless, from the body. As if as a reminder that the clarity of gesture which Sterne's characters occasionally discover is as·improbable and inimitable as the obsessions which regulate their speech, it is entangled with the methods and examples that others have used to describe expressiveness. *Tristram Shandy* is thick with reflections on the means by which wordless expression has been mediated, theorized, and put into words upon words.

The comparison between Walter's posture and that of Socrates in Raphael's painting is addressed to 'your connoisseurship', and it is the 'connoisseur', '*befetish'd* with the bobs and trinkets of criticism', who is imagined applying his 'rules and compasses' to Garrick's

---

[62] Letter to David Garrick, 1765: *Letters*, 236.
[63] See letter to David Garrick, Mar. 1762: *Letters*, 157.

soliloquy. The reader is presumed to know better than this pedant, blinded by a language of rules and precedents. Yet Sterne needs his own precedents: his attack on the 'Admirable connoisseur', practitioner of 'the cant of criticism' (III. xii. 182), is lifted from Joshua Reynolds's essay in *The Idler* of September 1759.[64] Both Reynolds and Hogarth, the other contemporary painter whose writings Sterne cites, use the 'connoisseur' as the model of a debased critic, their reliance upon the 'remembrance of a few names of painters, with their general characters' denying them 'any pleasure from the polite arts'.[65] Sterne is not expelling theories of visual representation from his text; he is using one theory to satirize others.

What Sterne exploits is a tactic common to the writings of both Reynolds and Hogarth. Reynolds lambasts the 'cant of criticism' and the slavish addiction of the 'connoisseur' to the norms which criticism has dictated, but his contempt is not for rules and precedents as such. In his artistic practice, as well as in his later *Discourses*, he dedicated himself to the justification and revivifying of classical models. Hogarth, although commonly supposed to have been Reynolds's theoretical antagonist (the passage from the *Idler* which Sterne lifts contains a veiled attack on Hogarth's *Analysis of Beauty*),[66] shares the habit of constituting a viewer unburdened by precepts as the best kind of reader of his theory. In *The Analysis of Beauty* of 1753, to which Sterne explicitly refers in *Tristram Shandy*, Hogarth declares that 'those, who have no bias of any kind, either from their own practice, or the lessons of others, are fittest to examine into the truth of the principles laid down in the following pages'.[67] His purpose is to 'teach us to *see with our own eyes*',[68] though it takes his expertise to achieve it—only one endowed with 'a practical knowledge of the whole art of painting' is fitted to pursue an enquiry into the 'grace and beauty' of pictorial representation.[69] The aspiration of sophisticated, opinionated theory and practice is to teach a supposedly unbiased vision, and theory becomes necessary to debunk what is falsely theoretical. It is a useful ideal for Sterne, for he is trying to create his own unbiased reader, assured of

---

[64] See Sir Joshua Reynolds, *The Idler*, No. 76 (29 Sep. 1759), in *The Yale Edition of the Works of Samuel Johnson*, vol. ii (New Haven, Conn., 1963), 236-7.

[65] Ibid. 236.

[66] See W.V. Holtz, *Image and Immortality: A Study of Tristram Shandy* (Providence, RI, 1970), 30-3.

[67] William Hogarth, *The Analysis of Beauty* (1753; rpt. Menston, Yorkshire, 1971), 6.

being judicious by not being the 'connoisseur'. Falsely learned criticism is always going to be the guarantee of the novel's 'sociality' with a desirably unprejudiced reader.

This does not mean that the references to Reynolds or Hogarth are given as unironical guidance. William Holtz has argued that Sterne refers to Hogarth's analysis in a spirit of 'genial criticism'—though 'genial' is what it has to be, as Sterne still persuaded Hogarth to provide two illustrations for his novel.[70] Holtz identifies, rightly, the inappropriateness of applying Hogarth's theory of pictorial composition to the postures of the likes of Trim, the point of which is their spontaneity; he detects 'Sterne's suspicion of Hogarth's theories', and of their pretensions 'to reduce nature to rules'.[71] It is true, as another critic has put it, that 'Sterne's main concern is not to create a visual effect but to play with a fashionable jargon',[72] but this is not simply to satirize that 'jargon'. *Tristram Shandy* cannot mimic the innocent spontaneity of its characters. Their gestures are swaddled in allusion and analogy because they are not immediately available; the devices which concentrate our minds on the dispositions of their bodies remind us that these come mediated by expertise which the inhabitants of Shandy Hall can never possess. The expertise may be questionable, but the innocence which allows the body to speak is unattainable. Thus it is that Sterne uses Hogarth unlike any of his contemporaries. Hogarth is referred to in the novels of Fielding and Smollett, but it is his art and not his theory that is used. In *Tom Jones*, for example, Fielding writes of Miss Bridget:

The Lady, no more than her Lover, was remarkable for Beauty. I would attempt to draw her Picture; but that is done already by a more able Master, Mr *Hogarth* himself, to whom she sat many Years ago, and hath been lately exhibited by that Gentleman in his Print of a Winters Morning, of which she was no improper Emblem.'[73]

In contrast, Sterne cites Hogarth the theoretician: not the pictorial equivalent to a verbal description, but the discourse which distances and abstracts the visual even as it attempts to define it.

---

[68] Ibid. 2.

[69] Ibid., p. iv.

[70] Holtz, *Image and Immortality*, 27.

[71] Ibid. 35.

[72] R. F. Brissenden, 'Sterne and Painting', in John Butt (ed.), *Of Books and Humankind* (London, 1964), 94.

In the *Analysis*, Hogarth's expertise is devoted to the representation of what is natural—an ideal for pictorial art, but an impossible one: 'Who but a bigot, even to the antiques, will say that he has not seen faces and necks, hands and arms in living women, that even the Grecian Venus doth but coarsely imitate?'[74] The artist is to strive, never with complete success, to reproduce naturally eloquent forms, an example of which is, significantly, taken to be the woman's body. When Sterne's search for natural gesture is pursued into his *Sentimental Journey*, that 'quiet journey of the heart in pursuit of NATURE' (p. 219), 'NATURE' is found in the untutored serving-women. The discovery produces an odd drama of erotic encounter, and I will return to this. It also extends *Tristram Shandy*'s provision of gestural expression as the prerogative of those who know no better: in *A Sentimental Journey*, the 'children' of 'Labour' (p. 268); in *Tristram Shandy*, the ingenuously speech-befuddled members of the Shandy household. If Sterne exploits Hogarth's *Analysis* wryly, it is because he shares Hogarth's perception of natural eloquence as that appreciated by those (not connoisseurs, but unbiased viewers) who know too much to be able simply to reproduce it. Spontaneity has to be constructed; the body's unlaboured attitudes take much labour to describe.

Tristram Shandy is not a text to aspire to pictorial immediacy. Everywhere it parodies the conventions of what B. Rogerson has called 'the pathetic style', 'an elaborate theory of the representation of the passions by their outward visible or audible signs'.[75] We can be sure that any such theory is at least questionable because it is the recourse of Tristram's father when he comes to reflect, with the usual displays of obscure and inappropriate learning, on the nature of the proper tutor for Tristram. In selecting the best candidate, he tells Toby and Yorick, he will look for 'a certain mien and motion of the body and all its parts, both in acting and speaking, which argues a man *well within*' (VI. v. 414). 'There are a thousand unnoticed openings, continued my father, which let a penetrating eye at once into a man's soul; and I maintain it, added he, that a man of sense does not let lay down his hat in coming into a room,—or take it up in going out of it, but something escapes, which discovers him.' He

[74] Hogarth, *Analysis of Beauty*, 66.
[75] B. Rogerson, 'The Art of Painting the Passions', *Journal of the History of Ideas*, 14 (1953), 70.

goes on to list all the bodily movements and facial expressions that he will not accept in the governor of his son, and Toby's response is for once appropriate: 'Now this is all nonsense again, quoth my uncle *Toby* to himself' (p. 415). Walter takes his specifications to an eccentric extreme, but he pursues a tendency which the text has already parodied when it has pretended to an impossible precision. '[Sterne's] technique verges on parody by virtue of its extreme movement towards the pictorial ideal. Detail is piled upon detail as Tristram makes discrimination after subtle discrimination, and the whole approaches unintelligibility.'[76]

The best-known example of what Holtz calls 'mock pictorial' delineation is the description of the attitude that Trim adopts to read Yorick's sermon[77]—what Brissenden refers to as 'the excessively detailed account' of his 'oratorical stance'.[78] As is the way of this text, the description is not just given, it is addressed to those too ignorant or pedantic to expect any irony:

He stood before them with his body swayed, and bent forwards just so far, as to make an angle of 85 degrees and a half upon the plain of the horizon;—which sound orators, to whom I address this, know very well, to be the true persuasive angle of incidence;—in any other angle you may talk and preach;—'tis certain,—and it is done every day;—but with what effect,—I leave the world to judge! (II. xvii. 122)

The text purports to explain 'The necessity of this precise angle of 85 degrees and a half to a mathematical exactness', though it cannot explain how Trim could have enacted eloquence so perfectly: 'so swayed his body, so contrasted his limbs, and with such an oratorical sweep throughout the whole figure,—a statuary might have modelled from it' (p. 123). The scene of Trim's oration was one of those illustrated by Hogarth, who could not have felt that the fact of Trim's adventitiously falling into an attitude 'within the limits of the line of beauty' (a phrase taken from his *Analysis*) was too mocking of his theory. After all, the passage makes its jokes out of a gap between the natural and the pictorial that Hogarth acknowledges. The description is a parody of pictorial precision, but this is parody to which Sterne is committed. If there is no original moment of unmediated demonstration—of gesture exactly transcribed—then parody is what is left.

[76] Holtz, *Image and Immortality*, 59.   [77] Ibid. 20.
[78] Brissenden, 'Sterne and Painting', 100.

Tristram Shandy makes an offer that only the self-regarding 'sound orator' or the bungling 'connoisseur' would be foolish enough to accept. It offers to freeze and make formulaic the gesture that it tells us is spontaneously eloquent. The irony of this offer is not usually to be discovered in novels of sentiment, which in even their less imitative versions precisely seek to make gesture repeatable and dependable—to make formulaic a symptom which can be recognized and translated. Even in the most whimsical liberties that it takes, Sterne's novel cannot pretend quite to capture the significance of what is without words. The drawing of Trim's 'flourish with his stick' (IX. iv. 604) is a moment of textual extravagance which seems appropriately to reflect the expansiveness of the gesture, but it is also an uncontrived, impromptu, simply momentary movement stopped and made reproducible. It looks like a sign of the inadequacy of words, but words (the concentrated premonitions of Toby and Trim about the effects of marriage) surround it and give it its meaning—'A thousand of my father's most subtle syllogisms could not have said more for celibacy'. We can refer to Hogarth again for an idea of how lines like the one Trim is supposed to create can be eloquent: 'having formed the idea of all movements being as lines, it will not be difficult to conceive, that grace in action depends upon the same principles as have been shewn to produce it in forms'.[79] Here he makes action and representation one, but Trim's flourish can be taken to show the impossibility of this conflation. It is not made according to 'principles'. The pictograph is Sterne's flourish, but it is a sign that gesture is unreachable and inimitable.

Sterne might derive humour from the non-fulfilment of a promise of meaning immediately available in a gesture, but this is fatalism rather than a destruction of the ideal of the sentiment which the body might speak. Where the failed attempt to make meaning visible is knowingly ludicrous, it also strives for poignancy. Again we have the running paradox: the bearers of feeling—Trim, Toby, Walter, even Yorick—are imagined as at once absurd and admirable. Take another example of 'the corporal's eloquence'. Upon the news of the death of Bobby, Tristram's permanently invisible brother, we are given the response of the servants—the tableau in the kitchen which echoes that in the parlour. At its centre is Trim, and his speech and

---

[79] Hogarth, *Analysis of Beauty*, 140.

gestures. Trim enacts the terrible truism of mortality by dropping his hat to the ground: ''Twas infinitely striking!' (V. vii. 361). His fellow servants burst into tears. We may suspect that those who weep are more ingenuous than we can be, but also that eighteenth-century readers willing to cherish the tale of Le Fever would not have found the tableau ridiculous. Indeed, the passage in which it is described was given in Enfield's *The Speaker* as another of those elegant (because sentimental) extracts that he took from Sterne.[80] What Enfield did not cite was what follows—the narrator's explanation of the impact of the 'eloquence' he has described. This explanation is in the habitual style of mock elucidation which is applied to pictorial detail elsewhere in the novel, and as such deflates the pathos of the scene. But it also implies its own inability to catch the gesture that signifies common mortality, and thus, in the very midst of comic deflation, discovers another kind of poignancy. Trim is supposed to be eloquent about loss, and the narrative has lost even the impression of that eloquence.

To be clear, here is the beginning of that reflection on the manner and effects of Trim's oratory:

Now as I perceive plainly, that the preservation of our constitution in church and state,—and possibly the preservation of the whole world—or what is the same thing, the distribution and balance of its property and power, may in time to come depend greatly upon the right understanding of this stroke of the corporal's eloquence—I do demand your attention,—your worships and reverences, for any ten pages together, take them where you will in any other part of the work, shall sleep for it at your ease. (V. vii. 361)

The hyperbole of this, and the mock solemnity of its address to 'your worships and reverences', encourage the discovery of bathos in the scene: Trim, 'falling instantly into the same attitude in which he read the sermon', is perhaps acting out a part which his fellow servants cannot see through. The discovery seems complete if we recognize that the exaggerated claims of this explanation echo those made by the fashionable lecturer on oratory Thomas Sheridan, whose theoretical writings were designed to puff his own lectures, and to assert that 'oratory' and 'elocution' were vital 'to the support of our constitution, both in church, and state'.[81] The text admits that there

80 Enfield, *The Speaker*, 243–4.

81 I owe this gloss entirely to the *Florida Edition*, iii. 355–6, which cites this phrase from Sheridan's *Course of Lectures on Elocution* and a similarly parallel passage from his *Discourse . . . Introductory to His Course of Lectures on Elocution*, and which

is 'nothing' in Trim's words: ' "Are we not here now, —and gone in a moment?"—There was nothing in the sentence—'twas one of your self-evident truths we have the advantage of hearing every day; and if *Trim* had not trusted more to his hat than his head—he had made nothing at all of it' (V. vii. 362) But if there is something that makes the sentence mean more than its words, the achievement of that meaning (to which the text sardonically directs the attention of 'Ye who govern this mighty world and its mighty concerns with the *engines* of eloquence') is still elusive. The narrative keeps repeating Trim's sentence, exhausting it in the apparent search for significance.

—'Are we not here now'—continued the corporal, 'and are we not'—(dropping his hat plum upon the ground—and pausing, before he pronounced the word)—'gone! in a moment?' The descent of the hat was as if a heavy lump of clay had been kneaded into the crown of it.—Nothing could have expressed the sentiment of mortality, of which it was the type and forerunner, like it,—his hand seemed to vanish from under it,—it fell dead,—the corporal's eye fix'd upon it, as upon a corps,—and *Susannah* burst into a flood of tears? (V. vii. 362)

The gesture is supposed to be sufficiently articulate, yet, in the narrative's usual mode of descriptive detail excessively or obstructively provided, it is characterized by *not* being one of a sequence of unimaginable alternatives ('had he dropped it like a goose—like a puppy—like an ass'). Its 'effect upon the heart' could be laughable; perhaps Trim's fellow servants are too easily coerced—'driven, like turkeys to market'. But it is rather the tyranny of explanation that is mocked, while, in the process, the ideal of expressing 'the sentiment of mortality'—that fact to which Trim at least has some response—slips away.

With all its layers of rhetoric—of pretended deference or implied confidentiality—*Tristram Shandy* can invite 'close reading'; it also, famously, parodies the complacent pedantry of commentators and critics. Even as the narrative lingers on the fall of Trim's hat, perhaps I have lingered on it too long. The ironies of the episode are, though, a guide to the ways in which the 'sociality' of this novel is used, and to the distinctiveness of Sterne's version of sentiment escaping words. In the introduction to his edition of the *Sentimental Journey*, Gardner Stout writes of *Tristram Shandy* that 'Walter, Toby, and

suggests that 'Sterne's readers may well have found the present passage an obvious allusion to Sheridan'.

the reader speak languages which are largely foreign to one another, but they do succeed in communicating their sensations out of their own spheres, largely through the mysterious operation of intuition and sympathy, aided by look and gesture.'[82] The 'operation of intuition and sympathy' is indeed a narrative necessity, but *Tristram Shandy* has to take on the cadences of parody (over-explanation, redundant analysis) to provide what is not spoken. Sentimental writing of the period typically employs a repertoire of signs: tears, sighs, blushes, the clasping of hands, the benevolent gaze. With the dropping of Trim's hat, or the waving of his stick, *Tristram Shandy* goes beyond the conventional deployment of gestures. The novel has accepted that the processes by which the characters can be thought to communicate with each other, and those by which the text communicates with its reader, must be incommensurable.

Tristram Shandy has other ways of distancing its reader from the displays of feeling that it presents. Like every novel of sentiment, it creates a special domain in which 'intuition and sympathy' can operate. It is conventional in the literature of the period for those possessed of sensibility to seek (usually rural) retreats, havens in which they can try to live on vegetables and sentiment. *Tristram Shandy* also idealizes a space in which sympathy can work, though it takes the idealization to the verge of absurdity. The bowling-green where Toby and Trim obsessively act out their war games is emblematic of the space that Sterne has created for his 'whimsical theatre': conflict innocently parodied and domesticated behind the yew-hedge. This conflict made harmless is surprisingly, fruitfully metaphorical. The language of the bloodless enactment of the War of the Spanish Succession becomes also the language of the courtship of Toby and the Widow Wadman, with her dangerous eye 'exactly like a cannon' (VIII. xxv. 577). Her 'attack' upon uncle Toby, like his upon the model of Dendermond, is a parody of ruses and battles which take place elsewhere—for Toby's wound and his innocence exclude even desire. In Toby's domain, innocence is the rule. He is safe from 'the world': 'The world is ashamed of being virtuous—My uncle *Toby* knew little of the world' (VIII. xxvii. 580). Even obsession and misunderstanding safeguard him and his fellows: what struggles can there be if each is content riding a different hobby-horse? Shandy Hall is where battles are always being parodied. Thus the

---

[82] *A Sentimental Journey through France and Italy by Mr Yorick*, ed. G. Stout (Los Angeles, 1967), Introduction, 35. See also Holtz, *Image and Immortality*, 72–80.

importance of symbolic male impotence ('nothing was well hung in our family'). A major conflict in the novels of Richardson, Mackenzie, and the rest is between the representatives of feeling and of desire. The formula is repeated in many of Sterne's letters, like that written to William Stanhope in September 1767: 'praised be God for my sensibility! Though it has often made me wretched, yet I would not exchange it for all the pleasures the grossest sensualist ever felt.'[83] What *Tristram Shandy* does is to exclude sensuality, and to emphasize the innocence, and so the inimitability, of those who can feel.

'The world' is that of which Toby knows little; it is also that to which Sterne's novel rhetorically abandons itself. When, in Chapter xx of the third volume of *Tristram Shandy*, we are belatedly provided with its 'preface', it commences thus: 'No, I'll not say a word about it, —here it is;—in publishing it, —I have appealed to the world, —and to the world I leave it;—it must speak for itself' (III. xx. 192). We know from biography, and many of Sterne's eighteenth-century readers would have known from reputation, that if 'the world' be the realm of fashion, prejudice, and prestige, the act of abandonment was neither ingenuous nor fatalistic. Even by the third volume (which meant the second instalment), the book had become a fashionable object. It was part of 'the world'. But 'the world' is a convenient fiction: it is everybody except the particular reader; it is critics and connoisseurs. Toby does not have to enter 'the world', and, by another act of exclusion, neither does the sympathetic reader. To read properly, cleverly (it is implied) is not to be one of those obtuse judges that the text invokes:

As for great wigs, upon which I may be thought to have spoken my mind too freely,—I beg leave to qualify whatever has been unguardedly said to their dispraise or prejudice, by one general declaration—That I have no abhorrence whatever, nor do I detest and abjure either great wigs or long beards . . . peace be with them . . . I write not for them. (pp. 202–23)

The absorption of and satire on antagonistic readings of his novel was the means by which Sterne fought a campaign against the critics. It is also a device for the text's coherence; the 'sociality' of reader and text is implied in the address to those for whom the book is *not* written.

The ways in which a reader of *Tristram Shandy* is cajoled,

informed, or flattered need to be considered if Sterne's sentimentalism is to be understood as something more subtle than a
pandering to the requirements of moralistic reviewers. Sterne's
liking for sentimental cameos has too often been seen by literary
critics as a weakening in the face of a vogue, a conventional
insincerity. The suspicion that in *Tristram Shandy* an
eighteenth-century reader might have found performers whom, as
John Traugott says, '*no one* would emulate, *least of all Sterne*' is well
grounded,[84] but then Sterne makes room for a reader who is expected
to be too knowing to suppose that emulation is an option. So it
would be equally misleading to characterize his sentimentalism as
(unfortunately, naïvely) sincere—a puzzle to be solved by the
biographer. We should be sceptical of attempts to discover in his
supposedly 'private' writings the trace of an emotionalism which
would explain the sentimental representations in his novels. Indeed,
his *Letters* and his *Journal to Eliza* are as liable to the accusation of
'insincerity' as either of the novels. Throughout L.P. Curtis's notes
to his edition of Sterne's *Letters* we find charted the borrowings,
repetitions, and opportunistic embellishments whereby Sterne
trades on his literary notoriety or adopts his declarations to one
female admirer to suit another. In the *Journal* the separation of
private feeling from deftly manipulated literary formula is, as Ian
Jack suggests, scarcely possible.[85] In the *Journal*, Sterne observes
that since Eliza's departure his only pleasure has been in 'writing':
'The Observation will draw a Sigh, Eliza, from thy feeling
heart—and yet, so thy heart would wish to have it—'tis fit in truth
We suffer equally'.[86] The production of all this 'emotion'—whether
sincere or not, whether for public or private consumption—depends
on the same conventional ideals as are exploited in his fiction: the
community of sentiments, the integrity of the 'feeling heart', the
sensibility whose privilege is both pleasure and pain. It all has to be a
kind of fiction—a 'pleasure' found best in 'writing', a satisfying
'sympathy' created in the composition of the *Journal* itself. In Eliza's
absence, mere 'conversation', Sterne writes, is insubstantial
compared to the ideal communion enacted in the *Journal*; but then

---

[84] J. Traugott, *Tristram Shandy's World: Sterne's Philosophical Rhetoric*
(Berkeley and Los Angeles, 1954), 75.

[85] Sterne, *A Sentimental Journey through France and Italy By Mr Yorick to which
are added the Journal to Eliza and A Political Romance*, ed. I. Jack (London, 1968),
Introduction.

[86] *Journal*, in the above edition, 145.

the *Journal* is a monologue, and its satisfactions those which Sterne offers to himself. It seems to have been the case that the impossible *Journal* was only abandoned, and then hastily, when the project of the *Sentimental Journey* arose to displace it. It would be appropriate that this supposedly private and infatuated writing be brought to an end not by any identifiable crisis in Sterne's emotional life but by another, and more captivating, kind of writing.

For it is writing, rather than the experience that it purports to record, that is truly 'affecting' for Sterne in his *Journal*:

> I gave a thousand pensive penetrating Looks at the Arm chair thou so often graced on those quiet, sentimental Repasts—and Sighed and laid down my knife and fork, and took out my handkerchiff, clapd it across my face, and wept like a child—I shall read the same affecting Account of many a sad Dinner which Eliza has had no power to taste of.[87]

The question as to whether these tears be 'genuine' does not have an answer. The claim that the *Journal* keeps making is to the integrity not of an experience but of a kind of writing—a style which, in its recourse to sentimental sighs and tears, can transform the banal or the ordinary into the significant. Conveniently, of course, it was a text used by eighteenth-century admirers of Sterne to prove that his fiction must have been well-intentioned—that he was not a purveyor of smut but a man of sensibility. But then Sterne's smartest use of fiction was always in the creation of his reputation, and the *Journal* could hardly be a better-calculated gift to posterity. Such a stylized exercise tells us about a writer whom Sterne fabricated, not about the original emotional condition of the person who wrote *Tristram Shandy*.[88]

The fabrication of a writer is the most complex effect of *Tristram Shandy*. Tristram, the narrator of his 'Life', writes from outside the household whose idiosyncrasies constitute the bulk of the narrative. Sterne has created a translator for us ('we must go up to the first springs'), and a persona who can rehearse the power of a sentimental episode to transport and possess. Via this writer, the effects of feeling are given as already vicariously experienced:

> For my uncle *Toby's* amours running all the way in my head, they had the same effect upon me as if they had been my own—I was in the most perfect

[87] *Journal*, 137.
[88] The *Journal* is treated as emotional revelation by Cross; see, for example, *The Life and Times of Laurence Sterne*, 460.

state of bounty and good will; and felt the kindliest harmony vibrating within me, with every oscillation of the chaise alike; so that whether the roads were rough or smooth, it made no difference; every thing I saw, or had to do with, touch'd upon some secret spring either of sentiment or rapture. (IX. xxiv. 629)

This passage introduces the encounter with 'poor Maria' and 'the full force of an honest heart-ache' (p. 630), one of those 'beauties' so admired by eighteenth-century critics. Sterne did try to provide the blend of 'pathos, refined sentiments, and chaste humour' which, as Gardner Stout writes, readers were coming to require;[89] but each sentimental episode comes via Tristram, a narrator willing, as the description of the 'state of bounty' induced by the story of Toby's 'amours' indicates, to be susceptible when the occasion is right. Feeling has already been mediated; the reader scarcely needs to be transported by empathy when the narrator that Sterne has created is quite capable of experiencing 'vibrations' on the reader's behalf.

Scenes of sentiment received few retorts from Sterne's audience, but the construction of a knowing and complicit reader could still provoke protests. The kind of objections mounted in the *Monthly Review* were to what *Tristram Shandy* compliments itself on as 'that ornamental figure in oratory, which Rhetoricians stile the *Aposiopesis*' (II. vi. 100). The impressive name is given to the device by which the text leaves the reader 'something to imagine'—the authoritative innuendo to which the critics objected. Walter and Toby discuss Mrs Shandy's antipathy to Dr Slop, the male midwife who comes on Walter's recommendation: '—My sister, I dare say . . . does not care to let a man come so near her ****. I will not say whether my uncle *Toby* had completed the sentence or not;—'tis for his advantage to suppose he had,—as, I think, he could have added no ONE WORD which would have improved it' (ibid.). Toby's pipe snaps and (perhaps) finishes his sentence for him. As so often, the marked omission which is the novel's pretence of tact actually compels the reader to supply the meanings it never quite specifies. This is not just suggestiveness, it is also the affectation of delicacy. It is hardly surprizing that the critics were exasperated; the novel does not just indulge in improprieties, it mocks the reader who might be determined not to find them.

I define a nose, as follows,—intreating only beforehand, and beseeching my

---

[89] *Sentimental Journey*, ed Stout, Introduction, 10.

readers . . . to guard against the temptations and suggestions of the devil, and suffer him by no art or wile to put any other ideas into their minds, than what I put into my definition. —For by the word *Nose*, throughout all this long chapter of noses, and in every other part of my work, where the word *Nose* occurs, —I declare, by that word I mean a Nose, and nothing more, or less. (III. xxxi. 218)

Vocabulary in *Tristram Shandy* is as if over-determined by its suggestive capabilities,[90] for words and things are made into symbols of the sexual activity in which the Shandy males cannot engage successfully. For the reader, there is 'a game of sexual discovering, recovering, uncovering',[91] yet *Tristram Shandy* is a text which avoids the dramas of passion and desire conventional in eighteenth-century novels. In Richardson's more dismissive phrase, it is 'too gross to be inflaming'.[92]

The suggestiveness of parts of *Tristram Shandy* binds the discriminating, private reader more thoroughly to the text's 'sociality' and parodies debates about how to read a narrative morally. It also enacts that avoidance of completion or fulfilment whose larger patterns run through the novel (from mis-conception to misconception). The novel that tried to be utterly, exhaustively moral (*Clarissa* is the model) was always striving for completion. Its ideal was that of the achievement of instructive intent, the reader who had been taught to read properly. Sterne, on the contrary, exploits the incompleteness that demands the reader's inferences. Which does not mean that these inferences are not already deter- mined; the problem of Sterne for the reviewers is that he takes his reader to be able and willing to supply them. 'Hast thou not played with sounds, and equivocal significations of words, ay, and with *Stars* and *Dashes*, before those whom thou oughtest to reverence?' asked the *Monthly Review*.[93] The likes of Richardson and Johnson worried about a reader who would know too little not to succumb to the false allurements of 'romance'; Sterne, as the reviewers realized, presumes a reader who will know too well not to provide the meanings which the text facetiously fancies itself too discreet to explicate. As the *Clockmakers Outcry* had it: 'If authors be answer-

---

[90] For a discussion of this phenomenon, see J. Berthoud, 'Shandeism and Sexuality', in Myer (ed.), *Laurence Sterne: Riddles and Mysteries*, 24–38.

[91] M. New, ' "At the backside of the door of purgatory": A Note on Annotating *Tristram Shandy*', ibid. 16.

[92] Cited in Howes, *Yorick and the Critics*, 32. See Carroll, 341.

[93] *Monthly Review*, 24 (Feb. 1761), 103.

able, as they certainly are, for the libidinous images which they excite in the minds of readers, how large must the author of TRIST- RAM's account be![94] The problem for such protestors was that the suggestive and the sentimental were next to each other; both types of representation in *Tristram Shandy* presume the same kind of reader.

*   *   *

I carry on my affairs quite in the French way, sentimentally.
(Sterne to John Wodehouse, August 1765).[95]

In *A Sentimental Journey* Sterne takes this further and conflates the suggestive and the sentimental. The *Sentimental Journey* goes out of its way to find scenes of erotic encounter, and thus seems to risk the production of outrage. It does this by interposing a body—the body of the narrator—whose sentimental whims sanction its erotic encounters. The eroticism of this body is at once innocent and knowing, coy and garrulous. It is a body which gauges sensibility, and whose vibrations register the pleasures of benevolence and of flirtation. Alone in a room with 'the fair *fille de chambre*', Yorick claims to feel 'a sort of a pleasing half guilty blush, where the blood is more in fault than the man', a 'sensation . . . delicious to the nerves' (*Sentimental Journey*, p. 234): 'But I'll not describe it.—I felt something at first within me which was not in strict unison with the lesson of virtue I had given her the night before' (p. 235). Through this body throb the vibrations of a finally conquerable erotic temptation—but also of benevolence, affection, sympathy. The pleasure of flirtation can be recorded because the body is taken to experience sentiments—fellow-feelings—which transcend 'carna- lity'. The presentation of each of Yorick's encounters as 'sentimental' renders it innocent, whatever our post-Freudian indictments might be. The *Sentimental Journey* produces its body not as a residue of desires but as a register of 'affections'—of 'feeling' refined by one who is determined to be a specialist in such matters. The contradic- tion taken to its logical conclusion in *Clarissa* was that the body was both 'sensible' and sexual; Sterne escapes the contradiction by making his narrator confess an utter susceptibility to feeling—by creating a narrator who can interpet every vibration as the symptom of a finally innocent sensibility.

The *Sentimental Journey* supplies 'pathetic' episodes, but always

[94] *Clockmakers Outcry*, 15.   [95] *Letters*, 256.

as part of Yorick's chronicle of his body's pulsations. He writes out his 'sensations', greeting the overflowing of sentiment with what Gardner Stout calls 'manifest self-approval' and what others have seen as a self-corrosive complacency:[96] 'I burst into a flood of tears—but I am as weak as a woman; and I beg the world not to smile, but pity me' (p. 103). This self-dramatization may now look to some as if intended to deflate sentimentalism, but it was not taken to do so by its eighteenth-century readers. (In popularizing publications like the *Sentimental Magazine* or the *Lady's Magazine*, the *Sentimental Journey* came to be taken as the ur-text for sentimental fiction.[97]) The confessional theatricality of Yorick's narrative undermines the interpretation of the *Sentimental Journey* as 'a text-book on feeling, an exposition of how, in any given set of circumstances, to behave in a sentimental and civilized mode';[98] it also obstructs the reader determined to find satire at the expense of sentimentalism. Yorick's capacities for feeling are refined beyond the possibilities of prescription or practicability, and his 'self-approval' is the means by which the novel allows its reader to recognize this. In a development of the narrative technique of *Tristram Shandy*, Yorick's body, one of the main topics of the *Sentimental Journey*, is made to get in the way of the story even as it communicates the effects of every episode: it is an instrument tuned to the influences of feeling; it is specialized to this purpose, defying the reader's identification with its extraordinary, private susceptibility.

We certainly cannot take it for granted that the vibrations and impulses of Yorick's body provide a consistent guide to any ethical model of action, though the benevolence which is a value in the *Sentimental Journey* is to be physically felt. On his first night in France, Yorick satisfies himself that he is well-disposed towards the French and their King:

—No—said I—the Bourbon is by no means a cruel race: they may be misled like other people; but their is a mildness in their blood. As I acknowledged this, I felt a suffusion of a finer kind upon my cheek—more warm and

---

[96] *Sentimental Journey*, ed. Stout, 25. For a version of the *Sentimental Journey* as a satire upon sentimental self-regard, see E. Dilworth, *The Unsentimental Journey of Laurence Sterne* (Morningside Heights, NY, 1948), and R. Putney, 'The Evolution of *A Sentimental Journey*', *Philological Quarterly*, 19 (1940), 349–69.

[97] See Mayo, *The English Novel*, 341–5.

[98] P. Quennell, *Four Portraits: Studies of the Eighteenth Century* (London, 1945), 183, cited in *Sentimental Journey*, ed. Stout, 26.

friendly to man, than what Burgundy (at least two livres a bottle, which was such as I had been drinking) could have produced. (p. 68)

Yorick himself provides the evidence for those who might want to attribute his 'suffusion' to a cause less noble than fellow-feeling, but then this is also, disarmingly, 'the evidence that he observes *himself* with comic detachment'[99]—the device by which Sterne's narrator is a move ahead of criticisms which could be directed at him. Yorick is not an unreliable narrator; on the contrary, he can be relied upon to draw attention to the irony of sensibility becoming a private experience. Having toasted the King of France, he contemplates dispensing the contents of his purse to some suitable 'object' of charity: 'I felt every vessel in my frame dilate—the arteries beat all cheerily together, and every power which sustained life, performed it with so little friction, that 'twould have confounded the most *physical precieuse* in France: with all her materialism, she could scarce have called me a machine—'(pp. 68-9). But this supposed instinct to benevolence is then thrown into relief by his failure to give generously to a mendicant monk until shamed into doing so by the presence of the lady from Brussels. An erotic attachment ('The pulsations of the arteries along my fingers pressing across hers, told her what was passing within me'—p. 97) corrects Yorick's sentiments. With this kind of attachment, the body is wholly given over to feeling, and churlish inclinations are conquered; the attachment is excusable because it is a matter of sentiment, of an innocent impulse which needs no greater satisfaction than two hands touching.

It is no doubt true that Sterne argued for the (limited) possibility of a life of benevolence. Certainly, in his *Sermons*, he opposes those (unidentified) 'moralisers' who contend that 'man is altogether a selfish creature' (though even here he sets against them the possibility not of an unproblematic benevolence but of a restrained practice of thrift and self-denial within the confines of the family).[1] But the self-induced throb which, in the *Sentimental Journey*, is the sign and pleasure of benevolence cannot easily be identified with any set of practical precepts or social obligations. Sterne's latitudinarian pronouncements as a preacher are not an immediate guide to the

<hr>

[99] *Sentimental Journey*, ed. Stout, 27.
[1] Laurence Sterne, *The Sermons of Mr Yorick* (7 vols. London, 1760-9), Sermon VII. ii. 12.

mingled self-attention and benevolent impulse that distinguish Yorick. In fact, Sterne encounters problems in his *Sermons* because, for didactic purposes, he has to attempt to project benevolence as a general human faculty. In the *Sentimental Journey* he avoids the difficulty of this by making it a minority experience. Many of the jokes in the novel, as well as the puzzling oscillation between the vanity and the self-deprecation of the narrator, stem from the fact that this has become a minority of one: Yorick experiencing benevolence through the very fibres and arteries of his body. He is a 'Sentimental Traveller' and writes against 'the whole circle of travellers'; his 'travels and observations will be altogether of a different cast from any of my forerunners' (pp. 81–2). His experience of the thrill of benevolence is, like the journey itself, *sui generis*.

Unlike the sermon, the novel can address its reader as if confidentially or exceptionally. When Yorick regrets his previous lack of charity, and the monk and the lady assure him that he is not one to act 'unkindly', we are told, 'I blush'd in my turn; but from what movements, I leave to the few who feel to analyse—' (p. 100). In this appearance of licence is a nice paradox. The text constitutes all who read as those who 'feel', those who are admitted to a complicity with the body's spontaneity, and are fitted to translate the vibrations of sentiment. Cleverly, as if a block to any who might want to find Yorick's record of his reactions ludicrously self-regarding, the text prompts us to infer Yorick's shame and his previous failures of benevolence. To understand all this is to be able to 'feel'. Yet the readers who can do this are also posited as 'the few', the exceptional. This is flattery of the polite (because inferential) reader, of course, a tactic which exploits the (not necessarily optimistic) association of sentiment and feeling with a quite uncommon refinement. But it is more than this. To feel is to enter into a special relationship with a narrative—to be a special kind of reader. The relationship between reader and text (that 'sociality') works because it can purport to be unique, and unrealizable outside the confines of the closet in which the book is read.

Sympathy as depicted by Sterne is not a model for behaviour; it is most likely to be an unusual and momentary privilege. It is not what Hume tried to make it: the natural pattern of a general principle. The novel and the moral philosophy are only directly comparable at the point at which both forms encounter the impossibility of generalizing sympathy and sociability—the unlikeliness of benevolence. 'Sterne's *Sentimental Journey* . . . made literary material of the concept of sympathy', says one critic;[2] on the contrary, the 'literary material' elaborates a sympathy confessed to be aberrant and eccentric—not the proof of a universal propensity, but the enjoyment of an unprecedented talent. Fewer writers than one might expect have discussed the relationship between sympathy as a term in moral and social philosophy of the period, and the sentimental representations in novels. When they have done so there has been a tendency to equate too easily the operations of the two kinds of text. John Traugott characterizes the tenets of what he calls sentimentalism thus:

By sensory apprehension of the behavior of other persons and by comparing that behavior by an association of ideas with our own, we conceive a sympathy with other persons . . . the concept ranged from the puerile elevation of vague benevolist feelings to a religious principle to Hume's carefully defined doctrine of sympathy.[3]

The congruence of philosophical doctrine and narrative pre-occupation is taken for granted. But in novels which rely on the depiction or demonstration of sentiment, sympathy is not that which is always and everywhere given. In the *Sentimental Journey*, it is the singular capacity of the ever-tearful Yorick and his blissfully responsive body. What could be an only self-regarding account is made communicative by the compliance of a reader, but this reader is made to realize that feeling is whimsical, quixotic, and simply unusual. It is not the currency of the world.

When Yorick contemplates, how seriously it is difficult to say, the possibility of his being imprisoned for not having a passport, it is an occasion for the conjuring of an idea of sympathy. Yorick begins to 'figure' to himself 'the miseries of confinement' and give 'full scope' to his 'imagination':

I was going to begin with the millions of my fellow creatures born to no inheritance but slavery; but finding, however affecting the picture was, that I could not bring it near me, and that the multitude of sad groups in it did but distract me,—

—I took a single captive, and having first shut him up in his dungeon, I

---

[2] K. MacLean, 'Imagination and Sympathy: Sterne and Adam Smith', *Journal of the History of Ideas*, 10 (1949), 399.

[3] J. Traugott (ed.), *Laurence Sterne: A Collection of Critical Essays*, Introduction (Englewood Cliffs, NJ, 1968), 4.

then look'd through the twilight of his grated door to take his picture. (p. 201).

This imaginary constitution of sympathy is finally Yorick's sympathy for himself, and comes through being 'in a right frame'. It is an exercise in 'feeling' and in the powers of 'imagination', which produce the 'affecting', out of nothing, as an intelligible and conveniently illustrative 'picture'. A modern reading tends to balk at this type of manipulation, this eliciting of the sentimental tears which close the exercise. But this is a sympathy which is not necessarily narcissistic and indulgent; it confesses itself to be inventive and purposeful: a necessary fiction. It confesses also that even the fiction requires the idea of a particular sympathy—that an undifferentiating fellow-feeling is scarcely imaginable. It is a resort to sympathy which has much more in common with the knowing and controlling strategy of Smith's *Theory* than with the absolute mutuality defined by sympathy in Hume's *Treatise*. For Sterne, as for Smith, pain can become a perfect pleasure, can serve as the necessary origin for the scenario of feeling. Sterne is not alone in the period in manipulating images of misfortune to provide an occasion for the display of sentiment; much literature of the eighteenth century reaches, as Maren-Sofie Rostvig writes, 'the paradoxical conclusion that happiness is to experience another's woe'.[4] But Sterne's (Yorick's) is an explicitly fictional act, and it is as such that sympathy can work. 'I burst into tears—I could not sustain the picture of confinement which my fancy had drawn' (p. 203): the text is mawkish here, certainly—although progressive on the question of slavery by the standards of Sterne's culture—but it is subtle about its own indulgence. It admits itself powerless to imagine benevolence as a general standard or experience it in a pressing and immediate form.

Yorick's journey, parodying the usual reports of foreign lands and avoiding the usual landmarks, is one which only a narrative can undertake. It is a journey to find the elision of the sentimental and the erotic. On Yorick's parting from Madam de L***, whose hand he has held for so long in the courtyard at Calais, he receives a letter promising to tell him 'her story . . . if my rout should ever lay through Brussels'. The promise evokes this exclamation, this fantasy:

---

[4] M.-S. Rostvig, *The Happy Man* (Oslo, 1958), ii. 244.

with what a moral delight will it crown my journey, in sharing in the sickening incidents of a tale of misery told to me by such a sufferer? to see her weep! and though I cannot dry up the fountain of her tears, what an exquisite sensation is there still left, in wiping them away from off the cheeks of the first and fairest of women, as I'm sitting with my handkerchief in my hand in silence the whole night besides her. (pp. 145–6)

The prospect has to be withdrawn for the sake of 'the pure taper of Eliza' (p. 147), but not before the 'moral delight', an almost erotic frisson, has been represented as the hearing of a particular narrative, a 'tale of misery'. Yorick's provision of himself as the perfectly sentimental, and perfectly excited, auditor, his entertainment and then retraction of the prospect, uses the titillating idea of a woman's pathos as another opportunity for the validation of sentiment. He gives himself, echoing a phrase from *Tristram Shandy*, an 'exquisite sensation': it is both explicitly far-fetched (it is all bizarrely, if keenly, imagined) and productive of a peculiar pleasure (conceived in the present tense, as if actually enjoyed). Listening to a story is the highest imaginable sympathetic pleasure. But the prospect is retracted; 'There was nothing wrong in the sentiment', but as 'sentiment', and not something more reproachable, it must remain. As long as the imagination is corrected, there can be no blame, and the wry justification of the whole episode can be a kind of boast: 'In transports of this kind, the heart, in spite of the understanding, will always say too much' (p. 148).

Yorick is after that moment of contact which sets the heart beating but is taken no further. 'He accepts in passing all the pleasures the ladies offer him, in the delicate shape of preludes to an always unfulfilled love which gets all its pleasure from the fleeting sensations of an awakening heart'.[5] Feeling triumphs in that suspended prelude: flirtatious and still polite; knowing, but innocently so. The text entertains the possibility of things going further in order to defeat it; true bliss is in the tiny yet suffusing warmth—the contact of hands—which restraint allows. In the face of the French count's 'indecent suggestion' that he might be interested in 'the nakedness . . . of our women', Yorick declares that he wishes only to 'spy the *nakedness* of their hearts': 'I have something within me which cannot bear the shock of the least indecent insinuation' (p. 217). This is ironical enough given not just the use of 'insinuation'

⁵ H. Fluchère, *Laurence Sterne: From Tristram to Yorick*, trans. B. Bray (London, 1965), 387.

in *Tristram Shandy*, but the proximity of innuendo in this novel: it ends, after all, with the most inciting example of 'that ornamental figure . . . the *Aposiopesis'*—'I caught hold of the Fille de Chambre's' (p. 291). But it is not marked down as a sham. Unalloyed sentiment cannot be enjoyed by those ignorant of its nearness to something improper; to guard against, and protest against, anything 'indecent' must be to know that it is always there—a temptation to be transcended.

Yorick tells the Count that his is 'a quiet journey of the heart in pursuit of NATURE, and those affections which rise out of her, which make us love each other—and the world, better than we do' (p. 219). It leads him 'through the Bourbonnois . . . in the hey-day of the vintage', and becomes 'a journey through each step of which music beats time to Labour, and all her children are rejoicing as they carry in their clusters' (p. 268). The pleasures of feeling are always liable to be enjoyed most readily with those untutored in the ways of sophisticated, unsympathetic society. The identification of labour and those who perform it as joyfully (and fortunately) innocent is a common enough ideological move in the eighteenth century, but here it is not quite repeated in the usual way. For it is only the 'sentimental traveller' who has access to such harmony, to such natural 'rejoicing'. It is only he who travels, unlike the conventional chronicler of names, dates, and places, 'with my affections flying out, and kindling at every group before me' who can finally join the dance in which 'simple jollity' is seen 'mixing' with 'Religion'. This traveller looks for neither 'foreign knowledge' nor 'foreign improvements' (p. 84). He says of the Paris salons, 'the better the *Coterie*—the more children of Art—I languish'd for those of Nature' (p. 266); his is a grand tour in search of innocence.

It is as if the *Sentimental Journey*, most graphically in the act of omission with which it concludes, dares its reader to find anything except innocence in its thrills and encounters. As Sterne declared to an admiring, aristocratic reader, 'If it is not thought a chaste book, mercy on them that read it, for they must have warm imaginations indeed!'[6] Attuned to contemporary ideas of reading as a moral (or immoral) activity, Sterne produces a narrative which 'is all quite innocent provided one takes it so'.[7] The sensitivity of a readership to

---

6 Letter of Nov. 1767: *Letters*, 403.
7 Cross, *The Life and Times of Laurence Sterne*, 461.

the notional suggestiveness of a novel is used to deflect attention on to the power of feeling to sanction pleasure and fantasy. In this sense, Sterne's fiction shows itself concerned with the moral implications of narratives. Yet his novels are not morally tendentious in the same way as Richardson's; they do not attempt to teach virtue by associating it with the capacity for feeling. In the writings in which he did tackle the relationship between this capacity and actual models of behaviour (the *Sermons*) there is an altogether less secure faith in the influences of sentiment and sympathy. When it comes to didacticism, and although Sterne wishes to avoid 'running into any common-place declamations upon the wickedness of the age',[8] 'generosity' and 'the tear of tenderness' cannot be proclaimed universal. The *Sermons* do trust to

something in our nature which engages us to take part in every accident to which man is subject . . . to find in such calamities . . . something then so truly interesting, that at the first sight we generally make them our own . . . from a certain generosity and tenderness of nature which disposes us for compassion, abstracted from all considerations of self.[9]

But alongside these are less optimistic perceptions. The parable of the Good Samaritan, on which the passage above is a commentary, illustrates a capacity for sympathy which is but rarely fulfilled.

So, in the *Sermons*, Sterne complains, as he never needs to in the novels, of the absence of moral standards from public life, especially 'amongst those whose higher stations are made a shelter for the liberties they take'.[10] So he hopes for a condition of 'society' different from the 'present state of vice',[11] and even lectures on the fate of a 'sinful people' which, ambiguously, may either be England as it is or England as it would be if it were not for 'the blessing of a protestant king'.[12] He is ready to talk not of public redemption but of the 'honest tear shed in private'; it is the most that can be expected.[13] The last three volumes of the *Sermons* were published posthumously in order to pay off some of Sterne's debts, and they certainly seem, in Brissenden's terms, less 'optimistic' than those which he himself prepared for publication. Sterne, of course, played his market for all it was worth, and no doubt realized that the easy lessons of his earlier sermons (though these were not necessarily written any earlier than

---

[8] *Sermons*, i, Sermon V. 131.
[9] Ibid. i, Sermon III. 54–5.
[10] Ibid. v, Sermon III. 65.
[11] Ibid. v, Sermon VI. 169.
[12] Ibid. viii, Sermon XIII, Preface.

those in the last three volumes) would prompt a more enthusiastic response among those who would expect the affability of address of the author of *Tristram Shandy*. But perhaps he also sensed that the closer his writings approached to prescription and prognosis—which is to say, the closer they approached to religion—the less able they would be actually to envisage benevolence or the society of sentiments. In the last sermons in the collection benevolence becomes a wishfully conceived vision. Could it prevail 'the world would be worth living in':[14] a conditional which is almost withdrawn as it is stated. The preacher who has to recommend, predict, or judge is not quite the comfortable latitudinarian often described; for him fellow-feeling is a less than tangible ideal.

Under the influence of R.S. Crane's essay on the 'Genealogy of the "Man of Feeling" ', sentimentalism in eighteenth-century novels has often been linked by critics to the habits of latitudinarian teaching, and both have been taken to articulate an 'optimistic' view of the sociable capacities of human beings. Indeed, the misnomer of optimism has been a reason for the comparative lack of interest shown, by literary histories at least, in the fashion for narratives of overpowering feeling and tremulous sensibility. Not to be the reader who can share such a putatively complacent view of social being is to begin to detect in the texts whimsicality, banality, or worse. Sentimentalism gets represented as a scarcely explicable foible of 'major' writers, and a paralysing obsession of 'minor' ones. But this version of the 'doctrine' behind the fiction is misleading. Sterne's uses of sentiment might equally well be taken to be fatalistic, atavistic, defensively playful. He does not describe a sociability that could ever be a practical model of being in society. His fiction substitutes its own 'sociality', its relationship with a knowing and exceptional reader, for any version of a wider social harmony. It is this retreat into the text's 'sociality' which is enough to align Sterne in critical canons with 'modern' novels: he becomes 'an inexplicable anachronism',[15] or his writings 'are perhaps better understood in some ways today than at any time since they first appeared'.[16] In fact, his interrogation of habits of reading is rooted in his own time and culture; his writing career is a series of confrontations with contemporary moral demands made of narratives, and the strictures of criticism provide him with crucial material.

[13] *Sermons*, iii, Sermon II. 50.   [14] Ibid. vii, Sermon XIV. 34.
[15] Traugott, *Critical Essays*, 1.   [16] Brissenden, *Virtue in Distress*, 188.

The *Sentimental Journey* takes its narrator's adventures to the brink of the immorality which critics and novelists condemned, but always to insist on the innocence of the sentimental inclination which leads him to each of his encounters. One of these is Yorick's meeting with the 'fille de chambre' on a Paris street:

'Tis sweet to feel by what finespun threads our affections are drawn together.

We set off a-fresh, and as she took her third step, the girl put her hand within my arm—I was just bidding her—but she did it of herself with that undeliberating simplicity, which shew'd it was out of her head that she had never seen me before. For my own part, I felt the conviction of consanguinity so strongly, that I could not help turning half round to look in her face, and see if I could trace out any thing in it of a family likeness—Tut! said I, are we not all relations? (*Sentimental Journey*, p. 190).

Clarissa hoped but forlornly that the world might be like a family; the members of the Grandison household tried to behave as if they were one large extended family; Yorick appropriately asserts his whimsical sociability in his ability to enjoy a mildly titillating acquaintanceship as if it is familial. We have learned to doubt the innocence of familial relationships, but the *Sentimental Journey* is particularly well adapted to the deflection of such scepticism. It substitutes feeling for desire, a scenario of gestures for any sexually provocative act. Where *Tristram Shandy* provoked its readers, and most of all its critics, with innuendo, the *Sentimental Journey* is knowing enough to provide episodes which only those with immoral intention would translate into 'carnality'.

Twentieth-century readers of the novel cannot be entirely willing to comply with Sterne by accepting the separation of sentiment from 'carnality', Eighteenth-century readers, more willing to find plausible the image of a sociability founded on feeling, made few objections, As Gardner Stout indicates, the book was 'generally praised' in 'fashionable circles' on its publication 'even by some who had consistently disparaged *Tristram Shandy*'.[17] The sanctioning of erotic encounter as sentimental innocence was generally acceptable to readers of the text in the eighteenth-century, despite contemporary concerns with the propriety of narratives. Aside from the *Critical Review*, which was perhaps smarting from Sterne's attack upon its former editor, Smollett, via the depiction of

[17] Stout, 21–2

Smelfungus, all the extant reviews of the *Sentimental Journey* greet the work with approbation. The *Political Register* of May 1768 praises the work particularly for 'the moral and the pathetic' instruction of 'our passions',[18] but perhaps the most telling reaction is that of Ralph Griffiths, the same reviewer who had previously bemoaned the indecency of much of *Tristram Shandy*. Writing in the *Monthly Review*, he delights to find most of the *Sentimental Journey* to be in the 'pathetic vein' which is his own preference. Commenting on the chapter in which Yorick has the pleasure of being accosted by the *fille de chambre* in the street, and declares the pleasure to be that of 'consanguinity', he exclaims: 'What delicacy of feeling, what tenderness of sentiment, yet what simplicity of expression are here! Is it *possible* that a man of *gross ideas* could ever *write* in a strain so pure, so refined from the dross of sensuality!'[19] Aware of the possibility of 'gross ideas' (he laments that Sterne's novel ends 'with a dash of *somewhat* bordering rather on sensuality than sentiment') Griffiths remains willing to take Yorick at his word. He, like others, is always ready to read 'for the sentiment'.

The frisson and the privilege of sentiment have become, with Sterne's final work, self-sustaining. The *Sentimental Journey* is sensitized to moralisms, but it does not strive, like Richardson's fiction, to outline a capacity for sentiment which is to be a model of moral responsibility. It does not even really celebrate a type of social being, but falls back on the invented voice of one dedicated to a specialized and eccentric experience of society. Sterne is no more an optimist than Richardson; he does not hold out a life of sentiment as a practical way of being in society. The gestures by which feeling is communicated are, in his fiction, the prerogative of those who cannot be imitated because innocence is inimitable. Sterne's fiction offers each exceptional reader the opportunity to recognize and approve the instincts in which such feeling originates, but its 'sociality' is always with this exceptional reader. This 'sociality' is its limit as well as its opportunity.

[18] Howes, *Sterne: The Critical Heritage*, 201.   [19] Ibid. 200-1.

5

Hypochondria and Hysteria: Sensibility and the Physicians

IN the novels of the mid-eighteenth century, it is the body which acts out the powers of sentiment. These powers, in a prevailing model of sensibility, are represented as greater than those of words. Tears, blushes, and sighs—and a range of postures and gestures—reveal conditions of feeling which can connote exceptional virtue or allow for intensified forms of communication. Feeling is above all observable, and the body through which it throbs is peculiarly excitable and responsive. The construction of a body attuned to the influences of sensibility is not, however, uniquely a project of the novelists. We find the same kind of body, and the same concentration on the gestural force of feeling, in the writings of many eighteenth-century physicians. These writings do not merely share a vocabulary with novels of sentiment; they also represent a capacity for feeling as ambiguous in similar ways. In the novels, sensibility can become excessive and self-destructive; it can declare itself reclusive, and retreat into the, sometimes histrionic, postures of melancholy. Comparably, the texts discussed in this chapter ponder a susceptibility to feeling which can be either a privilege or a weakness. They trace the shapes of a delicacy—an access to the pulsings of sentiment—which is seen as sometimes the omen of distraction, delirium, and defeat.

These texts concern themselves with the causes and symptoms of hypochondria, hysteria, and nervous disorder, but it is difficult now to categorize them exactly. They may have a place in the history of psychiatry, but they obviously pre-date what we might now know as psychiatric descriptions and procedures. They recommend a variety of cures for the ailments with which they are concerned, but also function to establish these putative ailments as fashionable and even, to some extent, desirable. A typical device for the explanation of such bizarre and contradictory strategies, strategies which I shall suggest should be understood in relation to the promises and recourses of a literature of sentiment or sensibility, has been the description of an insidious and ubiquitous 'irrationality'. A single step beyond the myth of an Augustan rationality (the 'Age of Reason', no less) is an apparently subversive but in fact perfectly conservative thesis. According to this thesis, the fashion for the discussion and representation of nervous disorder in the mid-eighteenth century is a symptom of a creeping 'unreason' which haunts supposedly triumphant 'reason'. A narrative of hardly articulate fears and obsessions is produced, to be set against one of confident order and poise.

Yet to describe 'the dark side of the Enlightenment', the seething realm of 'unreason', is to accept the myth of Enlightenment, the positivity of Reason. It is to substitute for an over-worked telelogy a comfortable paradox. In his 'The Madhouse, the Whorehouse and the Convent', Max Byrd writes of these places as serving 'the literature of the Age of Reason as symbolic prisons, where irrational energy was locked away from normal society'.[1] He sees a 'preoccupation with the obvious dangers of unreason, but also a certain barely disguised fascination with it . . . we see paradoxically in every case . . . constant traffic, unflagging and often obsessive, between the great world of Enlightenment society and the smaller, darker world of unreason that society denounces and yet secretly visits.' It is true that in this period pictorial and literary representations testify to a certain fascination with these places. But the opposition of 'unreason' to 'reason' cannot properly explain the deliberation with which images of susceptibility are described. Neither moral philosophy's recourse to a sympathetic transmission of sentiments, nor the increasingly conventional celebration of feeling in novels of the period, is simply indicative of a reversion to irrationalism. They evidence consistent projects of representation—consistent organizations of metaphor and rhetorical cadence. It is not that either of these types of writing is uninhibited by anxiety—but each expresses more than uncertainty about what the world considers reasonable. Both attempt to find a conventional language for the expression of values which are given as neither incoherent nor opposed to the claims of reason.

Equally, the writings concerned with hysteria, spleen, nervous

[1] *Partisan Review*, 44 (1977).

disorder—produced in a steady flow between about 1720 and 1770—are remarkable for the conventionality of the versions of cause and effect on which they rely. They do not testify to any insistent irrationalism: they seek to produce intelligible, repeatable, patterns of symptom and posture. In order to understand the purposes and the equivocations of this production, it is necessary to perceive both the dominance and inadequacy of the model of 'reason' versus 'unreason'. In its most sophisticated incarnation, this model haunts, via Horkheimer and Adorno, even Klaus Doerner's excellent *Madmen and the Bourgeoisie*,[2] and in its more characteristic form conditions George Rosen's account of 'Forms of Irrationality in the Eighteenth Century': 'when a rupture of the relations between the head and the heart led to a fundamental rift, the ensuing gap opened a way for the emergence of the dark, the weird, and the demonic—in short, the irrational—from the depths of the eighteenth century psyche'.[3] To attempt to move away from this schema is not to suggest that the doctors, authors, and administrators of the period did not practise strategies of exclusion, suppression, and imprecation. But it is to say that the discourses about nervous disorder, melancholy, and hysteria are not themselves disordered; that, with whatever difficulties, they elicit and arrange quite fastidiously the objects of their description.

Those who undertake such description are not usually obscure or socially marginal individuals. Richard Blackmore was physician to Queen Anne before he undertook his *Treatise of the Spleen and Vapours*. George Cheyne, perhaps the most renowned popularizer of ideas of 'Nervous Distemper', whose work *The English Malady* had reached its sixth edition within two years of publication, was physician to Samuel Richardson, was sought for advice by Johnson and, perhaps, David Hume,[4] and was personally known and admired by a large number of the notable social and literary figures

---

[2] Klaus Doerner, *Madmen and the Bourgeoisie: A Social History of Insanity and Psychiatry*, trans. J. Neugroschel and J. Steinburg (Oxford, 1981), Chapter 1.

[3] In H. Pagliaro (ed.), *Studies in Eighteenth-Century Culture: Irrationalism in the Eighteenth Century*, vol. ii (Cleveland and London, 1972), 256. See also G. Rosen, 'Enthusiasm "a dark lanthorn of the spirit" ', *Bulletin of the History of Medicine*, 42 (1968), for another version of the 'order' versus 'irrationality' model.

[4] This has tended to be presumed rather than proved. For the evidence to the contrary see E.C. Mossner, 'Hume's Epistle to Dr Arbuthnot', *Huntington Library Quarterly*, 7 (1944), 135–52.

of his time.[5] Later in the century, first Robert Whytt and then William Cullen become professors of the theory of medicine at Edinburgh University and the former was appointed first physician to George III in Scotland in 1761, three years before the publication of his *Observations on the Nature, Causes, and Cure of those Disorders which have been commonly call'd Nervous, Hypochondriac, or Hysteric.* These are some of the men to whom Roy Porter refers as 'a clutch of fashionable psychiatric doctors, friends to the Hanoverian order'.[6] They are fashionably placed in 'society' because, indeed, they have to be; for the most part they 'looked not to collective professional paths to glory, but to the personal favour of grandees'.[7] Like the poet, the physician needed his patrons. Successful physicians in this period are at the centre of the social and political life of the nation, as dictated and recorded by its ruling class.

The terms and categories which they deploy, initially reproduced from the seventeenth-century works of Willis and Sydenham, are common currency by the middle of the eighteenth century, but I shall hope to show that the use of these terms does not support the image of reason threatened and yet fixated by its supposedly sinister *alter ego.* Until the work of Whytt and Cullen, the many writings on hysteria, hypochondria, and nervous disorder are not intended for a particularly expert readership. They are generally written for all those who are educated, all those who might themselves suffer from such a 'Malady'. Blackmore's *Treatise,* in which the topic of 'the *English* Spleen' is distinguished from the 'Disorders of Mind, Lunacy, and disturbed Imagination' frequent amongst 'those nearer the Sun', those unable to aspire to the sensibility of the educated

---

[5] For the popularity of Cheyne's writings see G.S. Rousseau, 'Science Books and their Readers in the Eighteenth Century', in I. Rivers (ed.), *Books and their Readers in Eighteenth-century England* (Leicester, 1982), 217. For further discussion of the supposed recipient of Hume's own description of his 'lowness of spirits' see previous footnote, and *The Letters of David Hume,* ed. J.Y.T. Greig (2 vols., Oxford, 1932), i. 12; E.C. Mossner, *The Life of David Hume* (London, 1954), 67, and the second edition of this same biography (Oxford, 1980), 83–5.

[6] R. Porter, 'The Rage of Party: A Glorious Revolution in English Psychiatry?', *Medical History,* 27 (1983), 35–50.

[7] R. Porter, 'Laymen, Doctors and Medical Knowledge in the Eighteenth Century: The Evidence of the *Gentleman's Magazine'*, in Roy Porter (ed.), *Patients and Practitioners: Lay Perceptions of Medicine in Pre-industrial Society* (Cambridge, 1985), 287. See also N. Jewson, 'Medical Knowledge and the Patronage System in Eighteenth Century England', *Sociology,* 8 (1974), 369–85.

English patient,[8] declares itself to be written not solely for 'great Scholars, or Students in Physick' but for 'all intelligent Persons'.[9] Similarly, Cheyne's *English Malady* is not so much, in modern terms, a medical text as a work for 'my Fellow-Sufferers under these Complaints', for those who, like the author, see themselves as susceptible to such sufferings.[10] By the time of William Buchan's *Domestic Medicine*, published in 1769, the inclusion of 'diseases . . . of the nervous kind' under such a title is itself, perhaps, suggestive enough.[11] This is a book which claims to circumvent 'the nostrums of quacks and conjurers' on the one hand and the exotic 'poisons' of 'the daring empiric' on the other (pp. xii–xiii). Now aware, and suspicious, of the metropolitan fashion of certain types of ready diagnosis, the book seeks to teach 'the ladies, gentlemen, and clergy who reside in the country' to recognize their own symptoms, and if necessary to educate the 'ignorant rustic' (p. xiii). Even though this text confesses itself uneasy about the influences of too fashionable an appeal by the physician to a self-regarding readership, its *raison d'être* is still popularization. The physician may be a specialist, but he writes of 'nervous disorder' for all literate enough to comprehend.[12]

Both Blackmore and Cheyne, as well as presuming the accessibility of their speculations, produce the types of 'Malady' or 'Distemper' about which they write as symptoms of a peculiar privilege, of heightened faculties or unusual intelligence. It is this appearance of weakness and strength together—of special faculties which are manifested in illness—which is the most important description common to the medical text and the novel of sentiment. Writing specifically of men, Blackmore describes 'Hypochondriacal Persons' as 'endowed with a great Share of Understanding and Judgement, with strong and clear Reason, a quick Apprehension and

[8] Richard Blackmore, *A Treatise of the Spleen and Vapours* (London, 1725), p. v.

[9] Ibid., p. vii.

[10] George Cheyne, *The English Malady; or, a Treatise of Nervous Diseases of all Kinds* (first published 1733, 6th edn., London, 1735), p. ii.

[11] William Buchan, *Domestic Medicine* (Edinburgh, 1769), 508.

[12] Of interest here is John Monro's *Remarks on Dr Battie's Treatise on Madness* (London, 1758). Monro, like his father before him, physician to the Bethlem hospital, and threatened by Battie's emphasis upon the possibilities of treatment and cure, directs his attack against a fashion of *writing* about 'deluded imagination'. Instead of writing he would have 'observation' and 'the necessity of *confining*' (p. 37): his own trade.

Vivacity of Fancy and Imagination, even above other Men'.[13]
Despite the 'Obscurity and Confusion' which the malady introduces
to the 'intellectual Faculties', those prone to it are blessed as well as
cursed. Indeed, for Blackmore 'the lowest degree' of this 'Disease' is
'rather desirable than hurtful; and therefore no Skill or Remedies
should be employed to remove it'.[14] He repeats his assertion that
'Men of a splenetick Complexion . . . in whom no great and
considerable Symptoms appear, are usually endowed with refined
and elevated Parts . . . and in these Perfections they are superior to
the common level of Mankind'.[15] So too, 'many Hysterick Women
owe their good Sense, ready Wit, and lively Fancy, to the like
fountain'. Cheyne goes so far as to produce his own 'history', his
own 'valetudinariness', as that which sanctions his discussion of
'Nervous Disorders'.

The English Malady includes a record of the author's own
encounter with melancholy, and of his subsequent dietary
reformation.[16] For only those peculiarly privileged are liable to
'suffer' from this conventional ailment. In his letters to Samuel
Richardson, Cheyne diagnoses the novelist's 'Case' as 'Scurbutico
Nervose from a sedentary studious Life',[17] and assures him 'I have
been often under that Terror and Anxiety you mention'.[18] Cheyne's
assertion is made in order to substantiate the authority of his
descriptions. He repeats it in a letter of September 1735 to another of
his notable patients, the Countess of Huntingdon: 'All you describe I
have felt and gone through, even almost to distraction'.[19] A type of
susceptibility is the common experience of physician and patient,
and this enables Cheyne to write to Richardson, in May 1742:

You need not question that I am sufficiently apprized of and have felt the
Grief, Anguish, and Anxiety such a Distemper must have on a Mind of any
Degree of Sensibility, and of so fine and lively an Imagination as yours, and
it is happy for Mankind that they cannot feel but by Compassion and

---

[13] Blackmore, *A Treatise of the Spleen and Vapours*, 24.
[14] Ibid. 89.
[15] Ibid. 90.
[16] Cheyne, *The English Malady*, 'The Case of the Author', 325; and see Ilza Veith,
Hysteria: The History of a Disease (Chicago, 1965), 157.
[17] *The Letters of Doctor George Cheyne to Samuel Richardson*, ed. C. Mullett
(Columbia, Miss., 1943), 59: letter of Apr. 1740.
[18] Ibid. 92: letter of Apr. 1742.
[19] *The Letters of Doctor George Cheyne to the Countess of Huntingdon*, ed. C.
Mullett (San Marino, Calif., 1940), 50.

Consent of Parts (as one Member feels the Pain of another) the Misery of their Fellow Creatures of their Acquaintance; else Life would be intolerable.[20]

Cheyne classes himself and Richardson as 'serious, virtuous Valetudinarians'.[21] Their shared 'sensibility' renders them liable to the 'distemper' of which Richardson complains, but also allows them to communicate their 'feeling' to each other. Such communication is only possible between those who are properly sensitized.

In the writings of eighteenth-century physicians hypochondria, and, more ambivalently, melancholy are described as types of susceptibility which tend to be evidence of refinement and 'sensibility' and yet which can also be debilitating. Those who see such writing as the upsurge of an inefficiently censored irrationality do not account for the first element of this paradox. Those who see the interest in such forms of 'Malady' or 'Disorder' as constituting unproblematic signs of fashion ignore the second element.[22] The interest in nervous affliction is a vogue, but it is not just an easy or unworried self-attention. At certain points within the writings which I am discussing, there is a perturbation or ambiguity unresolved by schemes of nervous sensitivity. For the physicians, a susceptibility to the powers of feeling may be a token of refinement, but it is also the cause of disturbance. Here we have a paradoxical model similar to that developed in novels. That paragon of virtue, Clarissa, displays her sensibility, after all, most graphically in what Richardson's index refers to as the 'affectingly incoherent' 'rambling' of the 'fragments' that she writes after Lovelace has raped her (*Clarissa*, iii. 529). 'The lady's affecting behaviour in her delirium' is an enactment at once of integrity and disorder: virtue's triumph in the body's defeat. The paradox never achieves such fanatical symbolic clarity in the medical writings, but the myth that only those of particular merit are liable to become victims of nervous disorder is commonly resorted to.

The gender of such victims, of course, determines how they are to be described. Writers of the eighteenth century are generally agreed that, with the repudiation of the idea of a mobile womb which has classically defined the aetiology of a specifically feminine hysteria,

---

[20] *Letters to Richardson*, ed. Mullett, 94.

[21] Ibid. 109: letter of Sept. 1742.

[22] See, for example, G.S. Rousseau, 'Psychology', in G.S. Rousseau and R. Porter (eds.), *The Ferment of Knowledge* (Cambridge, 1980).

there is to be a male equivalent of hysteria which is designated as hypochondria. There is still a separation of male and female, a separation which allows for new forms of concentration on the woman, new ways in which she is constituted as disordered, inconstant, precarious. But even the privilege of male hypochondria is conditional or reticent. The basic formula is an old one. It quite specifically harks back to Burton and to Thomas Sydenham, who writes in 1682 of 'hysterical complaints', from which a specifically male hypochondria has not yet been absolutely separated, as constituting one sixth 'of the number of all chronic diseases'.[23] There is 'rarely' a woman 'who is wholly free' from these 'complaints', but some men too can be sufferers. These male hysterics, subject to the affliction of 'hypochondriasis', are 'such male subjects as lead a sedentary or studious life'. This theme is developed in the writings of the eighteenth century, and indeed a new translation of Sydenham's *Dissertatio . . . de Affectione Hysterica* is published in 1742, perhaps indicating the extent to which the fashion for such studies has taken root.[24]

Those males who become known as 'hypochondriac' are typically described as those who study, who write, who remove themselves from a world of trade, ambition, and 'business'. William Stukely, in a work which pre-dates more sophisticated analyses of nervous organization, writes in 1723: 'We know 'tis a common observation in our practice, that the modish disease call'd the vapors, and from its suppos'd seat, the SPLEEN, does most frequently attack scholars and persons of the soft sex most eminent for wit and good sense'.[25] For Stukely, this is to be examined and explained through surgical experiment and anatomical speculation, through an understanding of the supposed role of the spleen as the organ which governs the quantity and condition of blood in the body, 'the great *regulator* or watergage to the heart'.[26] By the time of William Smith's *A Dissertation upon the Nerves*, as the title suggests, the emphasis is upon a system of 'nervous fibres' as an explanatory model, but the truism remains to be repeated in another form: 'People of weak nerves are generally quick thinkers, from the delicacy of their

[23] Quoted by Ilza Veith, 'On Hysterical and Hypochondriacal Afflictions', *Bulletin of the History of Medicine*, 30 (1956).

[24] See R. Hunter and I. Macalpine, *Three Hundred Years of Psychiatry 1535–1860* (London, 1963), 221.

[25] William Stukely, *Of the Spleen* (London, 1723), 25.

[26] Ibid. 64.

sensitive organ'.[27] In a letter, the young David Hume describes himself as suffering from 'the Disease of the Learned', a synonym for the 'Distemper' which he calls 'the Vapors', a 'Weakness . . . of Spirits' deriving from 'profound Reflections' which prompts him to take 'Anti-hysteric Pills' and long daily rides.[28] Hume's self-description reproduces common categories and associations. In that great repository of precept, fable, and contradiction, Robert James's *Medicinal Dictionary*, we find, in the entry for 'HYPOCHONDRIACUS MORBUS', that 'Those are . . . in a peculiar manner, subject to this Disorder, who lead a sedentary Life, and indulge themselves too much in Study, continual Meditations, and Lucubrations. Hence the Disorder is very common among the *Literati*.'[29] This is produced as a classical formula now rejustified: 'Justly then did Aristotle observe, that melancholy Persons are endow'd with the greatest Capacities'.[30] In the *Dictionary*, 'Mania' can be induced by a 'Weakness of the Brain', but this is 'produced by intense Application of Mind, or too long protracted Lucubrations . . . Hence the Reason is Obvious, why the Literati, and Men of a studious Turn, are more Subject to Alienations of Mind than the common People.'[31] The domain of susceptibility is specialized: 'we must observe, that not only dull, stupid, and forgetful Persons, but also, and that more frequently, ingenious Men, Poets, Philosophers, and those charmed with the more deep and abstruse Parts of Mathematics and Algebra, are subject to Melancholy'.[32] One step from a privileged affliction, however, is something more dangerous—'Mania' and 'Madness'. It is the proximity of such excesses which complicates perceptions of learned melancholy.

If we return to Blackmore's *Treatise* we find the description of a 'Disease' which is privileged but which can pass into 'Lunacy': 'it is notorious, that many celebrated Men of Wit, that derive their superior Genius from an Hypochondriacal Constitution, have sometimes Spirits elevated to a degree above the Standard of sober and uninfected Reason'.[33] The problem of distinguishing a heightened sensibility from a dangerous disorder will continue to haunt those who associate hypochondria with specialized faculties

[27] William Smith, *A Dissertation upon the Nerves* (London, 1768), 191.

[28] *Letters of David Hume*, vol. i, Letter 3, Mar. or Apr. 1734, 13–14.

[29] Robert James, *A Medicinal Dictionary* (3 vols., London, 1743–5), s.v. 'HYPOCHONDRIACUS MORBUS'.

[30] Ibid., s.v. 'HYSTERICA'.   [31] Ibid., s.v. 'MANIA'.   [32] Ibid.

[33] Blackmore, *A Treatise of the Spleen and Vapours*, 166.

or abilities. This is an association which readily allows for the
ascription of a moral as well as an intellectual superiority to the
learned hypochondriac. In *Hypochondriasis*, which G.S. Rousseau
identifies as a particularly derivative text,[34] John Hill writes, 'Fatigue
of mind, and great exertion of its powers often give birth to this
disease . . . Greatness of mind, and steady virtue; determined
resolution, and manly firmness, when put in action, and intent upon
their object, all also lead to it.'[35] Those who are 'most subject to it'
are, inevitably, 'the grave and studious, those of a sedate temper and
enlarged understanding, the learned and wise, the virtuous and the
valiant'. So it does not in the least detract from, but instead
emphasizes, Boswell's reverence for Johnson that the biographer
should draw attention to the '"morbid melancholy", which was
lurking in his constitution, and to which we may ascribe those
particularities, and that aversion to regular life, which, at a very
early period, marked his character'.[36] According to Boswell,
Johnson, by the age of twenty, 'felt himself overwhelmed with an
horrible hypochondria, with perpetual irritation, fretfulness, and
impatience; and with a dejection, gloom, and despair, which made
existence misery. From this dismal malady he never afterwards was
perfectly relieved.' Boswell does not hesitate to write that Johnson
'was subject to what the learned, philosophical, and pious
Dr Cheyne has so well treated under the title of "The English
Malady". Though he suffered severely from it, he was not therefore
degraded.'[37] It is, it seems, an affliction liable to be visited upon a
man 'blest with all the powers of genius and understanding in a
degree far above the ordinary state of human nature'.[38] This type of
association of extraordinary 'understanding' with the danger of
affliction is common in the period. It is Mackenzie, the most
'sentimental'; of writers, who, at the end of his life, links the 'great
genius' of Collins and Cowper with the fact that they were 'both
nervous in constitution, and both having fits of low spirits
approaching to derangement'.[39] Specifically, hypochondria is seen

[34] See G.S. Rousseau, Introduction to John Hill, *Hypochondriasis: A Practical
Treatise* (1766; rpt. Los Angeles, 1969).
[35] Hill, *Hypochondriasis*, 6.   [36] *Life of Johnson*, 47.   [37] Ibid. 48.
[38] Ibid. 47–8. For an account of Johnson's disabling melancholia, see R. Porter,
'"The Hunger of Imagination": Approaching Samuel Johnson's Melancholy', in
W.F. Bynum, R. Porter, and M. Shepherd (eds.), *The Anatomy of Madness: Essays
in the History of Psychiatry* (London, 1985), 63–88.
[39] H.W. Thompson (ed.), *The Anecdotes and Egotisms of Henry Mackenzie*
(London, 1927), 165.

to be visited upon those for whom refinement, study, or 'imagination' involves solitude or retreat, the meditation which excludes all but the subjects of its fixation, the 'lucubration' which implies cloistered nocturnal reflection and the writing which comes out of it.

Indicative of this kind of association is the sobriquet under which Boswell wrote a column in the *London Magazine* between 1777 and 1783: 'The Hypochondriack'. Though he quarrels with the proposition that hypochondria is necessarily the affliction of 'men of remarkable excellence',[40] the very adoption of the pseudonym which gave its name to the column indicates that the association is still alive. Indeed, Boswell addresses his readers in terms reminiscent of Cheyne, with hypochondria assumed as a shared malaise and a shared privilege: 'I am so well acquainted with the distemper of Hypochondria, that I think myself qualified to assist some of my unhappy companions, who are now groaning under it . . . I have suffered much of the fretfulness, the gloom, and the despair that can torment a thinking being.'[41] Boswell repeats what he had said (almost proudly) of his disposition over a decade earlier, in the sketch for a brief narrative of his early life, written for Rousseau: 'I was born with a melancholy temperament. It is the temperament of our family. Several of my relations have suffered from it. Yet I do not regret that I am melancholy. It is the temperament of tender hearts, of noble souls.'[42] While, throughout the 'Hypochondriack', Boswell shows a desire to repudiate a vogue of melancholy and to assert the 'direful' and 'dismal' nature of an affliction personally experienced and thus not to be trivialized, he still treats hypochondria as that which defines a certain privileged understanding—which sanctions an autobiographical voice appealing to the reader as 'companion'.[43] However painful sensibility may be, 'insensibility of mind' is 'compatible only with ignorance'.[44]

---

[40] James Boswell, *The Hypochondriack*, ed. M. Bailey (2 vols., Stanford, Calif., 1928), No. 5 (Feb. 1778), i. 136.

[41] Ibid., No. 1 (Nov. 1777), i. 108–9.

[42] Boswell, 'Sketch of the Early Life of James Boswell, Written by Himself for Jean Jacques Rousseau, 5 December 1764', in F. A. Pottle, *James Boswell: The Earlier Years 1740-1769* (1966; rpt. London, 1984), 1.

[43] See *The Hypochondriack*, No. 30, Mar. 1780, i. 330, or No. 36, Sept. 1780, ii. 18.

[44] Ibid., No. 15, Dec. 1778, i. 207.

Reading Boswell's Journals, we cannot doubt the actual suffering involved in the 'low spirits' and 'melancholy' of which the author constantly complains. Of course there are the complications peculiar to Boswell: 'Gloomy doubts of a future existence';[45] the fear that he too will turn mad, like his brother John; drunkenness and guilt—lust sated and more guilt. His Journals are not the record of a sensitivity complacently and easily paraded. Yet there is something other than the description of depression and the desire for its alleviation. 'What misery does a man of sensibility suffer!' writes Boswell of himself; but if 'misery' was undesirable, 'sensibility' was to be prized.[46] Even as he records his malaise, Boswell recognizes this. On one occasion, after a night during which he has been kept awake by 'sounds which gave me a kind of fear', he gives us this account:

> I got up somewhat gloomy. Knowing that I would be immediately relieved when I got to town, I indulged hypochondria, which I had not felt of a long time. I called up into my fancy ideas of being confined all winter to an old house in the north of Scotland, and being burthened with tedium and gnawed with fretfulness.[47]

Safe in the knowledge that he has the distractions of Edinburgh to look forward to, Boswell abandons himself to meditations which are not simply painful—for the account ends with the reflection, 'As I would not wish to have my body of stone, so I would not wish to have my mind insensible'. If Boswell confesses himself subject to the power of fancy, which exerts itself in the period of melancholy, he does not describe merely a weakness: 'I am a being very much consisting of feelings. I have some fixed principles. But my existence is chiefly conducted by the powers of fancy and sensation.'[48] With his distinctive blend of guilt and candour, he describes his recognition of the ambiguous nature of his hypochondria: 'I did however perceive inwardly, at the very time, that I had a kind of pride in being melancholy and fretful like my grandfather'.[49]

To realize that there is a rhetoric of melancholy, eloquent and habitual, which is not reducible to the symptoms of illness or fatigue is not to doubt the sincerity of Boswell's confessions. It is to recognize that we cannot finally distinguish the experience of what Boswell, in deference to Cheyne, calls his *English malady*[50] from

---

[45] *Boswell: The Ominous Years. 1774-1776*, ed. C. Ryskamp and F.A. Pottle (London, 1963), 158.

[46] Ibid. 250.   [47] Ibid. 54.   [48] Ibid. 97–8.

[49] Ibid. 233.   [50] Ibid. 300.

conventional privileges of learning and sensitivity. David Hume does not just confess privately, in a letter, to the debilitating melancholy induced by 'profound Reflections'; he incorporates the voice of 'philosophical melancholy' in the product of those reflections, his philosophical work. Pausing, in the final Section of Book I of the *Treatise*, 'before I launch out into those immense depths of philosophy, which lie before me', Hume contemplates 'that forelorn solitude, in which I am plac'd in my philosophy' (*Treatise*, p. 264): 'This sudden view of my danger strikes me with melancholy; and as 'tis usual for that passion, above all other, to indulge itself; I cannot forbear feeding my despair, with all those desponding reflections, which the present subject furnishes me with in such abundance.' To set this against Boswell's account of his indulgence of hypochondria is to reveal a common narrative—a narrative which tells of the impediments to that 'commerce and society of men, which is so agreeable' (*Treatise*, p. 270). Boswell's capitulation to fancy, and Hume's to solitary 'reverie', are not pathological instincts: they are rhetorical evidence of a sensitivity which can never quite find satisfaction in the pleasures of society—which is felt to be a burden and a privilege.

I have argued that, in novels of the mid-eighteenth century, the apotheosis of feeling typically involves the representation of sensibility in retreat, segregated from a world impervious to it. Equivalently, the refined or studious hypochondriac is a necessarily exceptional figure, deriving both his status and his 'Distemper' from preoccupations and proclivities which remove him from 'the common People' or 'the ordinary state of human nature'. In novels of sentiment, the domain of sensibility—in Richardson that of a specifically feminine 'correspondence', in Mackenzie a precarious and idealized rural domesticity, in Sterne a knowing rhetorical playfulness—is constituted, in various ways, out of an opposition to a 'world' of masculine desire, commercial endeavour, and material ambition. This type of opposition also defines discussions of hypochondria and melancholy. Symptomatically, David Hume seeks a cure for his 'Distemper', which he sees as induced by 'Study & Idleness', in 'Business & Diversion', in the life and occupations of a 'Merchant'.[51] He writes, either to Cheyne or to Arbuthnot, that he hastens to Bristol with a 'Recommendation to a considerable Trader . . . with a Resolution to forget myself . . . & to toss about the

---

[51] *The Letters of David Hume*, i. 17.

World, from the one Pole to the other, till I leave this Distemper
behind me'.[52] Drawing on the same association, Samuel Johnson tells
Boswell, according to the latter's Journal, that 'employment and
hardships' alone stave off 'hypochondria' and 'madness'. He advises
Boswell to follow his father's career in the law: 'He . . . was of
opinion that I have such a mind that I must have my father's
employment, or one as busy, to preserve me from melancholy. I
must therefore be pretty sure of occupation in London before I venture to settle there.'[53] Outside the 'world' of specifically commercial
and practical activity are hypochondria, melancholy, nervous
disorder—but also sensibility, imagination, delicacy.

Some writers on hypochondria and melancholy, recognizing the
associations between such distempers and postures of reclusive or
specialized sensibility, would admonish any who permit themselves
such an indulgence. The unknown author of *A Treatise on the
Dismal Effects of Low-Spiritedness* of 1750, gravely warning of the
dangers of 'Vapours, Hippo, and Spleen', inveighs against their
'fashionable' status, seeing the forms of 'Indisposition' for which
they stand as rooted in a certain 'Laziness', a failure to become
properly involved in a world of business and trade, conversation
and resolve.[54] What in other texts is rendered as a necessary or at
least sensitive strategy is here described as damaging and morally
disreputable. Thirty years earlier, John Midriff, discussing cases of
'Spleen and Vapours' induced by the collapse of shares in the South
Sea Company in those financially involved, and despite his close
association of financial speculation *per se* with fear and delusion,
writes of a person whom he has treated, 'This Gentleman has been a
Valetudinarian from his Youth, which proceeded from a natural
Indolence, that ought to have been broke and overcome by
Business'.[55] If this is a moralism, it is a good deal more reticent than
the unattributed *Treatise on . . . Low-Spiritedness*. The more
exhortative attacks on the fashion of hypochondria are found in
texts written by men religiously employed and, by their own

[52] *The Letters of David Hume*, i. 18.
[53] *Boswell in Extremes: 1776–1778*, ed. C. Weis and F.A. Pottle (London, 1971),
169.
[54] *A Treatise on the Dismal Effects of Low-Spiritedness* (London, 1750), 22.
[55] John Midriff, *Observations on the Spleen and Vapours: Containing Remarkable
Cases of Persons of both Sexes, and all Ranks, from the aspiring Directors to the
humble Bubbler, who have been miserably afflicted with those melancholy Disorders
since the Fall of South-Sea and other publick Stocks* (London, 1721), 9.

accounts, religiously motivated. These texts, not written by physicians but committed to the vocabulary of symptoms and cures, continue to be produced until as late as the 1780s.[56] An early example is John Moore's *Of Religious Melancholy*, of 1692. In this work, which had reached its seventh edition by 1708, Moore, recently installed as Bishop of Norwich, understands melancholy in terms of preoccupations with redemption, sin, and religious duty, but also as a peculiar temptation. Against this temptation he writes, 'I exhort you not to quit your employment . . . For no business at all is as bad for you as too much: and there is always more Melancholy to be found in a Cloyster, than in the Market-place.'[57] These warnings are resumed, though perhaps not with such ideological clarity, by Edward Synge, Archbishop of Tuam, in Ireland, in his *Sober Thoughts for the Cure of Melancholy*, published in 1742: 'One Caution I must . . . give to all who are inclin'd to Melancholy; which is, that they never indulge, but always strive against it. For, although the Beginning of it to many has been very pleasant; yet, where it prevails, it seldom fails to turn into Bitterness.'[58] Discussions of nervous disorder, hypochondria, and melancholy are, for most of the century, shadowed by images of the pleasures and privileges that might come with such supposed afflictions. The pleasures and privileges are typically associated with kinds of retreat, variously rendered as evidence of 'Indolence' or of 'Sensibility', from worldly ambition and commercial activity.

So when Cheyne writes to Richardson 'you are a genuine Hyppo now with all its plainest Symptoms and Nothing earthly else, and I have told you the only Way on Earth to get rid of it',[59] he implies a compliment to Richardson's faculties of imagination and sensibility, as well as to his own powers of diagnosis. It was to be some time before 'hypochondria' came to indicate, as it does today, the unhealthy concern of a person with his or her imagined ailments. Cheyne is unapologetic about describing himself as a 'Valetudinarian', for to be such is to be especially empowered in the art of a particular kind of diagnosis. It is perhaps not until William Cullen's *First Lines of the Practice of Physick*, first published in 1777, that we find a clear identification of hypochondria in the sense in

---

[56] See Hunter and Macalpine, *Three Hundred Years of Psychiatry*, 253.

[57] Ibid.

[58] Edward Synge, *Sober Thoughts for the Cure of Melancholy* (London, 1742), 4.

[59] *Letters to Richardson*, ed. Mullett, 104: letter of July 1742.

which we now understand it. 'As it is the nature of men to indulge every present emotion, so the hypochondriac cherishes his fears, and, attentive to every feeling, finds in trifles, light as air, a strong confirmation of his apprehensions.'[60] For Cullen, the task of the physician becomes one of diverting the attention of the person being treated 'to other objects than his own feelings'. This task sanctions even the resort to 'the pious fraud of a placebo'.[61] A treatment of self-regarding anxiety that we can recognize.

It is a fact of biography that Richardson was, in this modern sense of the word, a hypochondriac—nervously and consumingly concerned with his own health. His correspondence speaks of his worries about 'nervous tremblings, catchings, and dizziness' and his theories about treatments: 'I have a great opinion of mustard. Be pleased to give me your process as to that.'[62] Cheyne's letters to him sufficiently register what must have been a constant pressure for reassurance. A biographer may plausibly find either sympathy or submerged impatience in the declarations that the physician has to make: 'I am heartily sorry for your continued Lowness and Indisposition which only Time and the Perseverance in the Means and Medicines I have suggested can Remedy'.[63] But more is at stake here than biographical detail. As Klaus Doerner and others have shown, there is, for much of the eighteenth century, a more general relationship between figures of susceptibility and nervous disorder on the one hand, and the conventional status of sensibility on the other. Richardson's 'case-history' illustrates this relationship.

It is not enough simply to see the interest in these forms of susceptibility as unthreatened signs of a fashion. Contradictions emerge not just in the representation of male hypochondria, but also in the discussions of hysteria, the depictions of feminine sensibility and disorder. There is no real symmetry between hypochondria and hysteria. The afflicted and yet self-consciously privileged 'Valetudinarian', armed with the fastidiously accumulated details of a specialized autobiography, never speaks with a woman's voice. The woman is, and continues into the nineteenth century to be, the object of a male scrutiny which is by turns suspicious, enraptured,

---

[60] William Cullen, *First Lines of the Practice of Physic* (3rd edn., 4 vols., Edinburgh, 1781-4) iii. 137.

[61] Ibid. 136.

[62] Letter to Rev. Skelton, Mar. 1751: Barbauld, v. 205.

[63] *Letters to Richardson*, ed. Mullett, 98: letter of May 1742.

and dismissive. Older dispensations according to which the woman is represented as inherently liable to internal disorder are constantly revisited and recomposed through the century. Robert Whytt, for example, in his *Observations* of 1765, writes at a time when ideas of the 'wandering womb' have long since been dismissed from the physician's repertoire, and rejects the description of 'the hysteric' and 'the hypochondriac disease' as 'different diseases'.[64] But then he writes this:

> It is true that in women, hysteric symptoms occur more frequently, and are often much more sudden and violent, than the hypochondriac in men; but this circumstance, which is only a consequence of the more delicate frame, sedentary life, and particular condition of the womb in women, by no means shews the two diseases to be, strictly speaking, different.[65]

The woman is still peculiarly 'delicate', still peculiarly subject to a disorder which cannot be dissociated from her reproductive capacities. The great majority of cases which Whytt produces as examples are of the abnormalities of female behaviour and affliction. 'WOMEN, in whom the nervous system is generally more moveable than in men, are more subject to nervous complaints, and have them in a higher degree.'[66] A putative feminine 'sensibility' exists on the edge of an abyss which is 'the too great sensibility of the nervous system', the excess which is dangerous affliction. The woman's body, collapsing or beyond control, is the very register of disorder: 'MANY hysteric women are liable to be seized with faintings, during which they lie as in a deep sleep . . . Others, along with faintings of this kind, are affected with catchings and strong convulsions.'[67] Not merely a precarious 'sensibility', but an inordinate suggestibility: 'It has frequently happened, in the Royal Infirmary here, that women have been seized with hysteric fits from seeing others attacked with them'.[68] Whytt, the physician of the Enlightenment, repeats, according to changing constraints, the old formulae.

But even within some such formulae is the hint of hesitation or ambivalence. If sensibility can be considered as the sign of a privileged susceptibility—to pain and to pleasure—then the

---

[64] Robert Whytt, *Observations on the Nature, Causes, and Cure of those Disorders which have been commonly call'd Nervous, Hypochondriac, or Hysteric* (Edinburgh, 1765), 10.

[65] Ibid. 105.   [66] Ibid. 118.   [67] Ibid. 231.   [68] Ibid. 215.

condescension of the physicians as they work and rework a picture of hysteria comes to seem problematic and perhaps anxious. Even in Bernard Mandeville's early *Treatise of the Hypochondriack and Hysterick Passions*, a work scarcely sophisticated in comparison to that of Whytt, and one which has little time for the pleasures of such 'Passions', we read that women 'are more capable both of Pleasure and Pain, tho' endued with less constancy of bearing the excess of either'.[69] Women are such that 'the Passions make greater impressions upon them, and sooner discompose their Bodies'. It is 'their tenderness' which disposes them 'to be Hysterick'.[70] In many of the novels of the eighteenth century which elevate sentiment, and most notably in *Clarissa* and *Sir Charles Grandison*, the investment in sensibility is an investment in a particular version of the feminine—tearful, palpitating, embodying virtue whilst susceptible to all the vicissitudes of 'feeling'. The very vocabulary which Richardson, for instance, uses in his delineation of this femininity and this resilient virtue is, at some points, exactly the vocabulary characteristic of eighteenth-century descriptions of hysteria: tenderness, sensibility, delicacy, disorder. Richardson deploys these terms in his portrayal of the woman as the object of an appalled and yet titillated scrutiny, and as the impossible paragon of virtue, the 'angel' that is Clarissa. Indeed, this investment in an image of femininity is such that some have seen *Clarissa* as a type of proto-feminist narrative, or at least as evidence of some 'feminization' of values'.[71] Terry Eagleton, having suggested that Richardson's novels are representative of a 'feminization of discourse'[72] qualifies his model of ideological effect: 'The "exaltation" of women, while undoubtedly a partial advance in itself, also serves to shore up the very system which oppresses them'.[73] This qualification refers us to the distinctive mythologizing of virtue in Richardson's novels; in the case of *Clarissa* figured in a silent and impossible femininity which triumphs only in death. The extrapolation from this construction of femininity of any proto-feminist political argument is a hazardous business.

Indeed, sensibility, for Richardson, is poised on the edge of excess;

---

[69] Bernard Mandeville, *A Treatise of the Hypochondriack and Hysterick Passions* (London, 1711), 176.

[70] Ibid. 175.

[71] T. Eagleton, *The Rape of Clarissa* (Oxford, 1982), 14.

[72] Ibid. 13.   [73] Ibid. 15.

this is particularly evident in the book which Richardson wrote in the attempt to construct a specifically masculine virtue, *Sir Charles Grandison*. Clementina's delirium and Laurana's suicidal despair are different forms of sensibility become excess. Pages of this novel read as if exploiting the categories and clichés employed throughout the century by those who write on hysteria. At one stage, Sir Charles writes from Italy to describe Clementina's 'malady', of which she declares herself to be 'sensible': 'Her eyes had then lost all that lustre which had shewn a too raised imagination: But they were as much in the other extreme, overclouded with mistiness, dimness, vapours; swimming in tears . . . These are usual turns of the malady' (*Sir Charles Grandison*, ii. 525). The male observes and diagnoses a self-conscious affliction, whose cause is also the promise of its cure: 'The Marchioness and I were extremely affected by her great behaviours: But tho' we were grieved for the pain her sensibility gave her, yet we could not but console and congratulate ourselves upon it, as affording hopes of her perfect recovery' (ii. 526). The drama of an afflicted feminine sensibility is played out as a repertoire of recognizable symptoms. The woman's sensibility is still privileged; in this case the narrative is laden with remarks about Clementina's 'greatness', her virtue and her perfect delicacy, about which the denizens of the Grandison drawing-room all agree. But her sensibility also leads, in particular circumstances—her Italian family and friends, her Catholicism—to temporary infirmity and delirium: 'O these hysterical disorders!' cries her governess, 'They tear her tender constitution in pieces' (ii. 568). She has been forced, by her very sensitivities, into what Richardson, using the old synonym for hysteria, has Sir Charles refer to as 'vapours'.

Sir Charles Grandison's letters from Italy in which he reports his diagnosis of, and his attempts to cure, Clementina's 'noble' malady perhaps constitute the clearest example of a literature quite directly informed by myths of the hysterical proclivities of women prominent in the writings of eighteenth-century physicians. But more importantly, they are further indication of the ambiguous status of sensibility, of a susceptibility which is part of the language of the physician as much as of the novelist. In one way, after all, the point of the representation, by Richardson and others, of sensibility as feminine is precisely its removal from the domain of power, action, availability. The preoccupation with hysteria as a disorder of women repeats itself through the writings of many of the authors whom I have already mentioned with an insistence which is testimony of this ambiguous status. Even comparatively late in the century, there is scarcely a separation between vocabularies of 'feeling' and 'passion', on the one hand, and of anatomically considered mechanism, on the other. In 1768, William Smith writes that, in women, 'variety of the quickness of the pulse, in a healthy state, is owing to the sensibility of the nerves in general'.[74] Susceptibility is naturalized in the coherence of the body. It is particularly the body of the woman to which the attention of the physician is drawn in order to describe the effects of passion and affection: 'Nothing produces more sudden or surprising changes in the body, than violent affections of the mind . . . Sometimes violent passions have thrown delicate women into a kind of . . . catalepsy.'[75] As women are supposed peculiarly susceptible to 'passion', so the control exercised by the spectatorial scrutiny of the (male) physician is threatened by the logic of his own construction; by, in the case of Smith's *Dissertation upon the Nerves*, the suggestion of an unknown pleasure—the woman's possibly subversive enjoyment of those palpitations which have been ascribed to her as the sign of her 'disorder'. As Michel Foucault writes, preserving almost too diligently the problematic relation between control and anxiety in eighteenth-century writings on hysteria, 'The entire female body is riddled by obscure but strangely direct paths of sympathy; it is always in an immediate complicity with itself, to the point of forming a kind of absolutely privileged site for the sympathies; from one extremity of its organic space to the other, it encloses a perpetual possibility of hysteria.'[76] This 'sympathetic sensibility of her organism' condemns the woman to the vapours.

Following the same logic as that which associated hypochondria with reclusiveness or scholarly obsession, women are declared to be more prone than men to nervous disorder because they are supposed to lead sedentary lives uninvolved in activity and the business of acquisition, and yet rich in the experience of 'Luxury'. Cheyne writes to Richardson in January 1742, 'I hope Mrs Richardson is not like the rest of her Sex or Kindred known to me who I fear would rather renounce Life than Luxury'. The renunciation of 'Luxury' was

---

[74] Smith, *A Dissertation upon the Nerves*, 147–8.   [75] Ibid. 176.
[76] Michel Foucault, *Madness and Civilization*, trans. Richard Howard (1967; rpt. London, 1977), 153–4.

evidently compulsory for the female members of the Cheyne household: 'My Female Family have been almost all forced into that Method to cure nervous and hysteric Disorder'.[77] The exclusion of the wives and daughters of the ruling class from economic activity and from the management of assets outside a narrow domestic realm has the unwarranted effect of rendering them more liable to such 'Disorders'. These, of course, are, like the domestic roles themselves, naturalized as unalterable dispositions. And as women are also excluded from the very language of symptom and diagnosis, they can even be held responsible for models of aetiology which are found wanting. So, James's *Medicinal Dictionary*, having defined hysteria as 'a spasmodico-convulsive Affection of the nervous kind, proceeding from a Retention or Corruption of Lymph, or Blood, in the uterine Vessels, which . . . influences all the nervous Parts of the Body', and having described the 'suffocating Interception of Respiration' to which it leads, writes 'whence many Women idly imagine, that the Womb ascends towards the Throat'.[78] The idle fancies of women are responsible, somehow, even for the outmoded models according to which their 'Disorders' have been constructed. They are not to be trusted to know their own bodies.

For the eighteenth-century practitioner of 'Physick', the female body is construed, like the bodies of Richardson's heroines, as an ever-visible corpus of signs given over to their practice of interpretation, but can also testify to the worrying obscurity of passion and imagination. Those who write to stress their claim as, precisely, practitioners—rather than theoreticians—tend particularly to emphasize the visibility of feminine disorder. Thomas Dover, in 1732, writes, 'I shall enter only on Hysterical Effects, because they are more common, and more visible in the finer Sex'.[79] This man's vaunted years of experience lead him to propose that 'the fair Sex' are more liable than men even to those types of 'distemper' not in themselves hysteric. This is because 'they are of a much finer Texture of Body than Men, they are more subject to the Passions of the Mind, which have often been the Cause of this Distemper'.[80] Dover is talking about 'Dropsy'. Richard Manningham, knighted by

---

[77] *Letters to Richardson*, ed. Mullett, 82.

[78] James, *Dictionary*, s.v. 'HYSTERICA'.

[79] Thomas Dover, *The Ancient Physician's Legacy to his Country* (London, 1732), 60.

[80] Ibid. 26.

George I and most famous 'man-midwife' of his day, similarly concentrates on a female display of symptoms when he discusses what is 'commonly called the *nervous* or *hysteric* Fever'. 'The *chief* of my Practice, indeed, has been among the *Female* Sex, who are generally of more *tender* and delicate Constitutions; and therefore such as are always *most* liable to this Sort of Fever.'[81] Nicholas Robinson, in his *New System of the Spleen, Vapours, and Hypochondriack Melancholy* of 1729, draws parallels between male 'Hypochondria' and female 'Hystericks', but almost all his actual descriptions of the appearance of the body are of women—visibly heaving, sweating, or palpitating.[82] The physician interested in the 'nerves' most often observes women.

The supposedly precarious condition of a feminine sensibility is sometimes rendered as a generic fickleness, an inconstancy seemingly designed to dupe even the physician himself. Nicholas Robinson declares that he shall confine his 'Observations' to 'the Fair Sex' on account of the fact that 'those Fits, vulgarly call'd the Hysterick Disease, are more frequently observ'd to affect their Habit, either from a stronger Impulse of their Passions, or a finer texture of their Nerves',[83] and proceeds to describe women suffering from this 'Disease' as 'constant to nothing but Inconstancy; always wavering, unsteady'.[84] James possibly draws upon this particular passage for the comment in his *Dictionary* that women suffering from hysteria 'know no Moderation, and are constant only in Inconstancy'.[85] In her article 'The Pregnant Pamela', Dolores Peters writes, 'A weak constitution rendered women's bodies and minds susceptible to disorder. Behaviour was intimately connected with anatomical susceptibility, and in some cases even determined by physiological disruption. Sensibility to disease frequently resulted in fickleness.'[86] But, as constituted in the study of hysteria, the female body is not merely 'connected' with disorder, it is the very visibility, at once the form and the formlessness, of that disorder. Because of the shifting nature of sensibility, both privilege and ailment, refinement and excess, this trembling body is appropriated by

[81] Richard Manningham, *The Symptoms, Nature, Causes, and Cure of the Febricula, or Little Fever* (London, 1746), pp. iv–v.

[82] Nicholas Robinson, *A New System of the Spleen, Vapours and Hypochondriack Melancholy* (London, 1729), 305.

[83] Ibid. 211–12.   [84] Ibid. 214.

[85] James, *Dictionary*, s.v. 'HYSTERICA'.

[86] D. Peters, 'The Pregnant Pamela', *Eighteenth-Century Studies*, 14 (1981).

eighteenth-century novelists, male and female, as the sign of a sentimental extravagance which may be either stubbornly virtuous or manifestly debilitating.

The ambiguity is preserved in the category of 'Imagination'. This faculty is not to be found 'in the rustick and meaner sort of person'.[87] But as it can mark an elevated status, so, in women, it can also bring about peculiar and obscure patterns of disruption. Under the heading 'IMAGINATIO', James's *Dictionary* provides at least three dozen supposed illustrations, drawn from other medical writings, to support his contention that 'The Desire . . . of the pregnant Woman is capable of marking the tender Infant with the Thing desired'. The entry in the *Dictionary* is, in fact, concerned *solely* with the dangers to which the pregnancy woman, always subject to 'the Power of the *Imagination* or *Fancy*', exposes her offspring. The improper and volatile 'Desire' raised in the woman by reading the wrong books or thinking the wrong thoughts intervenes in the process of the reproduction of a social order. The representation of pregnancy as incapacity, weakness, or illness is not, of course, unique to the period under discussion. At various times concerns with the reproduction of social order have manifested themselves in myths of pregnancy as a mysterious ailment. Such myths are still with us. What is peculiar about ideas of 'imagination' and female disorder in the early and middle eighteenth century is the relation between privilege and affliction, the ambiguity of sensibility.

As Foucault indicates, for example, a common theme of eighteenth-century writings on nervous disorder is the description of the arousal of imaginary desires, and thus the provocation of nervous ailments, through attendance at the theatre and the reading of novels.[88] Both physicians and novelists suppose women to be particularly prone to these diversions and these dangers. Whytt, indeed, gives as one of the characteristic causes of 'violent affections of the mind' in women the narration of 'doleful, or moving stories' which can 'often throw the person into hysteric fits, either of the convulsive or fainting kind'.[89] Women are supposed more susceptible than men to the persuasive powers of all forms of

[87] G. Baglivi, *The Practice of Physick*, translated from the Latin edition of 1696 (London, 1704), 178.

[88] Foucault, *Madness and Civilization*, 167.

[89] Whytt, *Observations*, 212.

narration and imaginative or illustrative fabrication; the dangers of
the reading which a woman undertakes were still considered worthy
of discussion in Pinel's *Genital Neuroses of Women* of 1798.[90] And
yet, in the works of novelists such as Mackenzie, Henry Brooke,
Sarah Fielding, and Richardson, the readiness to become excited and
affected by narratives of misfortune and suffering is a crucial sign of
the integrity of sentiment. To be sure, the very narratives which
celebrate sensibility and the willingness to shed a tear over a sorry
tale also, notably in the case of Richardson, warn against the lure
and dangers to young women of 'Romances'. But the distinction
between the flush of an improper excitement and the virtuous blush
of an entranced sensibility is a difficult and shifting one.

This is not to say that even upper-class women of the eighteenth
century are in any simple sense privileged over their fathers,
husbands, and sons. The figures of feminine susceptibility and
delicacy are not invented for the purposes of any political protest or
criticism. In general terms, the elevation of sensibility features in a
retreat from the implications of social difference and distinction,
from changing patterns of ownership and ambition; this retreat may
occasionally be idealistic, but it is never deliberately subversive.
Feminine sensibility is a *construction*. The novels which use it as an
incarnation of alienated sensitivity are not reports on social
conditions, and resist reduction to social history. If Clarissa's letters
were actually the letters of a young woman of the mid-eighteenth
century, we would have a document which was perhaps more
transparent and more radical, but not necessarily more significant.
For in both the novel and the description of hysteria, the
construction of femininity is not merely narrowly prescriptive—the
form of control and legislation—but also something less
authoritative: a wavering effort to construe value and significance.

In the myth of feminine sensibility are concentrated a culture's
anxieties about its capacity for sociability. Woman is made
metaphor. So it is misguided to read a text like *Clarissa* as an
innovating critique of sexual politics. Nor does it seem possible to
describe a satisfactory or convincing relation between the writings
on hysteria and the literature of sensibility in terms of the apparent
symptoms of 'characters' in certain of the works of that literature.
This type of description is sometimes attempted:

90 See Veith, *Hysteria*, 179.

Surely it was fashionable to be melancholic . . . Thus all types of socially mobile women, such as Moll Flanders in Defoe's novel, Miss Harlowe in Richardson's *Clarissa Harlowe*, and Elizabeth Bennett in Austen's *Pride and Prejudice* . . . may have developed their melancholy for purely social reasons, as 'signs' in the semiotic sense of a certain class consciousness, unaware that they were 'contracting' the awful condition.[91]

The notion of a character's conscious and unconscious motivations will only be a poor substitute for an analysis of what is a literary convention bespeaking a cultural obsession.

Whilst I have suggested that the function of categorizations of feminine disorder is not simply legislative (that these categorizations also evidence what Max Byrd would call 'fascination'), it is the case that where categories are threatened from within they often turn to the performance of legislative functions. As has already been mentioned with reference to Robert James's *Dictionary*, the (sometimes self-styled) physicians of the eighteenth century turn to admonition, especially the implied admonition of women, from the contradictions of their own constructions, the obscurities of their own myths. Thus the writer of the *Treatise on the Dismal Effects of Low-Spiritedness* unequivocally declares that each member of 'the Fair Sex' has a responsibility to reject 'Low-Spiritedness', as 'it is a physical Truth, as evident as the Sun, that the Mother must necessarily communicate to her Child, whatever Habits and Affections are predominant in her Disposition, at the Time of her Conception and Pregnancy'.[92] This is a habitually pessimistic rhetoric, though. For the condition of the woman which reveals itself in hysteria is, as characteristically described, an immutable fact of her nature. Diet and occupation may, as some writers suggest, be amended, but, for these same writers, some 'facts' cannot.

The primary fact in the aetiology of hysteria is menstruation. Doubtless Mandeville is repeating older slogans when he writes that

the want of Spirits in Hysterick Women may often be imputed to their Diet; in which the generality of them commit so many Errors: But besides these their idle Life, and want of Exercise likewise dispose them to the Disease, but above all the innumerable disorders, which upon account of the Menstrual Flux, and the whole *Uterus* they are so often subject to.[93]

---

[91] G.S. Rousseau, *Ferment of Knowledge*, 205.
[92] *A Treatise on the Dismal Effects of Low-Spiritedness*, 43.
[93] Mandeville, 172.

But as reference to the uterus disappears from discussions of hysteria through the century, menstruation is preserved as cause—and implicitly sign—of disorder. The irregularity or cessation of menstruation leads to nervous disruption. John Ball writes that when 'in the decline of life the menses cease, various nervous or hysteric symptoms appear', and bleeding and purges will be necessary.[94] William Cullen subordinates his discussion of the 'Interruption of the Menstrual Flux' to a general and lengthy section on 'Hemorrhagies', but still returns to 'Hysteria': 'In the female sex . . . the time at which it most readily occurs is that of the menstrual period'.[95] Pierre Pomme, in his *Traité des Affections Vaporeuses des Deux Sexes*, first translated into English in 1777, writes that 'The hysteric paroxism generally precedes the time of menstruation'.[96] The association between menstruation and hysteria is exactly that: not a clearly defined causal sequence, but an area of susceptibilities and equivalences. Menstruation is represented as an irregularity which takes the guise of a regularity; it is especially likely to signify a precarious condition in the bodies of those for whom womanhood does not mean the life of the fertile, domesticated, married female. Those particularly at risk are the unmarried, the ageing, and the sexually precocious. In his *Medical Precepts and Cautions* of 1751, Richard Mead begins his section 'Of the diseases of women' with 'those, which are often the consequences of a single life'.[97] Inevitably, 'the most frequent' of these is '*suppression of the menstrual discharges*'.

If the woman is to be cured, then, the most popular prescription is marriage. In discussing hysteria, so 'vexatious to the fair sex', John Ball acknowledges the necessity of returning to an old solution : 'if the patient be single and of a proper age, the advice of Hippocrates should be followed, who wisely says, that a *woman's best remedy is to marry, and bear children*',[98] while Baglivi suggests that 'Diseases arising from Passions of the Mind' are liable to be cured by 'Matrimony alone'.[99] In James's *Dictionary*, 'Women fit for

[94] John Ball, *The Female Physician; or, Every Woman her own Doctor* (London, 1771), 8.

[95] Cullen, *First Lines of . . . the Practice of Physic*, iii. 376.

[96] Pierre Pomme, *A Treatise on Hysterical and Hypochondriacal Disease* (London, 1777), 15.

[97] Richard Mead, *Medical Precepts and Cautions* (London, 1751), 280.

[98] Ball, *The Female Physician*, 11.

[99] Baglivi, *The Practice of Physick*, 179.

Marriage, and as yet strangers to the Matrimonial State' are particularly subject to 'the most violent Delirium'.[1] Whatever alleviating herbs, drugs, and applications might be listed, 'There still remains another highly natural and Efficacious Method of Cure, which is, that to be expected from Marriage. Reason, Experience, and the Authorities of the greatest Physicians, concur in pronouncing Matrimony highly beneficial in removing Hysteric Disorders.'[2]

Images of marriage as the resolving institution of a moral and material economy are prevalent in many different kinds of writing throughout the eighteenth century, and are crucial to the form of what we now call the novel. But in one way, the apparent ideological transparency of the emphasis upon marriage as resolution or cure is just too convenient. For, in the novel of sentiment or the discussion of hysteria, it accompanies an emphasis upon the young, unmarried female: repository of virtue, necessary cipher in the arrangement of inheritance and connection, bearer of possibly inordinate desires and unregulated passions. The most famous apotheosis of sensibility, *Clarissa*, of course ends without marriage—with the very impossibility of marriage. This is not because Richardson was seeking to criticize an institution. It is rather that the apotheosis of sensibility involves disturbance and excitation: the struggle of virtue. Sensibility is aroused through suffering, through narratives of others' misfortunes, and through the very impediments to the exercise of virtue. The body of the young woman, unresolved into matrimonial stability, becomes the site of an encounter between sentiment and adversity, the space in which sensibility can become visible. There is a general sense in which all narrative must necessarily proceed from types of disturbance upon which any resolution is predicated. In the novels of Richardson, Mackenzie, and others narrative is structured according to the excitement of sensibility by that which would seek to destroy it (male desire, acquisitiveness, worldly ambition). Such novels make a particular investment in the figure of a precarious and vulnerable condition, that of the young unmarried woman. They do not do so to construct any coherent opposition to themes of settlement, but because the specialization of sentiment and the triumph of sensibility can be traced only in an impossible movement of retreat, only outside the

---

[1] James, *Dictionary*, s.v. 'MANIA'. [2] Ibid., s.v. 'HYSTERICA'.

possibilities of certain kinds of settlement. The paradox, of course, is that to concentrate upon the palpitating, sensitized body of the woman caught in the difficult area between childhood and marriage is also to concede the dangers of this condition—those dangers which feature, in another form, in writings on hysteria. 'Sensible' virtue exists alongside the possible excess of sensibility, the threat of delirium, the dangers and delusions to which young women are subject who read too many 'romances'.

More is at stake, then, than a transcription of the terms of a 'medical' analysis in any of the novels of the period. It is at the level of such putative transcription that G.S. Rousseau offers a connection between the medical and the literary: 'Eighteenth-century literature is permeated with examples of women whose imaginations are "diseased", thereby illustrating more than casual interest of the literary man in the medical theories of the day'.[3] But what else do these 'examples' illustrate? They reveal the deeper equivalence of the different strategies operated by narratives and by 'medical' texts in the production of femininity. This femininity is on the edge of excess, exhibiting the precariousness of sensibility. The specialization of this femininity always returns to the construction of the body, the only possible object of the physician's scrutiny and, for the novelists, the only space where feeling can articulate itself unhampered by the spoken word.

Models of a sensitized body reach a higher level of sophistication in the 1760s and 1770s with the development of schemes of nervous organization. Throughout the century, however, the concept of 'sensibility' underpins observations of the body's internal integrity. It is 'sensibility', connoting both the involuntary action of organs and muscles and the susceptibility of men and women to shocks of passion or disappointment, which, in excess of anatomy, allows internal disorder to become observable. Disorder is represented in terms of an understanding of the body's order; but order is perceivable only in each manifestation of disorder. Mediating these two terms is 'sensibility'. Christopher Lawrence describes how Edinburgh physicians of the mid-century use the concept of sensibility

to provide a physiological and anatomical basis for one of their primary concerns, overall integration of the body functioning. This they did by using

[3] G.S. Rousseau, 'Science and the Discovery of the Imagination in Enlightened England', *Eighteenth-Century Studies*, 3 (1969).

the notion of 'sympathy'—which was no more than the communication of feeling between different bodily organs, manifested by functional disturbance of one organ when another was stimulated . . . Whytt was the first to give the term clearly defined structural and functional significance.[4]

It is through 'disturbance' that correspondence and organization reveal themselves. 'Sympathy' is the principle of coherence of those signs which possess the body to reveal the effects of passion and feeling.

But before Whytt, less clearly defined models of the body's coherence support discussions of hypochondria and hysteria. For Nicholas Robinson, it is in the internal coherence and 'Elasticity' of the body's structure that are found the true form and the true cause of intelligible 'Emotions'. For him, the ambiguous 'Elevation' of the 'Mind' depends upon the state of 'a System of Veins, Nerves, and Arteries': 'All those sublime Flights and extatick Visions, that elevate the Soul above itself, whereby it towers above the Clouds . . . owe their rise to this due Modulation of the Solids, to this happy structure of the Fibres.'[5] To confront unnatural or dangerous desires is to confront the body. For 'these strange and unusual Desires arise only from a perverted Motion of the Solids and Fluids . . . for if, by proper Applications, you recover these bodily Organs to their regular Standard again, these unnatural Desires, and strange unusual Fancies will vanish of their own Accord.'[6] The very standards of regularity enable the staging of an irregularity. Whytt writes 'we know certainly, that the nerves are endued with feeling, and that there is a general sympathy which prevails through the whole system; so there is a particular and very remarkable *consent* between various parts of the body'.[7] It is this 'sympathy' which integrates all parts of the body and allows the 'nervous disorder', which may originate in the most obscure recess of the body, to declare itself as a repertoire of signs. Yet, unlike physicians such as Stukely, Whytt asserts that 'the causes of nervous diseases' cannot always be reduced to anatomy—that in some cases 'no . . . morbid appearances have been observed in the body after death; it follows, that these symptoms may frequently proceed from causes, which,

---

[4] C. Lawrence, 'The Nervous System and Society in the Scottish Enlightenment', in B. Barnes and S. Shapin (eds.), *Natural Order: Historical Studies of Scientific Culture* (London, 1979), 27.

[5] Robinson, *A New System*, 56–7.   [6] Ibid. 69–70.

[7] Whytt, *Observations*, p. v.

eluding our senses, are not to be discovered by dissection'.[8] Whytt
has moved away from the account of the discoloured, decomposed,
or enlarged internal organ, produced as proof by the triumphant
dissectionist.[9] But still sensibility is revealed in what is at once the
discomposure and the coherence of the body's organization.

R.K. French describes Whytt's principle of 'general sympathy' as
'not a mechanism of bodily co-ordination as was the specific
sympathy, but an "awareness" of the sensible parts of the body by
each other':[10] that is, a principle of coherence which registers special
sensitivities and possible disorder. So 'nervous diseases' are regarded
as forms of 'pathological sympathy': 'it was by his rationalized
scheme of sympathy that his nervous diseases would be examined'.[11]
Sympathy is instrumental in the articulation of disorder, in the
iterability of its signs. Foucault characterizes this well: 'Diseases of
the nerves are essentially disorders of sympathy; they presuppose a
state of general vigilance in the nervous system which makes each
organ susceptible of entering in to sympathy with any other'.[12]
Disorder, in other words, is not that which is excluded, denied, or
censored for the sake of order. On the contrary, disorder and order,
susceptibility and nervous organization, are absolutely complicit,
each incomplete and unclear without the other. Disorder is not to be
repressed but to be coaxed into every possible expression, to be
endlessly discussed and recomposed, to be the topic for a fashion of
writing. The 'vigilance in the nervous system' is one version of the
body's readiness to offer up signs of passion, confirmations of
sensibility. This is a readiness which figures crucially in the novel of
sentiment, in a histrionic enactment whose special power is to
suggest that virtuous sensibility can finally be rescued from the
dangers of excess.

The novelists of sentiment and the writers on hypochondria and
hysteria have in common not merely a certain (voguish) vocabulary
('sensibility', 'sympathy', 'delicacy', 'passion'), but also a concern
with the organization of the body. The vocabulary which, in the
novels of Richardson or Mackenzie, refers a reader to the capacity to
experience and communicate ennobling feelings is employed, in the
language of the physicians, to describe the very workings of the

[8] Whytt, *Observations*, 222–3.
[9] For the influence of such an account see James, *Dictionary*, s.v. 'MANIA'.
[10] R.K. French, *Robert Whytt, the Soul, and Medicine* (London, 1969), 36.
[11] Ibid. 41–2.   [12] Foucault, *Madness and Civilization*, 153.

body. Equally, for a number of novelists, the privileging of sentiments over words depends on the body's expressiveness—its eloquence surpassing habits of inarticulacy, dissension, and compromise. The sensibility which is a privilege and the sensibility which might manifest itself in the disorder of internal organs are not to be separated. Christopher Lawrence emphasizes the fact that this deployment of 'terms such as "sensibility" and "susceptibility to impressions"' is directly facilitated by changing schemes of the body's organization. He describes how, by the middle of the century, notions of the body as 'a complicated hydraulic machine', employed most influentially by Boerhaave, had been displaced by ideas of 'the nervous system'.[13] But quite early in the century 'Nerves', though still thought of as the infinitely narrow avenues for the 'animal spirits', provide the organizing concept which makes homogeneous the body's set of effects. In Blackmore's *Treatise* of 1725, for example, the condition of the spleen is held responsible for hypochondria because in the spleen is to be found a concentration of 'Nerves'. So

when it is it self distempered, and contains inordinate, austere, and too acrid Juices, it may stimulate the Nerves dispersed through its Substance, and agitate the animal Spirits their Inmates, and so drive them into irregular and convulsive Motions, yet this is no more than what is common with it to all the rest of the Bowels, and less important Parts of the Body.[14]

The nervous connection of different parts and organs produces the body as an analysable whole. It makes sense of the scope of its sensitization. It is because of this connection that those 'irregular Flights and Agitations, as are observed in Hypochondriacal Patients' generate decipherable symptoms. Robinson in 1729 also describes a body articulated through a system of 'Nervose Fibres'. Disorder comes with 'a too great Dilation of the nervose Machinulae', when 'the Fibres of every Muscle are let down beneath their natural Standard'.[15] Despite Stukely's emphasis on the condition of the blood, for him too the 'nerves' play an important role in the making visible of an internal 'rebellion and misrule'. The nerves link the internal to the external, the 'bowels' to what is 'cognoscible in the face'.[16] Whether the 'nerves' vibrate or carry the 'animal spirits';

---

13 Lawrence, 'The Nervous System and Society', 25.
14 Blackmore, *A Treatise of the Spleen and Vapours*, 11.
15 Robinson, *A New System* 258.   16 Stukely, *Of the Spleen*, 76.

whether such 'spirits' are reckoned detectable or invisible: these are not for me the crucial issues.[17] Early theories of nervous organization are not identical, but all attempt to describe a body unified in its sensitivities. Every habit, every strain, every shock, must have its physiological equivalent.

Christopher Lawrence writes that, by the middle of the century, the 'physiological theory' of what he refers to as 'Scottish medicine' 'was characterized by its stress on the total integration of body function, the perceptive capacity or sensibility of the organism, and a preoccupation with the nervous system as the structural basis for these properties'.[18] More specifically, though, the 'nervous system' allows the body to be represented as, quite literally, a signifying system. Across the surface of this body are pursued the traces of speechless excitement and the premonitions of collapse. More often than not, these evidence passion—and here the ambiguity of what can be a resource or an affliction is repeated. Passion, visible in bodily symptoms, is no more indicative simply of disruption than sensibility is indicative purely of unnecessary weakness. Books on 'Regimen' in the eighteenth century conventionally name 'the Passions' (along with 'Air', 'Diet', and 'Exercise') as a category of the body's experience, and expect the individual who seeks health to moderate them precisely because they cannot be suppressed. John Armstrong's *The Art of Preserving Health*, for example, presumes that passion is a natural condition which must be regulated. It 'Inspires with health, or mines with strange decay / The passive body'.[19] Passion is not in itself disease, but it can produce the body's disorder.

Throughout eighteenth-century texts on hypochondria and hysteria, passion moves in complicity with bodily sensitivity and with internal mechanisms of cause and effect. Robinson analyses the phenomenon of nervous collapse thus: 'These Fits generally proceed from great Grief, Disappointments, unsuccessful attempts in Love, or some other huge Passion, that was too mighty for the weakly Mortal to encounter . . . they argue a Defect of Motion in the Blood

---

[17] But for discussion of them see E. Clarke, 'The Doctrine of the Hollow Nerve in the Seventeenth and Eighteenth Centuries', in L.G. Stevenson and R.P. Multhauf (eds.), *Medicine, Science and Culture* (Baltimore Md., 1968), and J.D. Spillane, *The Doctrine of the Nerves* (Oxford, 1981).

[18] Lawrence, 'The Nervous System and Society', 19.

[19] Dr John Armstrong, *The Art of Preserving Health* (London, 1744), Bk. IV, ll. 3-7.

of some principal Organ'.[20] Foucault for once seems to obscure the distinct ambiguity of passion for such writers when, describing how they treated madness as a disease 'of the body *and* of the soul', he asserts that, in this period, 'The possibility of madness is . . . implicit in the very phenomenon of passion'.[21] Certainly it becomes difficult to separate that passion which can lead to terminal disorder from the passion which can denote a heightened sensibility. This is a contradiction inherent in the elevation of sensibility, and those who fit Foucault's scheme by discussing the role of passion in the onset of madness concern themselves with only one of the elements in that contradiction.[22] The general interest in the analysis of passion does not represent simply a project of suppression nor of condemnation. Vigilance is recommended in the beguiling encounter with passion; the potential patient is advised to avoid not passion, but passion at the point of excess. As ever, the most convenient example is in James's *Dictionary*, where we find the definition of 'PASSIO' as 'A Passion, Affection, or Disease', and the argument that 'Nothing . . . is a more powerful Preservative against Melancholy and Madness, than a due Moderation and Subjection of the Passions; which will be easily obtained, if we take care not to indulge ourselves too far'.[23]

Passion can become disease, so it must not be indulged 'too far'—it must be not silenced but moderated. When Richard Mead attempts to reproduce the definition of passion as disease, he has to equivocate. He declares that 'The affections of the mind, commonly called *passions*, when vehement and immoderate, may be justly ranked among diseases; because they disorder the body various ways',[24] but a few pages later he enters the caveat that 'passions' and 'affections' are 'even necessary for keeping up society and connections between mankind'.[25] Here, indeed, we are close to the vocabulary of Hume's *Treatise*, in which 'passion' is part of the very currency of 'communication' and 'society'. In the medical version of its use, the tendencies which can enhance sociability can also turn the individual inwards and away from all society by becoming illness. It is indicative of the nature of the interest in passion that where we find a physician who enjoins his reader absolutely to suppress passion, it

[20] Robinson, *A New System*, 218.
[21] Foucault, *Madness and Civilization*, 88.
[22] See, for example, P. Frings, *A Treatise on Phrensy* (London, 1746), 26.
[23] James, *Dictionary*, s.v. 'MANIA'.
[24] Mead, *Medical Precepts and Cautions*, 269.   [25] Ibid. 279.

is in a work which presents an outmoded and atavistic theory of the body. James Mackenzie's *The History of Health*, of 1758, still adheres to an ancient scheme of 'humours' and dispositions, and advises that 'He who seriously resolves to preserve his health, must previously learn to conquer his passions, and to keep them in absolute subjection to reason'.[26] Because of the ambiguity of passion, such an injunction is rare in the medical texts of the eighteenth century.

Foucault describes how, as less faith was placed in schemes of humours and dispositions, 'the moral significance of "nervous complaints" was profoundly altered'.[27] What had been 'associated with the organic movements of the lower parts of the body . . . located within a certain ethic of desire' now proceeded 'from too much feeling; one suffered from an excessive solidarity with all the beings around one'. The emphasis upon 'feeling' and 'sensibility', and upon the body as a moral construction, is common to the sentimental novel. In novels, typically, what Foucault calls 'an excessive solidarity' can lead to a kind of physical disablement (the body beyond control—trembling, falling, fading away), but can also be the sign of a moral superiority. In *Clarissa* or *The Man of the World*, sensibility is at one with virtue, and is too good for the world. In *Madmen and the Bourgeoisie*, Klaus Doerner recognizes, in his discussion of the fascination with hysteria, that a susceptibility to feeling comes to be represented as desirable: 'With the establishment of this thesis of hysteria, one element of sequestered unreason—specifically the passions—became accepted as a vital component of bourgeois society, not simply as a dangerous evil crying out for rational control, but as a recognizable, physical, autonomous social, and moral force'.[28] But passion can take the path of excess. The sensibility which is celebrated by novelists is specialized, oppositional, set against the 'world'. It is not painlessly incorporated into any image of what Doerner calls 'bourgeois society'. If such a 'bourgeois society' is depicted in the novels of Richardson or Mackenzie, it is usually as that which would deny or destroy a virtuous sensibility. If virtue depends on sensibility, the moral logic of these texts is peculiarly pessimistic. They do not speak clearly of some triumphant 'bourgeois' model of social being; they

---

[26] James Mackenzie, *The History of Health* (Edinburgh, 1758), 388.

[27] Foucault, *Madness and Civilization*, 156.

[28] Doerner, *Madmen and the Bourgeoisie*, 30.

describe, however formulaically, a sociability whose fate is isolation.

Both Doerner and Foucault are right to say that the employment of 'delicacy' and 'sensibility' in the description of nervous disorder constitutes the body according to what Doerner calls 'moral categories'.[29] But this is not a new phenomenon that comes with a new physiological vocabulary. The body was always a 'moral' corpus. What has changed is that, by the middle of the century, a distinct ambivalence has become crucial; sensibility can produce either collapse or integrity, disorder or articulacy. In earlier writings, the emphasis upon moral implication is altogether more crude. In Mandeville's *Treatise*, for example, a great list of symptoms, from heartburn to insomnia, stomach ache to anxiety, is traced down to this:

now I hope looking back on the passages of your Life, you'll easily find out your self the Procatarctick Causes of your Distemper. The irregularities of your Youth having led the way by shaking the frame of your Constitution; The first I can accuse is your Marrying young, and being too much addicted to what you was pleas'd to call the *res uxoria*.[30]

The moralism of this address of physician to patient is a conditional severity, for Mandeville acknowledges there to be other causes of 'Hypochondriack and Hysterick Passions' than 'Excess of Venery' and youthful lack of moderation. But the signs which the body yields up and the physician transcribes tend, for Mandeville, to be the effects of moral as well as bodily failure. So the revelation of disease begins with a history, a narrative which tells of an ill-spent, dissolute, debt-ridden past.[31] This kind of narrative lingers on in the later writings of those who treat of sensibility as a privilege. For George Cheyne, self-confessed hypochondriac, the body's disorder can arise from moral failure, from types of excessive behaviour whose repercussions echo down the generations:

But as to the Disorders of the *Body* . . . they are naturally and philosophically to be accounted for, from *Accidents* only, *Debauches*, *Excesses*, and a *Mal-regimen*, gradually spoiling and destroying this *musical Instrument* . . . I can readily conceive how such a *Debauch* spoil'd, obstructed, or relax'd such a Set of *Glands*, *Nerves*, or *Capillaries* . . . how

---

[29] Ibid. 56.
[30] Mandeville, *A Treatise of the Hypochondriack and Hysterick Passions*, 142.
[31] Ibid. 3.

excessive *Leachery* [*sic*] dissolv'd, broke or unbended so many *Nerves, Fibres* and *Lymphatics*, and how the *crazy* Parents, from vitiated Juices, and rotten or unform'd Solids, brought into the World deform'd *ideotical* Children.[32]

Of course, for Cheyne, and for some of those whom he treated or advised, certain types of bodily distemper can indicate a heightened sensibility: learning, intelligence, sensitivity. The body is a moral body, but it can evidence either the defeat or the triumph of virtue.

This ambiguous potential renders difficult any attempt to relate descriptions of the body and its nervous disorders to any prevailing political or social concerns. One such attempt is made by Christopher Lawrence, who, in a discussion of Scottish medicine in the eighteenth century, links the formation of a 'concept of the body' with

the social interests and self-perceptions of the improving landed class that came to dominate Scottish culture . . . Through a theory of sensibility, physiology served to sanction the introduction of new economic and associated cultural forms by identifying the landed minority as the custodians of civilization . . . A related theory of sympathy expressed and moulded their social solidarity.[33]

But the ideological project has deeper incongruities than this elision of the physiological and the cultural can suggest. The monologue of the ruling class, designed to convince only itself, produces a sensitized but never absolutely reliable body. In *The History of Sexuality*, Michel Foucault describes a 'bourgeoisie' which is 'occupied, from the mid-eighteenth century on, with creating its own sexuality and forming a specific body based on it, a "class" body with its health, hygiene, descent, and race' (p. 124). This idea of the production of the body, of the social construction of its most private experiences, is important, but the proposal that the 'emphasis on the body should undoubtedly be linked to the process of growth and establishment of bourgeois hegemony' (p. 125) weakens when applied to the texts that I am discussing. The language in which the body and the 'theory of sensibility' is produced is also a language which tells of disorder and ambiguous susceptibility. The 'theory of sympathy' may be designed, as Lawrence suggests, to mould a 'social

[32] George Cheyne, *The Natural Method of Cureing the Diseases of the Body and the Disorders of the Mind depending on the Body* (London, 1742), 80–1.

[33] Lawrence, 'The Nervous System and Society', 20.

solidarity', but it also threatens to efface necessary distinction—to become indiscriminate, unregulated passion. The theory of sensibility acquired an unusual importance in Scotland because Scottish philosophy posited *feelings* as the basis of all human actions'[34]—but then 'feeling' is considered to be sometimes unreliable and not always universal. Firstly, feeling can overflow in disconcerting ways; secondly, medical, literary, and philosophical texts tend to describe the gift of feeling as special and exceptional—a privileged faculty which cannot be projected on to the world. It may have been that the most banal displays of sensibility became a well-worn fashion in the course of the century, but many of those members of 'society' who may have indulged themselves in weakness of spirits, ready tears, or pensive silence imitated the signs of what was not simply a hegemonic style. If it became fashionable to be possessed of sensibility, the enjoyment of that sensibility implied a metaphorical, wishful rejection of public being, 'business', the 'world'.

So the applicability of Lawrence's formula is limited. He writes that the 'theory of refined sensibility with its naturalistic basis in the nervous system and its corollary in a theory of the true custodians of civilized society, identified the natural governing role of the Edinburgh improvers, and sanctioned the cultural changes they were introducing'.[35] This must be conditional upon recognizing that the elevation of sensibility is not a clear indication of ideological confidence—that at the heart of such 'theory' is disturbance and hesitation. The identification of the writings on nervous disorder, or of novels which celebrate feeling, as evidence of the confident self-reflections of a dominant class cannot be accepted when the implications of figures of sensibility are so ideologically ambivalent. The general ideological significance of such figures is, as Doerner points out, conditioned by the quite practical distinction between the fashionable hysteric or hypochondriac and the mad pauper—the distinction between licence and incarceration. But even the logic of narcissism which Doerner tends to see in the study of nervous disorder is, in some sense, uneasy. For such a logic must work by confirming itself through images, through an observable repertoire of visible signs which implies a separation between observer and observed. In the space of this separation, in the necessity for order to be observed in the appearance of disorder, is the possibility of an

---

[34] Ibid. 25.   [35] Ibid. 30.

inordinate excitation, and the need for the physician to exercise his superiority over the object of his scrutiny. The symptoms of a nervous malaise, of hypochondria and hysteria, are not simply signs of being 'civilized'. A reading of the discussion of hysteria in the eighteenth century—a discussion both most authoritarian and most troubled—raises doubts about Doerner's description of a relationship between these writings and the ideological purposes of what he insistently refers to as a 'bourgeois society':

> from external, physical authority, society, self-reliant and at the same time following the market principle, was forced to orient itself in terms of itself. It did so via the sensations, passions . . . and opinions. Society learned how to suffer from them as though of something subjective, self-posited, while simultaneously making them the transmission belts of the social movement and of self-understanding. Hysteria and spleen had already established themselves in this circular motion by about 1750.[36]

Doerner himself has to admit the possibility of 'unnatural immoderation, with illness one of the possible punishments' opened up by such a strategy.[37] At no stage could either the physician or the sufferer be wholly at ease with the latter's sensibility.

In the novel of sentiment, and especially in the writings of Richardson and Sterne, sensibility is not necessarily credited as a possession uniquely of the educated and the property-owning. For these authors, certain servants or industrious members of the lower classes can have access to sensibility as natural, gestural expression. Culture's highest expression is the myth of a return to nature. But there can be that conflation of sensibility and class identity which Lawrence and Doerner expect. Cheyne, the most widely known physician of his age, firmly disposes of the notion that those involved in such an activity as labour can aspire to the delicacy and refinement which reveal themselves in nervous disorder. He divides the 'human race' into 'those whose Eminence and Dignity consists chiefly in their *Heads, Faculties* and *spiritual Nature*, and *those* whose great *Use* and *Design* is to excel in the Exercise and Use of their *Bodies, Limbs* and *material Organs*'.[38] The diet that he recommends for those of delicacy is 'proper for the *thinking, speculative,* and *sedentary* Part of Mankind, and not for the *active, laborious,* and *mechanical*'.[39] In a naturalization of the body as a confirmation of

---

[36] Doerner, *Madmen and the Bourgeoisie*, 51.   [37] Ibid. 59.
[38] Cheyne, *The Natural Method*, 82–3.   [39] *The English Malady*, p. iii.

social difference, Cheyne mobilizes an argument which fits exactly Lawrence's or Doerner's analyses. He writes that 'in one word, there are those *who govern*, and those who *are governed*, originally form'd and mark'd out by Nature, and their original *Frame* and *indelible Signatures*'.[40] The ruling class are those with 'more delicate and *elastic Organs* of *Thinking* and *Sensibility*'. Cheyne concedes that ambiguity which is fundamental to concepts of sensibility and delicacy. He acknowledges that those endowed with such faculties are liable to 'Sufferings', and affirms that 'all *nervous Hypochondriacal* and *Hysterical* Persons' are those whose sensibility has made them susceptible to, and which has itself suffered by, 'coarse Usage'. But then they are also liable to be '*Genii, Philosophers* and *Lawgivers*'. The picture is complicated by the presence of a '*Middle*' between the '*Extremes*' of manual labour and 'those *who govern*'. This class 'may sometimes produce a *false Hero, Conqueror*, or admirable *Mechanic* or Tradesman', if '*Chance*' intervenes, or if any of its members have 'some particular *Set* of *nervous Glands* and *Fibres* in the *Brain*, not quite spoil'd or relax'd by the Intemperance of their Parents'. Cheyne's recommendation of a meat diet for those who undertake 'Labour and Exercise' and vegetarianism for those 'whose Occupations require only *clear Heads*, great *Attention*, and a free and easy Exercise of their *intellectual Faculties*',[41] does not just reflect a confident class distinction. There is always disability. Those whose 'intellectual Faculties' are exercised are liable to be delicate; the attention they should give to their unreliable bodies is a safeguard against illness as well as a self-indulgence.

Even when a physician like Cheyne presumes the congruence of sensibility and social privilege, sociability itself cannot be taken for granted. We might say that the physicians' language of self-attention is limited and reductive, but its limits and reductions crystallize the paradoxes of the cult of sensibility. The best people become ill, their sensitivities visceral and privatized. In constructing this pattern of susceptibility, the medical texts dramatize the paradoxes of the vocabulary that they share with moral philosophers or novelists. For this is a vocabulary which elaborates society as a capacity of the self—a moral as well as semantic potential for which my

---

[40] *The Natural Method*, 83.
[41] Ibid. 86.

approximate word is 'sociability'—and, in the end, this capacity can achieve no expression which is not private and exceptional. There is no social space for sensibility. Illness is its appropriate metaphor.

Bibliography

Anti-Pamela (London, 1741).

ARDAL, P.S., *Passion and Value in Hume's Treatise* (Edinburgh, 1966).

ARMSTRONG, Dr JOHN, *the Art of Preserving Health* (London, 1744).

AUSTEN, JANE, *Sir Charles Grandison*, ed. B. Southam (Oxford, 1980).

BAGLIVI, G., *The Practice of Physick*, translated from the Latin edition of 1696 (London, 1704).

BALL, JOHN, *The Female Physician; or, Every Woman her own Doctor* (London, 1771).

BARKER, G.A., *Henry Mackenzie* (Boston, Mass., 1975).

BARNES, B. and S. Shapin (eds.), *Natural Order: Historical Studies of Scientific Culture* (London, 1979).

BARROW, JOHN, *Dictionarum Medicum Universale; or, a New Medical Dictionary* (London, 1749).

BATTIE, WILLIAM, *A Treatise on Madness* (London, 1758).

BEASLEY, J.C., *Novels of the 1740s* (Athens, Ga., 1982).

The Beauties of Sterne (London, 1782).

BENTLEY, G.E. (ed.), *Editing Eighteenth-century Novels* (Toronto, 1975).

BERTHOUD, JACQUES, 'Shandeism and Sexuality', in Myer, *Lawrence Sterne: Riddles and Mysteries*, q.v.

BLACKMORE, RICHARD, *A Treatise of the Spleen and Vapours* (London, 1725).

BOERHAAVE, HERMANN, *Aphorisms* (London, 1715).

BOSWELL, JAMES, *The Hypochondriack* (first published 1777-83), ed. Margery Bailey, 2 vols. (Stanford, Calif., 1928).

—— *Boswell: The Ominous Years. 1774-1776*, ed. C. Ryskamp and F.A. Pottle (London, 1963).

—— *Boswell in Extremes: 1776-1778*, ed. C. Weis and F.A. Pottle (London, 1971).

—— *Life of Johnson* (first published 1791), ed. R.W. Chapman (1904; rpt. Oxford, 1980).

BOUCE, PAUL-GABRIEL (ed.), *Sexuality in Eighteenth-century Britain* (Manchester, 1982).

BOWLES, G., 'Physical, Human and Divine Attraction in the Life and Thought of George Cheyne', *Annals of Science*, 31 (1974), 473-88.

BRAUDY, LEO, 'The Form of the Sentimental Novel' *Novel*, 7 (1973), 5-13.

BRAUDY, LEO, 'Penetration and Impenetrability in *Clarissa*', in Phillip North (ed.), *New Approaches to Eighteenth-century Literature* (New York, 1974).

BREDVOLD, L.I., *The Natural History of Sensibility* (Detroit, 1962).

BRISSENDEN, R.F., 'Sterne and Painting', in Butt, *Of Books and Humankind*, q.v.

—— (ed.), *Samuel Richardson, Clarissa: Preface, Hints of Prefaces, and Postscript* (Los Angeles, 1964).

—— (ed.), *Studies in Eighteenth Century Literature* (Canberra, 1968).

—— *Virtue in Distress: Studies in the Novel of Sentiment from Richardson to Sade* (London, 1974).

BROOKE, FRANCES, *The History of Lady Julia Mandeville* (first published 1763), ed. E. Phillips Poole (London, 1930).

BROOKE, HENRY, *The Fool of Quality* (first published 1764–70; London, 1906).

BROWN S.C. (ed.), *Philosophers of the Enlightenment* (Brighton, 1979).

BUCHAN, WILLIAM, *Domestic Medicine* (Edinburgh, 1769).

BUTT, JOHN (ed.), *Of Books and Humankind* (London, 1964).

—— and G. CARNALL, *The Mid-eighteenth Century* (1979; rpt. Oxford, 1980).

BYNUM, W.F., ROY PORTER, and MICHAEL SHEPHERD (eds.), *The Anatomy of Madness: Essays in the History of Psychiatry* (London, 1985).

BYRD, MAX, *Visits to Bedlam: Madness and Literature in the Eighteenth Century* (Columbia, SC, 1974).

—— 'The Madhouse, the Whorehouse and the Convent', *Partisan Review*, 44 (1977), 268–78.

CANTOR, G.N., and M.J.S. HODGE (eds.), *Conceptions of Ether: Studies in the History of Ether Theories* (Cambridge, 1981).

CARR, JOHN, *The Life and Opinions of Tristram Shandy* (London, 1760).

CARROLL, J. (ed.), *Samuel Richardson: A Collection of Critical Essays* (Englewood Cliffs, NJ, 1969).

—— 'On Annotating *Clarissa*', in Bentley, *Editing Eighteenth-century Novels*, q.v.

CASH, ARTHUR HILL, *Sterne's Comedy of Moral Sentiments: The Ethical Dimension of the Journey* (Pittsburgh, Pa., 1966).

CASTLE, TERRY, *Clarissa's Ciphers* (Ithaca, NY, 1982).

CHARKE, CHARLOTTE, *The History of Henry Dumont, Esq.* (first published 1755; 2nd edn., London, 1759).

CHEYNE, GEORGE, *The English Malady; or a Treatise of Nervous Diseases of all Kinds* (London, 1733).

—— *An Essay on Regimen* (London, 1740).

—— *The Natural Method of Cureing the Diseases of the Body, and the Disorders of the Mind depending on the Body* (London, 1742).

—— *The Letters of Dr George Cheyne to the Countess of Huntingdon*, ed. C. Mullett (San Marino, Calif., 1940).

—— The Letters of Doctor George Cheyne to Samuel Richardson, ed. C. Mullett, The University of Missouri Studies, 18 (Columbia, Miss., 1943).

CLARKE, EDWIN, 'The Doctrine of the Hollow Nerve in the Seventeenth and Eighteenth Centuries', in Stevenson and Multhauf, Medicine, Science and Culture, q.v.

CLIFFORD, J.L. (ed.), Eighteenth-century English Literature: Modern Essays in Criticism (Oxford, 1967).

The Clockmakers Outcry Against the Author of the Life and Opinions of Tristram Shandy (London, 1760).

COHEN, MURRAY, Sensible Words: Linguistic Practice in England, 1640–1785 (Baltimore, Md., 1977).

COMBE, WILLIAM, Letters Supposed to Have Been Written by Yorick and Eliza (London, 1779).

COOPER, ANTHONY ASHLEY, third Earl of Shaftesbury, Characteristics of Men, Manners, Opinions, and Times, etc. (first published 1711), ed. J. Robertson (1900; rpt. Indianapolis, 1964).

—— An Inquiry Concerning Virtue, or Merit (first published 1714), ed. D. Walford (Manchester, 1977).

COPLEY, STEPHEN (ed.), Literature and the Social Order in Eighteenth-century England (London, 1984).

CRAIG, DAVID, Scottish Literature and the Scottish People 1680–1830 (London, 1961).

CRANE, R.S., 'Suggestions Toward a Genealogy of the "Man of Feeling"', in The Idea of the Humanities (Chicago, 1967).

CROSS, WILBUR D., The Life and Times of Laurence Sterne (3rd edn., New Haven, Conn., 1929).

CULLEN, WILLIAM, First Lines of the Practice of Physic (first published 1777; 4 vols., 3rd edn., Edinburgh, 1781–4).

CURTIS, LEWIS PERRY, The Politicks of Laurence Sterne (London, 1929).

—— 'Forged Letters of Laurence Sterne', PMLA 50 (1935), 1076–1106.

DAICHES, DAVID, The Paradox of Scottish Culture (London 1964).

DAVIS, LENNARD, Factual Fictions: The Origins of the English Novel (New York, 1983).

DAY, R.A., Told in Letters: Epistolary Fiction Before Richardson (Ann Arbor, Mich., 1966).

DAY, W.G., 'Tristram Shandy: Locke May Not Be the Key', in Myer, Lawrence Sterne: Riddles and Mysteries, q.v.

DEPORTE, MICHAEL, Nightmares and Hobby-horses: Swift, Sterne, and Augustan Ideas of Madness (San Marino, Calif., 1974).

DIAMOND, A., and L.R. EDWARDS (eds.), The Authority of Experience: Essays in Feminist Criticism (Amherst, Mass., 1977).

DICKINSON, H.T., Liberty and Property: Political Ideology in Eighteenth-century Britain (London, 1977).

DIDEROT, D., *Éloge de Richardson* (first published 1761), in *Œuvres* (Paris, 1962).

DILWORTH, ERNEST, *The Unsentimental Journey of Laurence Sterne* (Morningside Heights, NY, 1948).

DOBREE, R., *English Literature in the Early Eighteenth Century 1700–1740* (1959; rpt. Oxford, 1968).

DOERNER, KLAUS, *Madmen and the Bourgeoisie: A Social History of Insanity and Psychiatry* trans. J. Neugroschel and J. Steinburg (Oxford, 1981).

DOHERTY, FRANCIS, 'Sterne and Hume: A Bicentenary Essay', *Essays and Studies*, 22 (1969) 71–87.

DOODY, MARGARET ANNE, *A Natural Passion* (Oxford, 1974).

DOVER, THOMAS, *The Ancient Physician's Legacy to his Country* (London, 1732).

DUNN, JOHN, *The Political Thought of John Locke* (Cambridge, 1969).

DUSSINGER, J.A., *The Discourse of the Mind in Eighteenth-century Fiction* (The Hague, 1974).

EAGLETON, TERRY, *The Rape of Clarissa* (Oxford, 1982).

EAVES, T.C.D. and B.D. KIMPEL, 'The Composition of *Clarissa* and its Revision before Publication', *PMLA* 83 (1968), 416–28.

—— and —— *Samuel Richardson: A Biography* (Oxford, 1971).

ELIOT, GEORGE, *The Yale Edition of the George Eliot Letters*, vi, ed. G.S. Haight (New Haven, Conn., 1955).

ENFIELD, WILLIAM (ed.), *The Speaker; or, Miscellaneous Pieces, Selected from the Best English Writers* (London, 1774).

ERAMETSA, ERIK, 'A Study of the Word "Sentimental" and of Other Linguistic Characteristics of Eighteenth Century Sentimentalism in England', *Annales Academiae Scientiarum Fennicae*, series B, 74 (Helsinki, 1951).

Explanatory Remarks upon the Life and Opinions of Tristram Shandy (London, 1760).

FERRIAR, JOHN, *Illustrations of Sterne* (London, 1798).

FIEDLER, LESLIE A., *Love and Death in the American Novel* (New York, 1960).

FIELDING, HENRY, *Joseph Andrews* (first published 1742), ed. Martin Battestin (Oxford, 1967).

—— *Miscellanies by Henry Fielding, Esq; Volume One* (first published 1743), ed. Henry Knight Miller (Oxford, 1972).

—— *The History of Tom Jones, a Foundling* (first published 1749), ed. F. Bowers (2 vols., Oxford, 1974).

FIELDING, SARAH, *The Adventures of David Simple* (first published 1744–7) ed. Malcolm Kelsall (London, 1969).

—— *Remarks on Clarissa, Addressed to the Author* (London, 1749).

FIGES, EVA, *Sex and Subterfuge: Women Writers to 1850* (London, 1982).

FISCHER-HOMBERGER, ESTHER, 'Hypochondriasis of the Eighteenth

Century—Neurosis of the Present Century', *Bulletin of the History of Medicine*, 46 (1972), 391–401.

FLUCHÈRE, HENRI, *Laurence Sterne: From Tristram to Yorick*, trans. B. Bray (London, 1965).

FORBES, DUNCAN, 'Hume and the Scottish Enlightenment', in Brown, *Philosophers of the Enlightenment*, q.v.

—— *Hume's Philosophical Politics* (1975; rpt. Cambridge, 1985).

FOUCAULT, MICHEL, *Madness and Civilization*, trans. Richard Howard (1967; rpt. London, 1977).

—— *The History of Sexuality: vol. i. An Introduction*, trans. Robert Hurley (London, 1978).

FRENCH, R.K., *Robert Whytt, the Soul, and Medicine* (London, 1969).

—— 'Ether and Physiology', in Cantar and Hodge, *Conceptions of Ether: Studies in the History of Ether Theories*, q.v.

FRINGS, P., *A Treatise on Phrensy* (London, 1746).

A Funeral Discourse, Occasioned by the Much Lamented Death of Mr Yorick (London, 1761).

GARDINER, H.M., *Feeling and Emotion: A History of Theories* (Westport, Conn., 1970).

The Gentleman's Magazine (London, 1731–1907).

A Genuine Letter from a Methodist Preacher in the Country, to Laurence Sterne (London, 1760).

GEROULD, G.H., *The Patterns of English and American Fiction: A History* (1942; rpt. New York, 1960).

GOLDBERG, RITA, *Sex and Enlightenment: Women in Richardson and Diderot* (Cambridge, 1984).

GOLDSMITH, OLIVER, *The Vicar of Wakefield, a Tale Supposed to be Written by Himself* (first published 1766; 1908; rpt. London, 1979).

——*The Vicar of Wakefield*, in Henshall's Ornamented Library of Classic Novels, vol. iv (Dublin, 1796).

—— *The Collected Letters of Oliver Goldsmith*, ed. K.C. Balderston (Cambridge, 1928).

—— *Collected Works of Oliver Goldsmith*, ed. Arthur Friedman (5 vols., Oxford, 1966).

GRAVES, RICHARD, *The Spritual Quixote, or the Summer's Ramble of Mr Geoffrey Wildgoose* (first published 1773), ed. C. Whibley (2 vols., London, 1926).

HAGSTRUM, J.H., *Sex and Sensibility* (Chicago, 1980).

HARTLEY, DAVID, *Observations on Man* (1749; rpt. London, 1791).

HARTLEY, LODWICK, *Laurence Sterne in the Twentieth Century: An Essay and a Bibliography of Sternean Studies 1900–1965* (Chapel Hill, NC, 1966).

HAYWOOD, ELIZA, *Love in Excess* (first published 1719; 4th edn., London, 1722).

—— *The History of Miss Betsy Thoughtless* (4 vols., London, 1751).

HILL, CHRISTOPHER, 'Clarissa Harlowe and her Times', *Essays in Criticism*, 5 (1955), 315–40.

HILL, JOHN, *Hypochondriasis: A Practical Treatise* (1766; rpt. Los Angeles, 1969). .

HIRSCHMAN, ALBERT O., *The Passions and the Interests: Political Arguments for Capitalism before its Triumph* (Princeton, NJ, 1977).

HOGARTH, WILLIAM, *The Analysis of Beauty* (1753; rpt. Menston, Yorkshire, 1971).

HOLLAND, R.F., *Against Empiricism: On Education, Epistemology and Value* (Oxford, 1980).

HOLTZ, WILLIAM, *Image and Immortality* (Providence, RI, 1970).

HONT, ISTVAN, and MICHAEL IGNATIEFF (eds.), *Wealth and Virtue: The Shaping of Political Economy in the Scottish Enlightenment* (Cambridge, 1983).

HOPKINS, ROBERT, *The True Genius of Oliver Goldsmith* (Baltimore, Md., 1969).

HORNE, THOMAS, *The Social Thought of Bernard Mandeville* (London, 1978).

HOWES, ALAN B., *Yorick and the Critics: Sterne's Reputation in England 1760–1868* (New Haven, Conn., 1958).

—— (ed.), *Sterne: The Critical Heritage* (London, 1974).

HUME, DAVID, *A Treatise of Human Nature* (first published 1739–40) ed. L.A. Selby-Bigge, 2nd edn. revised P.H. Nidditch (Oxford, 1978).

—— *Enquiries Concerning Human Understanding and Concerning the Principles of Morals* (first published 1748 and 1751), ed. L.A. Selby-Bigge, 3rd edn. revised P.H. Nidditch (Oxford, 1972).

—— *Essays, Moral and Political* (2 vols., 2nd edn., Edinburgh, 1742).

—— *Essays Moral, Political, and Literary*, ed. Eugene Miller (Indianapolis, 1985).

—— *Four Dissertations* (London, 1757).

—— *The Letters of David Hume*, ed. J.Y.T. Greig (Oxford, 1932).

HUNTER, RICHARD, and IDA MACALPINE, *Three Hundred Years of Psychiatry 1535–1860* (London, 1963).

HUTCHESON, FRANCIS, *A System of Moral Philosophy* (London, 1755).

—— *An Essay on the Nature and Conduct of the Passions and Affections with Illustrations on the Moral Sense* (3rd edn., 1742; rpt. Gainesville, Fla., 1969).

IGNATIEFF, MICHAEL, *The Needs of Strangers* (London, 1984).

IRELAND, JOHN, *Letters and Poems of the Late Mr John Henderson: With Anecdotes of his Life* (London, 1786).

JAMES, ROBERT, *A Medicinal Dictionary* (3 vols., London, 1743–5).

JEFFERSON, D.W. 'The Vicar of Wakefield and Other Prose Writing: A Reconsideration', in Swarbrick, *The Art of Oliver Goldsmith*, q.v.

JENNER, CHARLES, *The Placid Man* (1770; 2 vols., rpt. London, 1773).

JEWSON, N., 'Medical knowledge and the Patronage System in Eighteenth-century England', *Sociology*, 8 (1974), 369–85.

JOHNSON, SAMUEL, *The Idler* (first published 1758–60), in *The Yale Edition of the Works of Samuel Johnson*, vol. ii, ed. W.J. Bate, J.M. Bullitt, and L.F. Powell (New Haven, Conn., 1963).

—— *The Rambler* (first published 1750–2), in *The Yale Edition of the Works of Samuel Johnson*, vols. iii–v, ed. W.J. Bate and A.B. Strauss (New Haven, Conn., 1969).

KALLICH, MARTIN, *The Association of Ideas and Critical Theory in Eighteenth-century England* (The Hague, 1970).

KARL, FREDERICK R., *A Reader's Guide to the Development of the English Novel in the Eighteenth Century* (London, 1975).

KELLY, HUGH, *Memoirs of a Magdalen* (2 vols., 2nd edn., London, 1767).

KINKEAD-WEEKES, MARK, '*Clarissa* Restored?', *Review of English Studies*, 10 (1959) 156–71.

—— *Samuel Richardson: Dramatic Novelist* (London, 1973).

KNOX, VICESIMUS (ed.), *Elegant Extracts* (2nd edn., London, 1784).

KRAMNICK, ISAAC, *Bolingbroke and his Circle: The Politics of Nostalgia in the Age of Walpole* (London, 1968).

KYDD, R.M., *Reason and Conduct in Hume's Treatise* (Oxford, 1946).

LANHAM, RICHARD, *Tristram Shandy: The Games of Pleasure* (Berkeley and Los Angeles, 1973).

LAWRENCE, CHRISTOPHER, 'The Nervous System and Society in the Scottish Enlightenment', in Barnes and Shapin, *Natural Order: Historical Studies of Scientific Culture*, q.v.

LEAVIS, F.R., *The Great Tradition* (1948; rpt. Harmondsworth, 1977).

LEAVIS, Q.D., *Fiction and the Reading Public* (1932; rpt. London, 1965).

LEFANU, ALICIA, *Memoirs of the Life and Writings of Mrs Frances Sheridan* (London, 1824).

LENNOX, CHARLOTTE, *The Female Quixote* (first published 1752), ed. Margaret Dalziel (London, 1970).

Letters from Eliza to Yorick (London, 1775).

The Life of Dr Oliver Goldsmith: Written from Personal Knowledge, Authentic Papers, and other Indubitable Authorities (London, 1774).

LOCKE, JOHN, *An Essay concerning Human Understanding* (first published 1690), ed. P.H. Nidditch (1975; rpt. Oxford, 1979).

—— *Two Treatises of Government* (first published 1689), ed. P. Laslett (New York, 1965).

LOVERIDGE, MARK, *Laurence Sterne and the Argument About Design* (London, 1982).

McELROY, D.D., *Scotland's Age of Improvement: A Survey of Eighteenth Century Literary Clubs and Societies* (Washington, 1969).

MACFIE, A.L., *The Individual in Society: Papers on Adam Smith* (London, 1967).

MACINTYRE, ALISDAIR, *After Virtue: A Study in Moral Theory* (1981; rpt. London, 1982).

—— Introduction to *Hume's Ethical Writings*, ed. A. MacIntyre (New York, 1965).

MACKENZIE, HENRY, *The Man of Feeling* (London, 1771).

—— *The Man of the World* (first published 1773), in *The Works of Henry Mackenzie*, vol. ii (Glasgow, 1818).

—— *Julia de Roubigne* (first published 1777; London, 1805).

—— (ed.), *The Lounger* (first published 1785-6; 2nd edn., Edinburgh, 1787).

—— (ed.), *The Mirror* (first published 1779-80; 2 vols., London, 1794).

—— *Letters to Elizabeth Rose of Kilravock*, ed. H.W. Drescher (Münster, 1967).

MACKENZIE, JAMES, *The History of Health* (Edinburgh, 1758).

MCKILLOP, ALAN DUGALD, *Samuel Richardson: Printer and Novelist* (1936; rpt. Hamden, Conn., 1960).

MACLEAN, KENNETH, 'Imagination and Sympathy: Sterne and Adam Smith', *Journal of the History of Ideas*, 10 (1949), 399-410.

MANDEVILLE, BERNARD, *The Fable of the Bees* (first published 1714), ed. Douglas Gurman (London, 1934).

—— *A Treatise of the Hypochondriack and Hysterick Passions* (London, 1711).

MANNINGHAM, RICHARD, *The Symptoms, Nature, Causes, and Cure of the Febricula, or Little Fever* (London, 1746).

MAYO, R.D., *The English Novel in the Magazines* (Oxford, 1962).

MEAD, RICHARD, *Medical Precepts and Cautions* (London, 1751).

MERCER, PHILIP, *Sympathy and Ethics* (Oxford, 1972).

MIDRIFF, JOHN, *Observations on the Spleen and Vapours: Containing Remarkable Cases of Persons of both Sexes, and all Ranks, from the aspiring Director to the humble Bubbler, who have miserably afflicted with those melancholy Disorders since the Fall of South-Sea and other publick Stocks* (London, 1721).

MILLER, DAVID, *Philosophy and Ideology in Hume's Political Thought* (Oxford, 1981).

MILLER, NANCY K., *The Heroine's Text: Readings in the French and English Novel, 1722-1782* (New York, 1980).

MOGLEN, HELENE, *The Philosophical Irony of Laurence Sterne* (Gainesville, Fla., 1975).

MONRO, JOHN, *Remarks on Dr Battie's Treatise on Madness* (London, 1758).

MONTAGU, Lady MARY WORTLEY, *The Complete Letters of Lady Mary Wortley Montagu*, ed. R. Halsband and I. Grundy (3 vols., Oxford, 1977).

The Monthly Review, or, Literary Journal (1759-67).

MOORE, R.E., *Hogarth's Literary Relationships* (Minneapolis, 1948).

MORAVIA, SERGIO, 'From *Homme Machine* to *Homme Sensible*: Changing Eighteenth-century Models', *Journal of the History of Ideas* 39 (1978), 45–60.

MORE, HANNAH, *Sacred Dramas; Chiefly Intended for Young Persons: The Subjects taken from the Bible. To which is Added, Sensibility, a Poem* (Dublin, 1784).

MORICE, G.P. (ed.), *David Hume: Bicentenary Papers* (Edinburgh, 1977).

MORROW, G.R., 'The Significance of the Doctrine of Sympathy in Hume and Adam Smith', *The Philosophical Review*, 32 (1923), 60–78.

MOSSNER, E.C., 'Hume's Epistle to Dr Arbuthnot', *Huntington Library Quarterly*, 7 (1944), 135–52.

—— *The Life of David Hume* (1954; rpt. Oxford, 1980).

MYER, VALERIE GROSVENOR (ed.), *Laurence Sterne: Riddles and Mysteries* (London, 1984).

NEW, MELVYN, ' "At the backside of the door of purgatory": A Note on Annotating Tristram Shandy', in Myer, *Lawrence Sterne: Riddles and Mysteries*, q.v.

NORTH, PHILIP (ed.), *New Approaches to Eighteenth-century Literature* (New York, 1974).

OATES, J.C.T., *Shandyism and Sentiment* (Cambridge, 1968).

OWEN, DAVID, *English Philanthropy 1660–1960* (London, 1965).

PAGLIARO, HAROLD (ed.), *Studies in Eighteenth-century Culture: Irrationalism in the Eighteenth Century*, vol. ii (Cleveland and London, 1972).

PAULSON, RONALD, *Satire and the Novel in Eighteenth Century England* (New Haven, Conn., 1967).

—— and THOMAS LOCKWOOD (eds.), *Henry Fielding: The Critical Heritage* (London, 1969).

PETERS, DOLORES, 'The Pregnant Pamela', *Eighteenth-Century Studies*, 14 (1981), 432–51.

PHILLIPSON, NICHOLAS, 'Culture and Society in the Eighteenth Century Province: The Case of Edinburgh and the Scottish Enlightenment,' in Stone, *The University in Society*, q.v.

—— 'Hume as Moralist: A Social Historian's Perspective', in Brown, *Philosophers of the Enlightenment*, q.v.

—— 'The Scottish Enlightenment', in Porter and Teich, *The Enlightenment in National Context*, q.v.

—— 'Adam Smith as Moralist', in Hont and Ignatieff, *Wealth and Virtue*, q.v.

—— and ROSALIND MITCHISON (eds.), *Scotland in the Age of Improvement: Essays in Scottish History in the Eighteenth Century* (Edinburgh, 1970).

PIERSON, R., 'The Revisions of Richardson's *Sir Charles Grandison*', *Studies in Bibliography*, 21 (1968), 163–89.

POCOCK, J.G.A., *The Machiavellian Moment* (Princeton, NJ, 1975).
—— *Virtue, Commerce, and History: Essays on Political Thought and History, Chiefly in the Eighteenth Century* (Cambridge, 1985).
POMME, PIERRE, *A Treatise on Hysterical and Hypochondriacal Diseases* (London, 1777).
PORTER, ROY, 'Mixed Feelings: The Enlightenment and Sexuality in Eighteenth-century Britain', in Bouce, *Sexuality in Eighteenth-century Britain*, q.v.
—— 'The Rage of Party: A Glorious Revolution in English Psychiatry?', *Medical History*, 27 (1983), 35–50.
—— '"The Hunger of Imagination": Approaching Samuel Johnson's Melancholy', in Bynum, Porter, and Shepherd, *The Anatomy of Madness: Essays in the History of Psychiatry*, q.v.
—— (ed.), *Patients and Practitioners: Lay Perceptions of Medicine in Preindustrial Society* (Cambridge, 1985).
—— and M. TEICH (eds.), *The Enlightenment in National Context* (Cambridge, 1981).
POTTLE, F.A., *James Boswell: The Early Years 1740–1769* (1966; rpt. London, 1984).
[PRATT, S.J.], *An Apology for the Life and Writing of David Hume* (London, 1777).
PRESTON, THOMAS, *Not in Timon's Manner: Feeling, Misanthropy and Satire in Eighteenth-century England* (1975).
PRICE, MARTIN, *To the Palace of Wisdom* (Carbondale, Ill., 1964).
PRIOR, JAMES, *The Life of Oliver Goldsmith* (2 vols., London, 1837).
PUTNEY, RUFUS, 'The Evolution of *A Sentimental Journey*', *Philological Quarterly*, 19 (1940), 349–69.
QUINTANA, RICARDO, '*The Vicar of Wakefield*: The Problem of Critical Approach', *Modern Philology*, 71 (1973), 59–65.
RAPHAEL, D.D., *The Moral Sense* (Oxford, 1947).
—— 'The Impartial Spectator', *Proceedings of the British Academy*, 58 (1972), 335–54.
RATHER, L.J., *Mind and Body in Eighteenth-century Medicine* (London, 1965).
REEVE, CLARA, *The Progress of Romance* (2 vols., London, 1785).
RICHARDSON, SAMUEL, *Letters written to and for Particular Friends, on the Most Important Occasions* (first published 1741), ed. J. Isaacs (London, 1928).
—— *Pamela; or, Virtue Rewarded* (first published 1740–1; London, 1978).
—— *Clarissa; or, The History of a Young Lady* (1st edn. 1747–8), ed. Angus Ross (Harmondsworth, 1985).
—— *Clarissa; or, The History of a Young Lady* (3rd edn., 1751; London, 1978).

—— *The History of Sir Charles Grandison* (first published 1753–4), ed. J. Harris (Oxford, 1972).

—— *A Collection of Moral and Instructive Sentiments, Maxims, Cautions, and Reflexions, Contained in the Histories of Pamela, Clarissa, and Sir Charles Grandison* (London, 1755).

—— *The Correspondence of Samuel Richardson*, ed. Anna Barbauld (6 vols., London, 1804).

—— *Selected Letters of Samuel Richardson*, ed. J. Carroll (Oxford, 1964).

RIVERS, ISABEL (ed.), *Books and their Readers in Eighteenth-century England* (Leicester, 1982).

ROBINSON, NICHOLAS, *A New System of the Spleen, Vapours, and Hypochondriack Melancholy* (London, 1729).

ROGERS, KATHERINE, 'Richardson's Empathy with Women', in Diamond and Edwards, *The Authority of Experience: Essays in Feminist Criticism*, q.v.

ROGERSON, B., 'The Art of Painting the Passions', *Journal of the History of Ideas*, 14 (1953), 68–94.

ROSEN, GEORGE, *Madness in Society* (London, 1968).

—— 'Forms of Irrationality in the Eighteenth Century', in Pagliaro, *Studies in Eighteenth-century Culture*, q.v.

—— 'Enthusiasm "a dark lanthorn of the spirit"', *Bulletin of the History of Medicine*, 42 (1968).

ROSTVIG, MAREN-SOFIE, *The Happy Man* (2 vols., Oslo, 1958).

ROTHSTEIN, ERIC, *Systems of Order and Inquiry in Later Eighteenth-century Fiction* (Los Angeles, 1975).

ROUSSEAU, G.S., 'Science and the Discovery of the Imagination in Enlightened England', *Eighteenth-Century Studies*, 3 (1969).

—— (ed.), *Goldsmith: The Critical Heritage* (London, 1974).

—— 'Science Books and their Readers in the Eighteenth Century', in Rivers, *Books and their Readers in Eighteenth-century England*, q.v.

—— and ROY PORTER (eds.), *The Ferment of Knowledge* (Cambridge, 1980).

SALE, W.M., *Samuel Richardson: A Bibliographical Record of his Literary Career with Historical Notes* (1936; rpt. New York, 1969).

SCOTT, Sir WALTER, *Waverley* (first published 1814; London, 1982).

—— *The Lives of the Novelists* (first published 1821–4; London, 1910).

SEKORA, JOHN, *Luxury: The Concept in Western Thought, Eden to Smollett* (Baltimore, Md., 1977).

SENA, JOHN F., *A Bibliography of Melancholy 1660–1800* (London, 1970).

The Sentimental Magazine; or, General Assemblage of Science, Taste, and Entertainment (London, 1773–7).

SHERIDAN, FRANCES, *Memoirs of Miss Sidney Bidulph* (first published 1761–7; 5 vols., 5th edn., London, 1796).

SHERIFF, JOHN, *The Good-Natured Man: The Evolution of a Moral Ideal, 1660–1800* (University, Ala., 1982).

SITTER, JOHN, *Literary Loneliness in Mid-Eighteenth Century England* (Ithaca, NY, 1982).

SMITH, ADAM, *The Theory of Moral Sentiments* (first published 1759), ed. D.D. Raphael and A.L. Macfie (Oxford, 1976).

—— An *Inquiry into the Nature and Causes of the Wealth of Nations* (first published 1776) ed. E. Cannan (1904; rpt. Chicago, 1976).

—— *The Correspondence of Adam Smith*, ed. E.C. Mossner and I.S. Ross (Oxford, 1977).

SMITH, WILLIAM, *A Dissertation upon the Nerves* (London, 1768).

SMOLLET, TOBIAS, *The Adventures of Roderick Random* (first published 1748), ed. Paul-Gabriel Bouce (Oxford, 1981).

SPILLANE, J.D., *The Doctrine of the Nerves* (Oxford, 1981).

SPROTT, S.E., *The English Debate on Suicide: From Donne to Hume* (La Salle, Ill., 1961).

STERNE, LAURENCE, *The Life and Opinions of Tristram Shandy, Gentleman* (first published 1759–67), ed. J.A. Work (New York, 1940).

—— *The Life and Opinions of Tristram Shandy, Gentleman* (first published 1759–67), ed. M. New, R.A. Davies, and W.G. Day (3 vols., Gainesville, Fla., 1984).

—— *A Sentimental Journey through France and Italy by Mr. Yorick* (first published 1768), ed. Gardner Stout (Los Angeles, 1967).

—— *Letters of Laurence Sterne*, ed. L.P. Curtis (Oxford, 1935).

—— *The Sermons of Mr Yorick*, vols. i & ii (London, 1760), vols. iii & iv (London, 1766), vols. v, vi, & vii (London, 1769).

—— *The Journal to Eliza, A Sentimental Journey through France and Italy By Mr Yorick to which are added The Journal to Eliza and A Political Romance*, ed. I. Jack (London, 1968).

STEVENSON, L.G., and R.P. MULTHAUF (eds), *Medicine, Science and Culture* (Baltimore, Md., 1968).

STEWARD, DUGALD, *Biographical Memoirs of Adam Smith, of William Robertson, and of Thomas Reid* (1793; rpt. Edinburgh, 1811).

STONE, LAWRENCE (ed.), *The University in Society* (2 vols., Princeton, NJ, 1975).

STROUD, BARRY, *Hume* (London, 1977).

STUKELY, WILLIAM, *Of the Spleen* (London, 1723).

SWARBRICK, A. (ed.), *The Art of Oliver Goldsmith* (London, 1984).

SYNGE, EDWARD, *Sober Thoughts for the Cure of Melancholy* (London, 1742).

TANNER, TONY, *Adultery in the Novel: Contract and Transgression* (Baltimore, Md., 1979).

TAYLOR, J.T., *Early Opposition to the English Novel* (Morningside Heights, NY, 1943).

THOMPSON, H.W. (ed.), *The Anecdotes and Egotisms of Henry Mackenzie* (London, 1927).

—— *A Scottish Man of Feeling* (London, 1931).

THOMPSON, WILLIAM, *Sickness* (London, 1745).

THOMSON, DAVID, *Wild Excursions: The Life and Fiction of Laurence Sterne* (London, 1972).

TIMBURY, JANE, *The Story of Le Fevre* (London, 1787).

TODD, JANET (ed.), *A Dictionary of British and American Women Writers 1660-1800* (London, 1984).

TOMPKINS, J.M.S., *The Popular Novel in England 1770-1800* (London, 1932).

TRAUGOTT, JOHN, *Tristram Shandy's World: Sterne's Philosophical Rhetoric* (Berkeley and Los Angeles, 1954).

—— *Laurence Sterne: A Collection of Critical Essays* (Englewood Cliffs, NJ, 1968).

A Treatise on the Dismal Effects of Low-Spiritedness (London, 1750).

Tristram Shandy's Bon Mots, Repartees, Odd Adventures and Humerous Stories; All Warranted Originals (London, 1760).

VAN GHENT, DOROTHY, 'On Clarissa Harlowe', in Carroll, *Samuel Richardson: A Collection of Critical Essays*, q.v.

VAN MARTER, SHIRLEY, 'Richardson's Revisions of *Clarissa* in the Second Edition', *Studies in Bibliography*, 26 (1973), 107-32.

—— 'Richardson's Revisions of *Clarissa* in the Third and Fourth Editions', *Studies in Bibliography*, 28 (1975), 119-52.

VEITH, ILZA, 'On Hysterical and Hypochondriacal Afflictions', *Bulletin of the History of Medicine*, 30 (1956), 233-40

—— *Hysteria: The History of a Disease* (Chicago, 1965).

WARNER, WILLIAM BEATTY, *Reading* Clarissa: *The Struggles of Interpretation* (New Haven, Conn., 1979).

WATT, IAN, *The Rise of the Novel* (1957; rpt. Harmondsworth, 1970).

WHYTT, ROBERT, *Observations on the Nature, Causes, and Cure of those Disorders which have been commonly call'd Nervous, Hypochondriac, or Hysteric* (Edinburgh, 1765).

WILLIAMS, RAYMOND, *The Country and the City* (1973; rpt. St Albans, 1975).

WINCH, DONALD, *Adam Smith's Politics: An Essay in Historiographical Revision* (1978; rpt. Cambridge, 1979).

WOLFF, CYNTHIA, *Samuel Richardson and the Eighteenth-century Puritan Character* (Hamden, Conn., 1972).

WOODS, SAMUEL, 'The *Vicar of Wakefield* and Recent Goldsmith Scholarship', *Eighteenth-Century Studies*, 9 (1976), 429-43.

—— *Oliver Goldsmith: A Reference Guide* (Boston, Mass., 1982).

WRIGHT, JOHN, *The Sceptical Realism of David Hume* (Manchester, 1983).

Yorick's Skull; or, College Oscitations (London, 1777).

Index

Printed in the United Kingdom
by Lightning Source UK Ltd.
124390UK00001B/154-159/A